Your Inner Child Has Rights, Too

A Common Man's Quest To Become One With God

By Joe Mittiga

Published by:
Spirit Walkers Publishing
Atlanta, Ga
Edited by:
Denise Hmieleski

ISBN 979-8-9915568-1-1

Contents

Acknowledgements iv

Introduction v

Part 1
Chapter 1: Where is All Begin 2
Chapter 2: Seeking Help 9
Chapter 3: Living Euphoria. 18
Chapter 4: Starting Over 25
Chapter 5: The Ego vs. the Loving Adult 29
Chapter 6: Healing Your Inner Child 35
Chapter 7: Creating a Safe Environment 39
Chapter 8: Creating a Dialogue with Your Inner Child 53
Chapter 9: The Courage to Feel Again 68
Chapter 10: The Miracle Happens 83

Part 2
Chapter 11: Denial 99
Chapter 12: The Magic of Anger 109
Chapter 13: Loneliness and Aloneness 121
Chapter 14: Grief 130

Part 3
Chapter 15: Integration of Create Spirit 139
Chapter 16: Self-discovery 163
Chapter 17: Repairing the Past 172
Chapter 18: Seeking Your Purpose 180

Part 4
Chapter 19: To Dream Big Dreams. 190
Chapter 20: Trust 199
Chapter 21: "I am" Statements. 210
Chapter 22: The Spiritual State Abundance 223
Conclusion: 228

Acknowledgements

I want to thank my sponsor / counselor (who chooses to remain anonymous) for all of her love and support through this era of my life. Many of the following exercises were taught to me by her. Today I want to freely share with you what was freely shared with me.

I also want to thank my friend Jacqueline for her love and continual encouragement during the creation of this book. Jacqueline's limitless patience allowed me the external reality I needed to complete such a monumental project. Thank you, Jacqueline. You truly are my twin soul.

I thank Great Spirit for giving me the words I needed to share during the writing of this book. I take no ownership of the content of this publication I was only a channel for God to write through me to communicate with you. My hope is that God's words guide you in some loving way.

Finally, I want to thank myself and my editor for having the courage to follow our hearts as we have taken these words and brought them to you.

The 12 steps are adopted with permission of Alcoholics Anonymous world services inc. (A.A.W.S.). Permission to adopt the 12 steps does not mean that A.A.W.S. Has reviewed or approved the content of this publication or that A.A.W.S. Necessarily agrees with the views expressed herein. A.A. Is a program of recovery from alcoholism - use of the 12 steps in connection with programs and activities which are patterned after A.A but which address other problems or in any other non – A. A. Context does not imply otherwise.

Introduction

Dear Friend,

I thank you for the opportunity to share my experience, strength and hope with you today. I am very humbled that you have followed your inner guidance and have chosen to purchase this book.

My name is Joe Mittiga and I am a 36-year-old single man who is walking the same self-discovery path as you are. My intention is to share with you, through my experience that self-love can heal all wounds. As you read about my life's challenges and the depth of spiritual bankruptcy in which I lived perhaps you will be able to say to yourself, "If he can heal, so can I."

Today my life is filled with love, hope and the grace of Spirit in my heart. I talk my walk as well as walk my talk. My life was totally transformed into a spiritual reality as a consequence of learning and acting on the self-loving techniques I'm about to share with you throughout this book. I am a teacher not a preacher my friend so please feel free to take with you any aspect of this book that works for you and willfully leave the rest.

My desire is to paint the picture of my personal despair as clearly and as intimately as I can. This is called my experience. I will teach you the self-loving techniques I learned that allowed me to feel what I needed to heal. This is called my strength. I will share with you how I gained the courage I needed to follow my heart's desire and to pursue a life and career filled with love and abundance. This is called my hope.

My promise to you is that I will be as honest and as accurate as I possibly can throughout this book in order to gain your trust as well as your friendship. My dream is that one day our paths will cross, and you will share with me how in some small way my gifts from God have enhanced your life.

PART ONE

This book is based on the actual experiences in my life and the lives of friends around me. We are neither doctors nor psychiatrists. We are just common people like you; questing to heal, questing to love and be loved, and questing to be all that we can be.

CHAPTER 1

Where it All Begins

As I stood in confusion and terror, I asked God to take away my sixteen-year need for drugs and alcohol. Seven days before I made this request, I sat with a friend in the basement of his home. Getting stoned and drunk was an everyday event for us. The only difference on this afternoon was the content of our conversation. My friend was telling me of his inability to go ninety days without drinking, as was suggested to him in his first exploration into the Alcoholics Anonymous program. My immediate thought was how anyone could possibly go ninety days without any mind-altering or body-altering substance. This idea seemed totally impossible to me.

As our conversation about alcoholism continued to progress, the rationalizing voice in my head got very loud and strong saying, "I don't drink very much anymore, so there is no problem with me; it's just my friend's problem." Then I took another sip of my beer.

At this point on my path I still thought that outside sources were the cause of all of my internal feelings. As I looked into his eyes, I saw the tremendous amount of guilt and shame he was experiencing so I, in turn, blamed all of his feelings on the A.A. program. Never once had I thought these feelings were already in existence inside of him.

We continued our conversation and our personal inebriation became more and more intense. I started to wonder what it would be like not to drink or smoke marijuana every day. The thought of this, like in a dream, seemed so far-fetched that it was hard to hold on to. Reflected in the eyes of my friend, how- ever, were my own potential feelings of guilt and shame. I was convinced in that moment that sobriety was about experiencing all of these feelings, so I wanted nothing to do with it.

As we continued drinking, my mind wandered back in time. I remembered my childhood, which had very little alcohol in it. The occasional glass of wine my father drank at dinner seemed appropriate to me. I also witnessed moderation in drinking by both of my parents in celebration situations, which also seemed harmless. My parents fit in well in all social situations, so it seemed quite normal to see them with a drink in hand.

Following in my parents' footsteps, my own drinking also seemed very normal. Everywhere I went I, too, seemed to fit in with a drink in my hand. As time went on, and my alcohol and drug consumption increased, my feelings of isolation and false sense of purpose also grew. I began to understand the meaning of the term "liquid courage" because only with some type of chemical substance in my body did the false feelings of being protected from the world become strong. My need for this protection was so great because of my paranoid belief that everyone and everything was out to get me. With alcohol and drugs in my system, my perception of the world was that of a very scary, very dark place.

My need for this liquid courage seemed to grow every day. My fear of the world seemed to consume me as if a blanket were being pulled over my body. The more fear I felt, the more I needed to drink to experience this false sense of protection. It was like a never-ending cycle. The more I drank and drugged for courage, the more my insecurities grew.

Looking back, I now realize that drugs and alcohol were protecting me from feeling the deep fear and grief in my heart. Though not unlike any false belief, time is the only variable until it just doesn't protect us anymore.

Throughout my entire life, it seemed "protectors" or "ego parts" (drugs, alcohol, sex, etc.) had saved my life. Back in my drug-filled days, I felt I needed these protectors to live. Sitting on the couch, back in the reality of my basement dwelling, I started to realize that it had been many years since I had gone consecutive days without some type of numbing substance in my body.

My mind continued to wander back to high school days where the standing challenge of who could drink the most alcohol was a daily ritual. It seemed as though whoever could drink the most liquor was recognized as the king of the world; and for me, being on top of the world was exactly where I felt I belonged. Little did I know that this type of extreme arrogance and attitude only enhanced my protector parts to drink and smoke more heavily. For me, the definition of a good time was going out with my friends, getting drunk, and raising hell. Life was nothing but a big party.

When I was eighteen years old, during the spring break of my senior year, several of my closest friends and I headed to Florida to broaden our drinking and partying horizons. The first thing we did upon entering the city limits of Daytona Beach was to head straight for a liquor store. You can imagine the feeling of freedom we felt being in a city where we were legally able to drink. As I walked into the liquor store, I felt like a kid in a candy shop. I bought three large bottles of alcohol, thinking this might last a day or two. I visited the liquor store several more times that week trying to satisfy my need to numb myself.

Now on that particular weekend, our rival high school happened to be in the same city on the same portion of beach. My ego's false need to show the world that I was a "real man" was very great. So when I was challenged to guzzle a quart of whiskey, of course I accepted immediately. Within minutes of this challenge, it was my turn to start drinking. I opened a full bottle of whiskey, poured it into an empty beer pitcher, and proceeded to drink the entire bottle in one breath. As I finished, and everyone in the room yelled and screamed at my accomplishment, I felt on top of the world. My ego would tell me over and over that I was a big man because I could drink so much alcohol.

As my challenger started his pursuit to victory, he opened his full bottle of whiskey, threw the lid on the floor, and proceeded to drink the entire content straight from the bottle. I felt an extreme sense of defeat because he could guzzle from the bottle and I could not. My ego then took me from the top of the hill to the bottom of the gutter. I felt like such a loser because, in my mind, I had lost my reputation as the best drinker in town.

The only thing I can remember from the rest of that insane night was walking on the beach with a friend and vomiting most of what I had drunk. *(Looking back on it now, fifteen years later, it is very clear to me that Great Spirit was taking care of me that night, and that is the only reason I did not die from alcohol poisoning. The sole reason I share this story is to demonstrate how powerfully insane our ego and addictions can be in our lives.)*

My mind continued its wandering, drifting on to my college years where I saw the same patterns happening for me. Drinkers and party-goers seemed to be attracted to me like metal shavings to a magnet. If there was a party with drugs and alcohol present, I always seemed to be attracted to it. The biggest difference, though, between my college years and my high school years was that for the first time in my life, I started to experience the deep feelings of loneliness and abandonment associated with my changing life.

During my senior year in high school, my father had moved one thousand miles away from home to seek the "Promised Land." He was on a mission to find his family's new future in the south. Although this seemed a noble act, it left me feeling extremely alone and afraid.

As my college days came and my path led me to change, the empty feelings in my stomach and heart began to grow. At this point in my life, I felt very uncomfortable and lonely most of the time. I seemed to be experiencing life as an outsider looking in. My obsession to be with my father grew every day. As a consequence of this personal obsession, all of my summers and all of my school breaks were spent traveling a thousand miles away from my home to be with him. The rest of the time, on weekends or midweek breaks, my abandonment issues and unreleased grief took me north to visit my mother and the girl of my dreams.

Regardless of whether I traveled north or south, I never felt I belonged. Growing in me every day was the desire to be "fixed" by someone or something outside of myself. No matter where I was or with whom, I always felt very lonely, with an emptiness inside me.

As my college years passed, my substance abuse grew. My fear of authority and having a boss led me into business for myself. With no experience or direction, I started a roofing company on sheer commitment and determination. I had dreams of filling the empty hole inside of me with a successful business. However, with years of hard work and difficult learning experiences, I never felt this hole ever filled. It was like a vicious circle; the more I worked, the more stress I created for myself. With this self-induced stress came more fear, and with the fear came a higher level of substance abuse. Even though my external life seemed very functional, I still felt very, very empty inside. In fact, stress I created for myself. With this self-induced stress came more fear, and with the fear came a higher level of substance abuse. Even though my external life seemed very functional, I still felt very, very empty inside. In fact, no amount of work, drugs, relationships, or sex seemed to give me any relief.

At this stage of my life, I never thought to ask Great Spirit for any guidance and support because I "knew" in my mind God would want nothing to do with me. It felt very hypocritical for someone like me–who was partying and drinking and smoking and chasing women all week long–to then go on Sunday and ask God for help. It seemed especially so when I knew so well that on Monday I would be right back behaving exactly as I had the week before. At this point on my path, I wanted no part of this thing called God, and I decided He could want nothing to do with me, either.

Again my awareness was brought back into my basement dwelling. As I was sitting on that couch that particular afternoon, I started remembering my thinking patterns during my middle twenties. I remembered how I used to wonder how my life could have gotten any worse. Even though my external life seemed fine, my internal world was full of holes and I was very lonely.

Then one day late in 1989, my life hit a new emotional bottom. A phone call came from my relatives back home telling me that my grandmother had been in an accident and wasn't doing very well. In a state of panicked confusion, my entire immediate family rushed north to care for my grandmother; however, my own work responsibilities did not allow me this freedom.

I remembered sitting in fear and anticipation, waiting to hear of her health condition. As time went on, and I was able to talk to her, she reassured me that she was okay. My grandmother was the one person in this world I truly loved, and I knew she loved me. Throughout my entire life she listened to me and advised me. She gave me a home during my toughest years and was always there for me. She was the one and only stable thing I had in my world. I felt as though I owed her so much in return for loving me.

The last words I heard from her mouth were, "Joe, thank you for calling me." I never imagined she would pass on. I never considered the possibility of her leaving me; but on September 1, 1989, she did just that.

When I heard the news about her death, the emptiness inside of me became overwhelming. I was so angry and so sad that she had left me, some days I couldn't see straight. The pain inside became so great that my need for substances to numb my feelings increased dramatically. During the week before her funeral, I consumed two quarts of whiskey a day to alleviate my pain.

I had no conscious awareness of what emotions were, let alone how to nurture them. My path led me to two DUIs and one weekend in jail.

My obsession to fill my enormous wounds inside actually led me to break into a friend's parents' home just to wait for her to arrive. I felt an extreme need just to be hugged and held by her. The insanity of the situation was that she wanted nothing to do with me. My thoughts were, "Maybe if she sees me she will change her mind." The reality was, my uninvited presence in her home scared her to death, and she ran out the door yelling for help!

The emptiness inside of me at this point was so big, it totally ran my entire life. The consequence of my choice to enter my friend's home uninvited was to be thrown in jail. I was issued a court order not to call, write, or be within five hundred yards of this young woman. However, the pain inside was so great I disobeyed the law and still made contact. I would have done anything to relieve my internal pain.

One day my father looked me straight in the eyes and said, "Have you lost your mind? You are going to jail if you keep contacting her." I was in such a daze that I could not comprehend anything he was saying. All I knew was that I needed relief. My God, I just needed relief.

They say that time heals all wounds. In my case, the wounds just festered! My drug, alcohol, sex, and work addictions all escalated to an every day occurrence. I changed geographic locations several times in hopes of some relief, though nothing seemed to help. The agony I felt inside was overwhelming.

Sitting on that couch in my friend's basement, I remembered the feeling of living in total hopelessness and abject despair. I had realized, even back then, that something was wrong with me, although I had no idea what it was.

Then one day I was sitting in my mother's house feeling lonely and depressed, with tears streaming from my eyes, and I thought, "I NEED HELP!" Later I realized what I was actually feeling was grief and fear. Back then I was so emotionally closed down that I did not even realize I was crying. In fact, I did not know that emotions are standard and normal characteristics of who we really are as human beings.

I sat there that day crying and asking for help; and help is what I got. For the first time in my adult life, I felt like things might be okay. This is when I was introduced to my inner child for the first time.

My inner child was an aspect of me that I never knew existed. I was twenty-six years old when I started my inner emotional quest for peace. Even though this was only the first step of my emotional path, it was certainly the largest step I had ever taken. With this step, I literally went from a totally unconscious lifestyle to living a life where conscious choice became my reality. I realized that the wounds I was feeling were inside of me, and now for the first time, I had hope they could be healed.

Soul Mate

As we journey down our paths of life, We often times cross
paths with a spirit of
Great importance to us.
We often times know right away that this person Is someone
very special in our journey.
Daily growth allows us to feel and experience a similar love and
Compassion for each other, as though
Acquired years and years ago.
We come to understand this experience To be a soul mate
relationship.
This relationship is cherished for a lifetime.
Deep love is created on a daily basis.
Love that sometimes leads the relationship to separate, Though
never dwindle apart.
Soul mates are inner lovers, life after life after life. It is a
blessed day when you happen upon a friend You call soul mate.

Soul Mate

CHAPTER 2

Seeking Help

Seeking help was not something that was easy for me at all. I was raised in a very traditional Italian family where the man was taught to be the strong one and the leader. In my reality, men were supposed to be tough and fearless. I also totally believed in the social paradigm that if a man shows any emotion, he is a sissy; if a woman shows any strength, she is a bitch. I grew up believing that to be in control of my emotions was to be in control of my entire life. I needed such extreme control because without it, my world seemed totally unbearable.

I also lived in a family where it was not okay to be angry. In fact, you were taking your life into your own hands if you expressed any type of anger at home. My father grew up with a rageaholic mother, so in turn, all he knew was personal trauma in regard to expressing anger. He forbade any expression of anger in our home and as a natural consequence of this rule, every time I felt this emotion inside myself, I also experienced deep feelings of shame and guilt. At my core, I knew I was a bad seed, the evil one; or better yet, just totally crazy because I was so angry all of the time. Since I was never taught how to express my anger in a healthy way, it would boil up until it was time for me to explode.

I remember one experience when an old girlfriend of mine was meeting a male friend of hers at a bar where I was drinking. When I spotted them together, all I saw was red. As I watched them go outside to talk to each other, I followed them very quickly. In my pursuit, the only feeling I held in my heart was rage. As I approached the exterior doors of this huge hotel lobby, I remember hitting them with one rage-filled blow, knocking them entirely off their hinges. I stepped through the opening and grabbed the young man by the neck, pinning him up against a brick post. By that time I was screaming at my ex-girlfriend, totally unaware I was choking this young man into submission. My internal stuffed rage was so great, and my inability to express my emotions in a healthy way was so meek, that very often in fits of rage, I would vomit all of this stuffed inner pain onto anyone in my path. That's exactly what I did that night.

I've shared this story to illustrate how my life really was. This was not an extreme case for me, but an example of an every day occurrence. I want to make it clear that finding and healing our inner child wounds IS NOT ABOUT BLAMING our parents, siblings, or our environment, although throughout this book I will describe the emotional harm that has been done to us as a natural consequence of emotionally growing up in a dysfunctional world.

The truth is, our parents did the best they could. Being brought up in an unconscious world themselves, they had no basis for how to raise their children in any other way. It remains a case of the blind leading the blind, where no one gets very far emotionally. Our parents, and all parents, have done the best they know how to do.

We, however, are the GENERATION OF CHANGE. We have the internal emotional ability to be different from the generations that preceded us. We have the ability to love differently, to act differently, and to live differently. In order to make these lifetime changes, though, we need to be willing to do whatever it takes.

For me, I needed to seek outside therapy and an outside loving support system to help me through my journey toward serenity. When I first got started on this emotional quest, to actually seek support was extremely terrifying for me. Looking back, this is one of the first times I could understand that God was doing for me what I could not do for myself.

It takes a tremendous amount of courage to seek and learn about oneself. Left to my own devices, I could never be here at this conscious level. I know today that Great Spirit is the source of all of my internal courage. I thank God every day that I was at a place to be able to receive and act on this God-given gift of inner wisdom and inner courage.

The idea of consciously seeking a therapist on my own was totally foreign to me back then. In fact, the very act of calling my first therapist in a small town near my home was almost impossible for me. My fears of people, places, and things were so great that I was paralyzed in my own terror at the thought of making this call. (It's important to share that I was an owner/operator of a small business with ten employees at the time. So please don't let the ego statement, "I've got a job, so I must be okay," stop you from seeking emotional support, like I did.) The first several appointments were actually made and paid for by my mother.

Meeting Mary, my therapist, literally saved my life. Up until this point, I never knew this type of healthy environment even existed. My interpretation of a therapist was a guy with short hair, tiny glasses, and a funny accent. My new friend, Mary, was none of these. She was nice, gentle, and very understanding with me. She created an environment where I could talk to an individual with a non-biased opinion; where I was never judged, just listened to. She never told me what to do; she only made suggestions. She never criticized me; she only spoke loving words of encouragement. Because of her loving behavior, I noticed a tangible difference in how I felt each time I would visit her at her office.

Week after week, month after month, we would sit and talk about my general problems. Then on one magical day, as if by an act of God, Mary started teaching me about my inner child. As she spoke to me, I had no idea intellectually what she was talking about, although I seemed to relate to everything she said. At this point on my path I was not consciously aware of the aspect of a self who could totally relate to Mary's every word, but I do know it all seemed to feel true.

Her explanation of the inner child was very simple. She said that as we mature in a dysfunctional world, a part of us called the inner child, does not receive the emotional support it needs to thrive and survive. She said that through hypnosis and imagery work of the mind, we can reeducate this aspect of ourselves to believe that everything is okay. I thought what she said seemed really cool, and I was game to continue if she was.

Our first session of imagining the child within me was very simple. She told me to relax by taking several deep breaths in and out—you know, those full, slow breaths you feel deep in your stomach. I did this several times over and over. Then she said to allow my mind to wander into my childhood. She told me not to pick a time, just allow it to come up for me. Eventually I saw a little boy playing Little League baseball. (Later in this book, I will explain in detail the entire meditation technique I used to reconnect to my little boy.)

He was standing out in left field wearing a Minnesota Twins baseball uniform. He seemed to be continually looking around, paying little attention to the game. Then I sensed the little boy was at this game all alone. Mary asked me to describe in detail what I saw, and then she asked me to walk up to the little boy and say hello. As I did this, I got the feeling I knew him, but for the life of me I didn't know from where. Then it hit me! I just knew it! The vision I was seeing in my mind's eye was me—my little boy inside; lost, alone, and very afraid.

I didn't know what to do at this point and became very confused, so I lost the image. Disappointed in losing it, I felt a sense of shame. Mary was very loving and understanding with me as she confirmed my understanding. She told me that this vision was my inner child and I could reach him at any time I chose.

My session ended and as I left Mary's office, I felt excitement mixed with confusion. My mind was racing. My ego kept saying to me, "This can't be true. How could any of this stuff help me?" As I drove away, I thought that all of this "inner child stuff" is baloney. So I turned on the radio as a distraction.

While driving, I became more relaxed and my mind started wandering back to that little boy inside of me. Now, though, the vision was that of a child sitting all alone in anticipation, as though he were waiting for something. I kept driving, only giving brief thought to this new vision.

That evening, while talking to a friend and getting stoned, I saw this little boy again in my mind's eye. He still seemed to be waiting for someone, although I didn't know who. Then it hit me, as if by another act of God–this little boy wasn't waiting for just anyone, he was waiting for me! A feeling of reality hit my inebriated body as never before. I knew in that moment that Mary was right; connecting with my inner child would help me. I had no idea how or why, but I truly felt this newly discovered connection would help.

◆ ◆ ◆

For the sake of clarification I want to stop my story for a moment and explain in more detail what I mean when I refer to the aspect of self called the inner child; who and what the inner child is, and where he/she resides. What I am about to explain is information I learned through years of personal experiences well after this point in my story.

The inner child is the emotional aspect of self which resides in all human beings. It is the part of self that feels the basic emotions of anger, happiness, sorrow, and fear (mad, glad, sad, and scared). It permits us to dream again just as we did when we were children, allowing us to be spontaneous and full of life. It is a reconnection to our childlike faith in God, as well as all of the true wisdom of the universe.

The inner child is the natural connection with true compassion for other human beings and all the beings in God's creation. When we reconnect with the inner child in us, we begin to feel totally whole inside. For me personally, it is in this wholeness that I have remembered my connection to my Higher

Power and to Great Spirit. It is deep inside our inner child that we will find our natural feelings of vulnerability, humility, and a deep sense of inner peace. The inner child allows us to close the gap between our personal emotion of love and the love of Great Spirit.

Now of course, on some level, we all know that the above-mentioned reality is truly what we desire. So the question is, if we all have an inner child, why don't we all live in the truest sense of inner peace? The answer is that we all have the ability to feel these wonderful loving aspects of life, though most of our personal, internal peace is buried deep inside ourselves under layers and layers of inner wounds.

Very few of us have known how to develop or nurture our inner child. In fact, most of us have been raised in an environment where the little kid in ourselves was not only neglected, but shamed into complete seclusion.

Let me share with you a few examples to illustrate my point. When you were a child perhaps you heard these words, "Stop that crying or I will give you something to cry about," or "You should have known better," even though you were only seven years old. Perhaps you grew up in a household where it was not okay to express anger. In my home, the only people allowed to get angry were my parents, and my mother could only express her anger when my father was not around because he refused to allow anger to be expressed. So whenever I felt angry, I had to suppress this natural emotion, thereby suppressing my inner child. As if this external reality wasn't hurtful enough, my ego reinforced this untrue belief that the emotion of anger was not okay. Therefore, every time I felt angry, not only did my surrounding world shame me into sub- mission, my own ego voices learned how to shame me, too. I would say to myself, "I am angry, but anger is not okay, so I must not be okay."

As a consequence of this false belief, I always felt like something was wrong with me. In fact, the effects of this internal false belief were totally devastating to me because the consequence of this internal shame caused my little kid to close down completely. Another false belief that totally invalidates the inner child of males is the belief that big boys don't cry. That statement to me is total baloney, though it has been projected on us men since the beginning of time.

Intellectually then, let us stop and think about this unloving reality for a moment. If every time in our life when we were angry and needed to express this rage, or if we were sad and needed to express our grief, and we were not allowed to do so, where did this energy go? The answer is that all this unexpressed emotion is still suppressed inside of us, and it is covering up our inner child's true love and joy one layer at a time.

Here are a few more examples of the different ways in which our inner child or our emotional self has been hurt and buried over the years. Any type of physical, verbal, psychological, or especially sexual abuse to us as actual children will create an internal reality for our inner child that will cause him/her to be buried under layers of grief, fear, and anger. Also, any type of personal invalidation or shaming us as children can cause a tremendous amount of harm to our inner child in later years.

As children, in order to develop our emotional selves, our primary inherent needs are to be validated and loved by our environmental source figures. For most children, these source figures are our parents. So if we were raised by parents who were emotionally unavailable, or who did not know how to verbally communicate or show their love, then naturally, an environment was created that inhibited the emotional development of our inner child. As a consequence of this type of limited emotional availability, a child will grow up very confused because deep inside each child's heart is the intuitive knowledge that love and validation are needed for healthy growth.

When outside loving support is not given to us as children, our only means of protection is to close down our vulnerable inner self. To perpetuate the closing down process, our inner voices start to say, "I know I need to be loved by my parents, but since they don't give me this love, there must be something wrong with me." As a consequence of the internal false belief that there is something wrong with us, our inner child will close itself down to protect itself, hiding under more and more layers of anger and grief.

The amazing thing for me is that the entire process of human emotional development can be summed up in this passage from the Bible, "...visiting the iniquity of the fathers upon the children, and upon the children's children to the third and the fourth generation," (Exodus 34:7). What this means to me is that as parents we emotionally end up raising our own children the exact same way our parents emotionally raised us, even though we promise ourselves a thousand times we will never treat our children the way our parents treated us. I have always wondered why this happens. I believe it is because as children, in order to protect ourselves, our ego parts had to cover up the truth of our need for love and support from outside sources. So over time, the natural human development of these unloved ego parts creates a reality which eventually runs our lives and all of our choices. As a consequence of this development, the same unloving voices that are running our lives are the exact same voices that were running the lives of our parents. Hence, the emotional awareness of the father is passed on to the son. The bottom line is that emotionally you are going to interact in your world of today exactly the same way you emotionally experienced your world as a child, unless you consciously choose to change.

My hope is that I can show you, step-by-step, how I healed my inner emotional self and how in turn, the fear-based ego that used to guide my life has transformed into my Higher Self. As a natural consequence of this internal healing, I now live in a world filled with peace, love, and serenity. By healing the wounded parts of me, my feeling of wholeness is absolutely tremendous. For me, the natural consequence of this newly-found wholeness has not only been the creation of a deep connection with Great Spirit, but the realization that I live in complete freedom of all my fear-based ego voices. I hope that you will acquire the tools you need to create your own sense of this magical freedom.

As I now continue with my story using the terms inner child, little kid, or emotional self, you will have a clearer understanding of who and what I am talking about.

◆ ◆ ◆

I went several weeks without even a thought of this inner child vision, let alone my little kid himself. The family business I owned kept me working seventy to eighty hours a week because of the illusion, "If I had a lot of money, I would be okay." In addition to my work schedule, I also exercised five to six nights a week because of the false belief system that said, "If my physical body were big and strong, then everybody would love me."

I also had a girlfriend who was just as addicted to sex as I was. I could have sexual interactions at least nine or ten times a week because of the false belief system that says, "sex equals love." So when you add drinking five nights a week and smoking marijuana every day, it's no wonder I didn't have any time for my inner child.

I was addicted to everything in an extreme way and never knew why! Then one day I was sitting in a session bitching and complaining that my dad did this, and my girlfriend wasn't good enough to be loved, and my workout partner was a drug addicted loser. Mary, my therapist, stopped me and said, "Joe, that which we see or judge in others is a true description of ourselves on some level." After she said this, it finally became clear to me what she was actually talking about. For the first time in my life I could truly say that I understood what she meant about criticizing other people. She had made the exact statement to me before, but on that day I became aware of its true meaning.

I realized that as I am judging and criticizing other people, I am actually describing my own unconscious interpretation of myself. So if I think someone else is a drug addicted loser, then in actuality some part of me, deep inside, feels as though I am a drug addicted loser, also! Or if I think my girlfriend is not good enough to be loved, then some aspect of myself feels as though I am not good enough to be loved, either. For the first time on my path I became aware of the actual reality of being a multi-dimensional human being. The truth is, even though we are not consciously connected to our own inner wounds, that does not mean those wounds do not exist.

I remember saying to Mary, "You mean to tell me that all of the horrible things I see in other people are truly inside of me?" Mary never spoke; she only nodded her head in an affirmative way as I sat there in shock. The truth is, I was totally unaware of how much pain I had inside myself. I just never knew! I left Mary's office that day confused and very afraid. I kept saying to myself, "How can I possibly have all of that pain inside of this perfect body?" My ego was so big that I had convinced myself for many years that I really didn't have any pain at all. How could I? I felt like I was a god and since a god is perfect, so am I.

That night, though, while I was listening to the tape that Mary had given me during our session, I saw my little boy again. This time, however, unlike my other experiences, I just walked up to him and sat down. I was too afraid to say anything, and my little boy would not voluntarily look up. So we just sat there. I finally felt myself coming down off of my daily marijuana buzz, feeling extremely frightened and alone. I realized I was in a lot of internal pain, but did not know what to do about it. I was lost, and alone, and full of fear.

It was on this night that I became aware for the first time in my life that I was truly paralyzed in terror. I lay there that night helpless in my own fear, not being able to move or talk. As the night wore on, all I could hope for was to fall asleep; and after shaking with terror for three or four hours, sleep finally came.

To Embrace Our Fears

There is no light without darkness, no life without death, No
love without fear.
To embrace our fears is to give love to the unknown Parts of
ourselves that are still hidden.
To love the dark side of who we are Takes tremendous amounts
of courage.
In life we so very often walk to what we know Because seeking
the unknown creates change. Even though change is the most
feared event Life puts in front of us,
Change is also very necessary for our growth.
So as we face our fears, we create a personal growth in love.

Love is that unconditional feeling of abundance That we create
as we connect inside.
The connection to the child within
Brings us trust and faith in our Spirit throughout.
Embracing our fears means loving ourselves unconditionally.
Embracing our fears means to grow Where no one has grown
before.
Embracing our fears is to feel the love of Spirit, And know who
we truly are.
Embracing our fears—what a challenge.
It takes courage from a deep unknown place.
Embracing our fears means we live in the love of
Who we truly are.

To Embrace Our Fears

17

CHAPTER 3

Living in Euphoria

In some ways my life became better as the years continued, but in other ways it became worse. My intellectual understanding of the inner child concept grew each day. I realized that by just spending a little time using this concept on a daily basis, my knowledge surrounding my inner child grew more extensively. My external life, however, was not getting any better at all. I was still working eighty or more hours a week, lifting weights, and getting stoned daily. My biggest dilemma at this point in my life was trying to figure out why my business would not grow. I knew in my heart that if I could make more money, I would feel better. I just knew it!

My addiction to marijuana had become an every day, every hour, and every minute experience. I smoked marijuana like most people smoked cigarettes. My ego was so massive that I would walk around in public places smoking a joint, rationalizing it to myself by saying, "No one would ever expect this to be marijuana out here in broad daylight. And anyway, if anyone says anything to me, I will just beat the shit out of them." To tell you the truth, all of my thoughts and actions during those days were totally insane. Looking back, I realize that it was because of this insanity that my business had no chance to grow and prosper.

There was an extreme void in my life at this point. All I did was work, smoke, and play pool in strip clubs. Then one day my life was changed forever. I looked across the room, saw a waitress, and fell in love at first sight. She had waist-long blond hair, blue eyes, and a smile that was absolutely incredible. I knew in that moment that I had to meet this beauty. A friend of mine who worked with my "new love" told me that her name was Angel and that she could arrange for us to meet.

A few days later, as I was sitting at a table drinking beer, Angel walked up to me and as she touched my shoulder she said, "You need to sit in my section." I knew by this first touch that she loved me as much as I loved her, and that my life would never be the same.

◆◆◆

Now before I go any further, I want to describe my illusion of love more clearly, to show how addicted to love, sex, and relationships I truly was. The truth of this situation was that I was sitting in a bar with a hundred naked women, drunk and stoned, THINKING that I was feeling the sensation of love at first sight. To make the scenario even more insane, later I found out that Angel had a husband who was living in Los Angeles. For me, though, my addictions to love, sex, and relationships were so massive I did not consider Angel's marital status to be an issue that would hinder our relationship at all. At that point in my life, I honestly believed that I had found and connected with the love of my life; so nothing was going to stop me from pursuing our experience together.

◆ ◆ ◆

The next two months for me were absolutely euphoric. I was in love with a beautiful girl who loved me, too. Seven days after Angel and I met, I moved into her apartment with her because I knew my problems were over. I was so in love with this girl I even tried to give up smoking marijuana because she did not like it. My good intentions did not last very long, although I did try because of my illusion of love for her. For me life was great! Our relationship together was new and the sex was fantastic and alive. In fact, we spent hours together in the shower just talking about anything that life had to offer us. All of my senses told me that this was the girl I was going to marry.

Angel and I were alike in many ways. She enjoyed drinking, talking, and having sex as much as I did. In fact, looking back, she filled every hole I had. As far as I was concerned, Angel was absolutely perfect for me, and I knew I was going to spend the rest of my life with her.

I was so in love, I didn't even care that my business was in trouble. To be honest, nothing mattered to me in my outside world because of this newly-found illusion. I remember thinking to myself that God had finally blessed my life because he had led me to the woman of my dreams in that strip club that night. Everything in my world was great because I lived in the euphoria of "cloud nine" for two or three months. I even remember talking to Mary about Angel and expressing to her my hopes and dreams of creating a lifelong relationship.

Now at this point in my internal process, I had gained an extremely keen intellectual understanding of the inner child concept. My understanding was that all I had to do was use my imagination and bingo, there was my inner kid. In fact, during the beginning years of creating this new inner knowing, I felt as if that was exactly what I was doing—just using my imagination.

I knew that my inner child was inside of me, although to tell you the truth, he always felt very separate from me. And even after working with Mary for over three and half years, I still felt as though there had to be something more. The cliche " fake it till you make it" just was not working for me anymore.

The idea of leaving Mary never entered my mind, even though I was seeking more.

My life with Angel seemed to solidify itself when she, too, started visiting Mary in the hopes of learning more about her inner child. The woman of my dreams was also seeking out her inner child and I was absolutely elated!

My external world seemed to be going very well, even though my internal world still felt restless and lonely. I just did not understand why I still felt so terrible inside. (Today I realize nothing outside of myself can fill my internal holes. I also understand that to fill my internal holes, I have to create an internal healing process for myself; although I did not understand this back then.) What happened for me next on my path dropped me to my knees in my own overwhelming reality of inner pain.

My relationship with Angel seemed to be going extremely well except for three things. First, I tried to stop smoking marijuana for her, but I could not. Without drugs in my system, I was much too scared and insecure in my life. So I kept smoking, but began lying to Angel about it. The reason I lied was because of my codependent need to get her approval and love. My dishonest illusion lasted for a little while until over time, my lies caught up with me and caused us a tremendous amount of trouble.

The second aspect of our relationship that really bothered me was that Angel would call her husband in Los Angeles and ask him for money. Of course, I never shared my concerns with her because I was too cool to admit I was jealous.

The third aspect of our experience together that hurt our relationship was when Angel started staying out of the apartment, partying later and later into the night without me. Several times she even stayed out the entire night without telling me where she was. I knew something funny was going on, but I did not want to know the truth because my addiction to this dream relationship was so strong that no unloving behavior was going to stop me from working things out between us.

I never shared my problems about Angel with Mary because I figured I could handle our situation by myself. Mary and I only talked about my relationship with my father and why I felt so abandoned by him. Then one day during work, I became consciously aware that my father had never really been there for me throughout my entire life. So when Mary and I saw each other the following week, we talked about this new awareness in detail. That day in session, Mary asked me to imagine my father with a baseball uniform on, playing catch with me. At this place on my path, this new mental vision actually lifted my spirits.

♦ ♦ ♦

The imagery work I completed during those three and half years of my life taught me how to intellectually understand my inner child's wounds. Even though this imagery work probably saved my life, it did not heal the internal wounds of my inner child that I was feeling in my heart. The reason is because mental imagery work is done in the mind, and internal wounds are in the heart. So by definition, most mental imagery work only acts as a bandage over the wound that is growing in our heart! Now for me, this bandage was exactly what was needed during the process of healing my inner child, although eventually it would no longer work.

♦ ♦ ♦

That session truly changed my life! I rushed home with excitement to share this new experience with Angel, but she was not there. I was back on "cloud nine" with this new image in my mind, but my heart really hurt because Angel was not there to share it with me.

The next day I confronted Angel about where she had been and what she had been doing the previous evening. After a couple of hours of consistent and aggressive badgering, she finally admitted to me that she had had sexual relations with her separated husband, as well as an old boyfriend. I was absolutely stunned as she blurted out the truth! The energy of this admission knocked me straight back onto the floor where I sat in shock. The love of my life had cheated on me not only once, but twice. I couldn't believe it!

I was in so much pain the next couple of days that I tried to get her to tell me she had been lying to me; but of course she hadn't. Then when the truth settled in and the shock wore off, the pain in my heart and soul increased to a level I never imagined possible. Every old wound that Angel had filled over the previous four months was now open and festering. Every feeling I had thought was true, I now found to be an illusion. Every dream I had held of a beautiful wife and a white picket fence was now smashed. For me, my wonderful illusion was over with one simple statement, "Joe, I cheated on you." I fell into a deep state of darkness and depression, and moved out of Angel's apartment the following week. I was completely confused. I didn't know if it was day or night, and I really didn't care. Even alcohol and drugs would no longer numb my inner pain. Renting a room from a strange man, I spent most of my time inside the confines of those four walls with my head under a pillow. My world as I knew it was destroyed, and again my life was riddled with fear. I remember checking my business pager one day and seeing twenty-seven messages for me to return. I could not bring myself to make these calls because I was too terrified to talk with anyone. Again my life was paralyzed in hurt, anger, and terror.

Over the next couple of months time passed, but nothing really changed for me. I felt totally betrayed and alone again. Parts of me wanted Angel back, although other parts literally hated her. I knew I had to heal, but I had no idea how.

I had a birthday coming up and I was about to turn thirty years old. For my entire life I had looked forward to this birthday because a part of me always fantasized about having a beautiful birthday experience with a beautiful woman. My dream was to sail off into the sunset with someone who loved me, drinking champagne and eating great food. Soon, though, the dream was over and the actual day arrived. The truth is, that day I did spend time with Angel, although it was just long enough for her to tell me that she was going to Florida with an old boyfriend to visit the ocean and to party. I also was able to drink champagne that night, but it was at a smelly, hard-core rock-and-roll bar where I knew no one.

At this point, I recognized something was very wrong with my life. I also remember asking for God's guidance that night for the very first time in my adult life. I had always believed in God even though I honestly did not think God wanted anything to do with me. All alone, with a broken heart, I said these words, "Please help me to see a better life." I never used the word God even though I did ask for a little help.

The next three days were spent in bed with my head under the covers. My fears had totally paralyzed me, and I had a massive struggle going on inside my head because a part of me wanted Angel back, while a larger part didn't. I stayed in bed those three days shaking with terror until I finally realized that the pain I was feeling was not just from my broken heart over Angel. I consciously became aware that the pain I was feeling was in every cell of my body. I was finally able to see that what I was experiencing was not just about Angel's choice to leave me, but it was also about a lifetime of suppressed feelings and fears surrounding all of my abandonment issues.

Three days after my thirtieth birthday, I had what I called my womb experience in Mary's office. During our session that day, I realized on a very deep level that I had felt personally alone and abandoned ever since I experienced living in my mother's womb. It was this womb experience that took me out of my head and into my body for the very first time. I realized in that very moment that my work with Mary was finished. Everything she had taught me had probably saved my life and even though I had a deep sense of gratitude and commitment to her for all she had given me, I knew it was time to move on. I recognized that the time had come for me to actually feel my inner child's pain, not just intellectualize his needs.

One week later, Angel moved back with her husband. Again I found myself frightened and alone, grieving the loss of two very important people in my life. The sorrow I felt over these separations was tremendous, but I knew in my soul it was for my greater good. So here I was, in my heart for the first time, all alone and grieving the sorrows of my entire lifetime.

The Sorrow of Separation

When the path of a loved one Is suddenly changed
And you find yourself physically alone, Often times the sorrow
of separation is great!
Be it by a death or by choice,
The internal feeling of loss is tremendous.
Even though we know that the soul cannot flourish If the heart
does not grieve,
These times in our life are still very difficult and lonely.
Looking inward for the answer,
We sometimes ask ourselves the question, "Why?" The answer
is always the same,
And never seems to get any easier.
The answer is growth.
With grief comes joy. With loss comes abundance.
With all fear comes courage.
My spirit aches with the loss of a friend.
My heart closes
As my soul grieves for a death inside, Knowing all along that
the sorrow of separation
Always brings the glory of wholeness.
Today my heart aches and My soul grieves.
Today my path is clear, Though very thick.
Today I live in pain, so tomorrow my spirit will flourish.

The Sorrow of Separation

CHAPTER 4

Starting Over

The sorrow of my new separations took me emotionally to a place I never knew existed. Being a man, I never felt it was appropriate behavior to cry or feel lonely. I had no basis of past healthy experiences on which to compare these feelings. Quite honestly, my life felt hopeless to me because I was terrified and alone, and had no one to turn to in my time of need.

My own definition of addictive behavior is to actively partake of any action, substance, or internal belief system that alters our true feelings of the moment. Our addictions take us out of our true spiritual state of being, and discount our little kid's needs. Our addictive self is cunning, baffling, and powerful. It will go to any lengths to lie to us and keep us in these unloving behaviors.

Addictions will also do everything they can to protect us from our deep, inner wounds; so in turn, they will fight and scream as they hold on for dear life in hopes of controlling us one last time. In fact, some addictions are so powerful that relief can be obtained only as a natural consequence of the internal realignment with a spiritual act of self, integrating with our Higher Self.

For me, these spiritual acts only happened as a consequence of learning to be a loving adult to my inner child who was able to heal as I allowed the child within me to feel love, comfort, and peace. As a natural consequence of my inner child healing, my inner holes went away and my addictive ego protector parts were also transformed from within, shifting and changing into a loving vibration.

Let's take a moment to identify different parts of our whole self in order to understand the different aspects of self which reside in each of us. We must first comprehend that all human beings—man or woman, black or white, Protestant or Catholic, Democrat, or Republican—are made up of four basic elemental aspects: mental, physical, spiritual, and emotional. The mental and physical aspects of self relate to our masculine side and are our "doing" energies. The spiritual and emotional aspects of self relate to our feminine side and are the "being and allowing" energies.

The objective of conscious growth is to identify and learn from each of these God-given parts, with the ultimate intention to create the perfect balance between all of these aspects. The natural consequence of this balanced integration is a total feeling of oneness with Great Spirit. In this newly-found place of oneness, we will live life with a grand sense of inner peace, love, and serenity. We will be able to act in total love toward all of mankind.

Here is a diagram of your male side and female side: Mental/ Physical and Spiritual/Emotional.

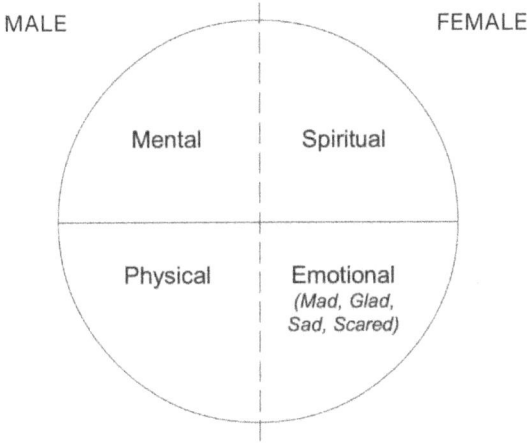

```
        MALE                                    FEMALE

                  Mental  |  Spiritual

                  --------+--------

                  Physical |  Emotional
                           |  (Mad, Glad,
                           |  Sad, Scared)
```

Mental/Physical Characteristics: assertiveness, action steps, thinking, rationalization, choices, working with numbers, exercise, diet, etc.

Spiritual/Emotional Characteristics: feelings (mad, glad, sad, scared), oneness, vulnerability, humility, openness, receiving, communication, etc.

Most people, including myself, are familiar with the masculine side of our reality. As a society we live in the male-dominated world of "doing" and the false illusion that the more we think and do, the more power we have. We also foster the false belief that in order to deserve love and attention, we must be physically attractive.

Our governments and religions are also perfect examples of societal institutions that are based on the hierarchy of ego-based male energy. The false belief system that says the more bombs we have, the more power and control we have is all based on the male energy of doing. Also, the doctrine of any church that says if you don't do what the church says you're supposed to do, then you're going to burn in hell as a sinner is a perfect example of a fear-based ego energy that is trying to manipulate and control its society.

I share these examples not in disrespect for our government or any religion, but to give examples of massive organizations that use fear-based male belief systems to control their worlds. It's important to also understand that dominating male energy is not just isolated to the behaviors of men. The women's rights movement of the '60s and '70s is a perfect example of how women used their aggressive male energies to get what they wanted.

Another expression of male energy has to do with parenting. For example, when we, as parents, tell our children what to do rather than show them how to act, we are using our male energy. Manipulative choices of our fear-based ego include threatening, shaming, or striking our children in order to control their behaviors.

An example of fear-based male energy is when we try to manipulate or control another human being by using fear, guilt, or any other type of shaming technique. I remember several times in the past whenever a girlfriend would break up with me, I would use all of these techniques to try to get her back into my life. My codependent behaviors during these years were so prevalent that I would do or say anything to get what I wanted. For example, I would send my old girlfriend cards to try to manipulate her back into my life using guilt; or I would threaten with physical force any man she was around to try and scare her back into my world. I also would continually call her on the phone to tell her how she made me feel loved and secure.

My internal wounds were so big that I would try to shame her by telling her over and over again that because I loved her so much, she was crazy not to be with me. I would tell her that no one else would ever be able to make her as happy as I did. In fact, I even went as far as to say, "We might be separated now, but in three or four months you will realize you have made a big mistake, and you will beg me to let you come back into my life."

My addictive need for control over another human being was so great during that period in my life that I would behave in any manipulative manner that might get me my own way. The reason my desire to have this person in my life was so all consuming was because, in my mind, I really thought I was in love with her. The truth is, my codependent protector parts were so big because I had such a huge hole inside my wounded little kid revolving around abandonment issues and neglect. In reality I was not in love, but because of my wounds I was trying very hard to fill my inner holes with the presence of someone else in my life.

Now for those of you whose egos are introverted, maybe you've played the unconscious role of martyr to control your world. Or possibly you totally lost yourself and your desires surrounding your own needs to get your way. For example, you might have had sex with a partner when you really did not want to in order to manipulate your world. This fear-based manipulation takes place because the ego has us thinking, "If I don't have sex or give love to my partner, he or she might leave me." So even if we don't feel like participating, we do it anyway out of fear of being abandoned or left behind. The inverted ego will also say to us that to be a loving person, we must please our partner even though we are hurting ourselves. The truth is, there is nothing loving about any relationship in which either partner is being hurt.

I have a friend, Sue, who was very excited about her upcoming marriage. However, when she was asked what she wanted in her future, she responded with, "John wants to move to Savannah," or "John wants to start a new business," or "John wants to have three kids," or "John wants a house in the country," etc.

My reply to her was, "Sue, that is nice, but what do you want?" Her only answer was, "All I want is to support John's life."

Sue had totally lost herself and her personal desires out of the fear of losing John, and was calling this love! The truth is, her cunning and powerful fear-based ego was lying to her about the essence of this relationship, because when we lose our self in a relationship, there is no real love.

It should be evident now that we all fit into one or more of these fear-based male energies. The question is, what action steps can we take to create a more loving environment in our actual world? The answer is to heal the wounds inside us by first learning and admitting that these wounds exist. Next, we must identify our own unloving behaviors associated with each of our wounds, so in turn, we can change our personal life choices. Finally, we need to reconnect emotionally with the inner child inside us in order to fill our internal holes from the inside out.

I know in the beginning that all of this probably seems like a very tall order, but if I can do it, so can you. It isn't only about identifying your behaviors; it's primarily about becoming empowered in such a way that you, too, can feel the natural consequence of healing your inner self. My hope is that you will be able to identify the different aspects of yourself that you would like to change, and allow me to take you step-by-step toward the creation of each of these loving changes.

CHAPTER 5

The Ego vs. the Loving Adult

There are many different aspects of our fear-based ego. So far I have explained the behaviors and actions of the ego, unloved adult, protector parts, and addictive parts. Now I will explain to you what they actually are and why they are in us all.

I use all of these terms interchangeably because during my own process, I felt more comfortable with specific terminology at different stages of growth. For me, ego and addictions were two words I internally struggled with for a long, long time. These words sounded ugly and horrible to me because I felt a deep, paralyzing shame inside of me each time I even thought of myself as being addicted to anything. So in order to protect myself from this feeling of shame, my ego would say to me that I had no addictions at all. As a consequence of this high level of denial, the circle of pain in my life continued to grow larger and larger. My ego was lying to me and in fact, my addictions were running my life.

As a natural consequence of living in addiction, my inner child was totally denied and left alone one hundred percent of the time, causing even more wounds. Because of this additional pain, my ego and addictive parts had to work even harder using more alcohol, drugs, sex, and anything else to keep me out of my deep, inner child pain.

It was not until I met my new counselor, Sandy, that I truly understood the hurtful dynamics of this vicious circle. The more pain I felt inside, the harder my protectors, or addictive parts, had to work to keep me numb from my inner wounds. It was a noble idea of protection, although the opposite effect was actually the truth. My addictive parts weren't helping me anymore; they were hurting me.

Over time, I began to see how my addictive parts were trying to help me cope with life by keeping me shielded from my deep, internal pain. With a new awareness of these addictive aspects of myself, I felt more comfortable in labeling them protector parts.

I also began to realize that these wounded parts were running my life. These protector parts or unloved adult parts were in control of all of my decisions and actions. I became aware that the unloved adult's grandest solution for protecting me from my inner pain was to do, do, do.

My unloved adult's belief was that if I kept busy enough, I would not have to feel my inner pain. This aspect of self is also where I took on the false belief that the answer to my serenity was outside of myself.

It was my unloved adult's voice that kept saying, "If I just had more money, I would be okay," but each time I earned a tremendous amount of money, the feelings of emptiness in my heart were still there. My unloved adult also said, "If I had the right woman in my life, I would be okay," and even though the "perfect women" came and went, the horrible feelings of emptiness remained with me.

Another continuous suggestion from my unloved adult was, "If I lived in a different city, I would feel better." Now of course, that did not work either. It did not matter who I was with or where I was, I still had to take myself with me!

Then on one magical day, in the depths of incredible pain, I became totally aware that the solution to all of my internal pain was inside of me, not outside in the world. To be honest with you, this was my first real awareness of personal empowerment because I realized in that moment that I did not have to be a total victim of my surroundings. I realized that the solutions to my life's problems were inside my heart and my soul, not outside myself. I began to understand on a deeper level that all of my answers to life and love were inside of me. It was a glorious day on my life's path when I came into this new awareness. It was finally clear to me that I was being given an opportunity to heal my deep, inner emptiness.

To tell you the truth, though, I was both excited and scared. Until this point in my life, I always had something or someone else to blame for my own inner pain. I had come to the realization that the only way to heal my internal pain was to nurture myself through it. I had no idea what tomorrow was going to bring, but I did know it would be totally different from today. I was walking in blind faith back then, not having a clue of where my life was taking me. I knew I could no longer blame anything outside of myself for the emptiness I was feeling in my heart. This new awareness had a profound meaning for me, even though I really did not know what it was. The one thing I did know was that from that day on, my world would never be the same.

Wisdom of Uncertainty

As we look at life through the eyes of another, We often will
determine our own destiny.
So often we get stuck in the misery of a confused moment,
Rather than experience the wisdom of uncertainty.
Never knowing what will happen next Allows us to enjoy bliss
in this moment of time.
So often we live in fear of tomorrow Because of our unconscious
ability
To look outside ourselves for life's pleasures.
Living in fear of tomorrow is impossible Because tomorrow
never comes.
We only have this moment.
Living in the wisdom of uncertainty
Allows us to always live with excitement, as well as
anticipation.
Joy flows from the heart, as does fear. Living life in the wisdom
of uncertainty
Allows us to look at each moment with the intent to learn.
Each moment we learn exactly what Our spiritual path wants
us to learn, If we just take time to look and listen.
To live with wisdom is to live each moment With the intent to
grow.
To grow we have to be able to allow the Uncertainty of the
moment
To be filled with love and joy.
Therefore, to live in the wisdom of uncertainty Is to allow each
moment a lesson,
Each feeling a joy,
And all experiences to be that of love and growth!

Wisdom of Uncertainty

I felt I had come to a major revelation, and in fact, I had. The next question that came to mind was, "Now what do I do with this new awareness?" I could see that all of my pain was inside of me, as was the solution to stop the pain, but what was my next step? This question provoked a need to learn about the concept of creating a loving adult aspect of self. Without a clue of what having a loving adult inside really meant, it took me a long while to learn about this internal behavior.

My new counselor, Sandy, taught me that our loving adult is the aspect of self that needs to be nurtured and integrated into our new internal reality. She told me I needed to "unlearn" everything I had ever learned in regard to my own personal, internal behaviors. This would allow my loving adult aspect to be developed.

When I asked her why I needed to have an inner loving adult aspect, she explained that the loving adult is an aspect of each of us, and through its kind words and gentle actions, the inner child can feel safe enough to come out and heal. Our loving adult is the part of each individual that creates a safe environment for us to live. The loving adult is also the part that, over time, allows the ego and addictive aspects to feel safe enough to let go and transform. I now could see this very clearly, so my next desire was to do something about it.

◆◆◆

I am going to stop my story again and describe what and who the loving adult, Higher Self, and female aspects are. Now remember, at this point on my path, I had no concept of what any of these aspects were, so what I am about to share was learned from experience, over time. Because I use these three terms interchangeably throughout the rest of the book, I feel it is important to interject this information so you can consciously understand what I'm talking about. The loving adult aspect of myself was very hard for me to develop because I had such strong and controlling self-hatred voices. At first, those boisterous ego voices always dominated my internal dialogue, so to even hear a loving voice was almost impossible. I was bound and determined, however, to rediscover this loving part of myself. So I started listening to my thoughts and attributing to my ego any voice that was shaming or hurtful. Then I determined that any voice that was soft and loving must be my loving adult or Higher Self.

Later on in the book, I will explain in more detail how and why I did this exercise.

Our loving adult is the aspect of our self that is totally connected to the love of Great Spirit. It is deeply compassionate during our times of grief, as well as supportive and congratulatory during our times of joy and accomplishments. It is our loving adult who listens to our little kid when he/she needs to be heard and supported. It is the part that holds our little kid when he/she needs to cry, and is also the aspect of self that reassures our little kid when he/she needs to release anger. This part of us teaches the inner child appropriate healthy behaviors for expressing this anger. Our loving adult also allows all aspects of self to be exactly who and where they are moment by moment, even if in that moment a particular aspect is scared or lonely. Our loving adult is an aspect of self that merely needs to be developed for some of us; however, for others, this concept is a totally new discovery.

Most people have a naturally intuitive loving adult available to them, so quite often this part is used in nurturing other people instead of nurturing themselves. The trick is to find the balance between self-caring and helping others.

I have a friend whose loving adult part of her has been extremely apparent to me since the first day I met her. Her ability to set healthy boundaries, to take care of herself, and to allow herself to dream was amazing to me. Over a very short period of time she was able to see and experience how her extreme caring for other people was hurting herself as well as hurting them. As she consciously observed these hurtful behaviors, her loving adult was quickly able to change them in order to increase her own self-love.

My friend, always remember that the degree to which you love yourself is the degree to which you can love someone else. So as we develop our loving adult aspect more and more, our love for others and ourselves will naturally grow.

◆ ◆ ◆

Because I had no idea what this loving concept meant, I had to learn from scratch how to be a loving adult to myself. I was so accustomed to mentally beating myself up every day, that to love to myself was totally foreign. So I decided the easiest way for me to learn more about my loving adult was to learn more about the unloved adult part; and that is what I did. Whenever I heard an unloving statement in my head, I would write it down. This exercise helped me identify how many unloving voices were actually in my head.

The next question I asked myself was, "Why do I have so many unloving voices?" I discovered that the number of unloving voices screaming in my head was in direct proportion to the depths of the inner child wounds in my heart. I remember the day I consciously became aware of this new reality. I realized that because I had so many voices in my head, my little kid inside of me must have been dying with pain. As time went on and my quest to heal continued, I realized that this new reality was exactly my truth.

My next question to myself was, "Okay, if my little kid is so wounded inside of me, then what do I do about it? I mean how do I really heal myself?" The answer, I was taught, goes as follows: First, I had to have the internal desire and intention to want to heal my inner child.

Second, I had to create a safe, healthy environment at home and with a support system of loving friends to allow my inner child to feel safe enough to surface and express his repressed feelings of grief, fear, anger, and joy.

Third, it was important for me to create a dialogue with my inner child so he could feel heard and safe as he quested to heal himself.

Fourth, I needed to muster the courage to have the willingness to feel and express the deep feelings associated with my wounded inner child.

Fifth, I had to stop numbing myself so I could feel what I needed to heal.

When I first heard all of this, it seemed very easy except for the fifth step, because at this point in my life I had no intention at all to stop drinking, smoking, or doing anything else that was a normal part of my life. So I figured I would start at the top and move forward one step at a time.

CHAPTER 6

Healing Your Inner Child

Having the internal desire and intention to heal my inner child was easy for me. Luckily, I connected with this concept very quickly. I was able to see the wounded little boy inside of me and would repeat over and over to myself, "This little boy deserves to heal. He deserves it!"

At that point on my path, I began developing the desire to heal something separate from myself. My little kid did feel separate from me, so in turn, it was very easy to see his pain. What I continually saw, in my mind's eye, was myself as a little boy dressed in a baseball uniform, wishing that my daddy were with me at my ball game. This child in me always looked so rejected and so let down. It was because of this internal picture that my desire to heal my inner child grew every day.

A lot of the world's "questers" direct their healing focus toward stopping the critical voices of the unloved adult, instead of healing the wounds of their inner child. They believe if they could just stop these critical voices in their head, their world would be okay. This is a true statement; however, the voices are not the source of their inner pain. The critical voices of our unloved adult are the natural consequence of the wounds of our inner child. Because of focusing in the wrong place, I have seen many people spiral in their own shame because they cannot stop the critical voices in their head, no matter what they do.

One example of this is a friend of mine who meditates with deep breathing techniques for two or three hours every day. During this time, she emotionally leaves her true reality behind and takes herself to a very quiet, serene place inside herself to seek the peace and quiet in her head. This technique is fine for temporary relief, but as soon as she comes back to normal reality and back into her body, her critical voices come right back into her head in full swing. Why does this happen? It's because these voices are not the original source of her pain. The critical voices in her head are a natural consequence of a wounded little kid underneath them.

Another example of what I see people doing with their unloving voices is trying to learn how to accept them by blaming their source on anything but the pain of their inner child. Some people will say, "I have all of these crazy thoughts just because I am an alcoholic." They try to rationalize their critical voices as a malady of their disease.

Other people just deny the voices altogether. In public they talk and act one way, but behind secret, closed doors they act in some totally perverse manner. As a consequence of this choice of reality, many people can literally create two totally different personalities and lives. For instance, most child molesters live two separate lives; one life denying the voices and one life acting on the voices.

An additional way people try to rid themselves of their unloving voices is through mental imagery work. This work literally teaches an individual how to convince the mind that the voices don't exist. My first counselor used hypnosis to teach my mind how to discard the truth of my past and to create a different image.

For example, as a child in Little League baseball, I always wanted my father to come with me to my games. Since he never chose to show up, I always felt abandoned and rejected. Another big desire for me as a child was for my father to play catch with me, but he never did. So my first therapist, using imagery work, would have me imagine myself at nine years old, wearing a Minnesota Twins baseball uniform, playing catch with my father who was wearing the same uniform.

For me, this technique did mask my pain and the voices in my head for a little while, but eventually my "not good enough" and "abandonment" voices, along with all the grief associated with them, returned. I began to realize, though, that whenever I remembered the truth of my emotional relationship with my father, that was the time to feel my grief.

In plain English, trying to trick your mind into thinking that certain emotional events did not happen to you as a child does not work over the long term because your emotional wounds are in your heart, not your head. For me, the only way I was able to relieve my abandonment voices was to actually feel and express my emotions surrounding my lifetime of abandonment issues.

Another illusion used to try and stop our critical voices is called "positive affirmations." This is a futile attempt to retrain the mind to quiet our unloved, critical thoughts. Saying things like I am abundant, I am lovable, I am wealthy, I am whole, I deserve a loving relationship, etc. is well and good, and I do believe that it cannot hurt you. However, you can say to yourself till you're blue in the face, "I am abundant," but if your emotional inner child is feeling lost, alone, and full of grief, you're going to feel anything but abundant.

The saddest thing for me when teaching people about positive affirmations is when someone is convinced that affirmations will cure them, and they work really hard over and over to silence the voices by using this technique. However, the voices will naturally come back because the child within is still very wounded. Unfortunately, as this happens, most people just spiral in their own shame saying to themselves, "There must really be something wrong with me because the positive affirmations aren't working."

In actuality, there is nothing wrong with them. Through my own experiences I have found that to stop the voices in my head, I had to go to the source of why the voices existed in the first place. The original source of my critical voices was the wounded kid inside of me who was yelling, screaming, and even begging me to please hear him. In trying to only stop my voices, I was truly only masking my pain. Again, focusing on the voices is just like focusing on the bandage instead of the cut underneath it.

So for me, this first step of having a genuine intention and desire to heal my inner child was very important. Also, as a consequence of these internal intentions to heal my inner child, everything else just naturally seemed to fall into place. At this point on my path, I began to use these unloving voices as emotional red flags. These voices literally became like indicator lights to warn me of my inner child's needs.

I will give you a few examples of how my unloving voices indicated to me the true inner pain of my child within. Every time I felt lonely and alone, the voices in my head would say, "It is time to find a woman so I can love her and have sex with her, and then I won't feel so lonely anymore." The truth was, by using this voice as a red flag, I found out that my little kid inside was feeling lost and scared, and needed extra attention from me. My old pattern, though, was to follow the voices instead of nurturing my inner child. As a consequence of this old choice, I ended up abandoning myself even more, which caused my internal pain to grow even larger.

Another voice I heard in my head happened every time I felt angry. I was extremely terrified to feel anger in my earlier years. So the voices protecting me from my fear would say, "Let's just get stoned, drunk, have sex, etc., and then I won't have to feel anything." In reality, though, I was denying my real internal feelings with this old choice, which in turn, caused even more anger to manifest inside of my little kid.

So remember, whenever we choose to neglect our true feelings inside ourselves, we are actually neglecting the emotional well-being of our own inner self. As a natural consequence of this present-day neglect, we will also continue to feel abandoned, abused, and emotionally void. To heal and change these unloving experiences, we need to allow our little kid inside to truly feel and express all of his suppressed emotions.

The pain of your inner child is only represented by the unloving critical voices in your head. So having the actual intention and desire to heal your inner child really means having the desire to learn how to nurture yourself through your pain, and in turn, heal that pain. Also remember, as a natural consequence of allowing your inner child to feel and express what he needs to heal, all of your critical voices in your head will eventually transform effortlessly.

CHAPTER 7

Creating a Safe Environment

Creating a safe environment for our inner child and ourselves is very important because for most of us, our little kid inside is a very scared, very vulnerable aspect of self which has been hidden deep inside for many years. So the environment in which we choose to live needs to be safe and loving in order for our inner child to feel safe enough to heal.

To help you identify where you are living at this time, I'll offer some examples of unsafe environments. Any environment that has any type of abuse in it is not safe for you or your inner child. Emotional abuse is created from any verbal, physical, sexual, or psychological situation in which your personal boundaries are being crossed. For example, verbal abuse is a relationship or environment where someone else is constantly yelling at you or putting you down. Verbal abuse is present when someone blames you for everything and/or belittles you. Any environment in which someone else is taking his or her verbal anger out on you is verbal abuse and is not safe for you or your inner child.

Physical abuse includes being slapped, hit, cut, kicked, shoved, pinched, or bitten. Choosing to stay in a physically abusive relationship with anyone is very damaging for you and your inner child. Physical abuse might not happen all the time in a relationship. For example, it might only happen when your spouse or friend gets drunk and then gets mad at you. No matter what the situation, you don't deserve abuse–physical or otherwise.

Sometimes our ego will try to rationalize abusive situations by saying something like, "I must have done something wrong, and that is why he hit me," or "I deserve to be hit by my wife because I was a bad boy today." These types of statements are damned lies! Your ego is lying to you! There is no reason ANY person deserves to be physically hurt by another human being. No reason!

In the majority of all physically abusive adult relationships, at least one of the individuals was almost always physically abused as a child. The important key in healing this old pattern is to get past the voices that are telling you, "You deserve it," and to heal the little kid beneath this illusion who confusingly believes the same thing.

Again, I emphatically state that no person has the right to physically abuse another human being, and there is no reason ANY person deserves to be physically hurt by another human being.

No reason!

So if physical abuse is happening to you, and you really have the desire to heal your inner child, you have to make the choice to leave this unloving environment. The only way to heal your inner child is to leave.

Sexually abusive environments are created in relationships when the sex drive of one of the partners is so demanding that nothing else seems to matter except sex. If you are being forced by physical strength or emotional guilt to have continual sex with your partner or someone else, this is not a safe environment for you or your inner child.

Perhaps your ego voices are saying things like, "This is my husband/wife and I owe it to him/her to have sex regardless of my personal desires," or "It would be selfish not to have sex with my partner," or "If I don't have sex with my partner then he/she might leave me or reject me."

I assure you that none of this is true! You have the right to choose when and with whom you have sex. It is not selfish to set self-loving boundaries regarding your own needs. We are being self-loving when we have the courage to say no when we don't choose to have sex. And remember, when we give ourselves love, we are also loving our inner child. As a consequence of our little kid feeling loved by us, our wounds will heal over time, and all of our unloving ego voices will go away. Of course, the other side of this experience is when you are the individual in your relationship who just can't seem to get enough sex. This endless sexual desire is also a red flag.

My own sexual addiction was an extremely powerful one because it rationalized very easily. My ego would continually say, "Sex is a natural aspect of me, so I deserve to have it all the time." Perhaps your ego tells you, "I'm a man/woman and I have to have sex to survive," or "I can't control myself; I have to have it!"

I have a friend whose addiction to sex was so powerful that one time he was in bed with a prostitute who had to smoke crack cocaine before they could perform. Because my friend was a recovering crack cocaine addict of three years, he was putting his entire recovery process on the line because his sexual addiction was so massive.

Imagine how terrified his inner child must have felt inside, knowing that crack cocaine almost killed him in the past, and now he was choosing to be in bed with this person just because his ego said, "I have to have sex to survive!"

Another common example of sexual abuse happened with another friend of mine. This woman was in a situation with her husband where every day, two or three times a day, 365 days a year, he used her for sex! There was no emotion, no compassion, no lovemaking at all. She just provided the friction needed so he could feed his high libido. She also told me that each time she had sex with this man, he physically hurt her. For twelve years she allowed this behavior to continue because her unloving ego voices told her that good wives were supposed to sexually satisfy their husbands. How scared do you think my friend's little girl was? The answer is—terrified!

If any of the sexual behaviors or environments I have just mentioned push any personal buttons for you, then I suggest you allow your inner child to heal by looking at yourself and striving to change your own unloving sexual behaviors. I personally chose to go without sex for a couple of years so I could consciously learn more about the unloving behaviors associated with my own sexual addiction. This allowed my inner child to feel the safeness he needed to heal the internal issues covered up by my sexual desires.

Psychological abuse is probably the most difficult unloving environment to identify because it can be so subtle. For example, you are experiencing psychological abuse if you are in a relationship with someone who is shaming you, putting you down, neglecting or never listening to you, or continually trying to put you on a guilt trip. All of these environments are unloving and very hurtful to you and your inner child.

The reason these unloving behaviors are so difficult to personally identify as abuse is because we have become so familiar with this type of unloving interaction with other human beings that we are not even consciously aware of how hurtful it is for us. When we fail to recognize the abuse of people who chose to treat us with unloving behaviors during our childhood, often we can't see that the unloving behaviors of our current environment are also abusive. In other words, we have become so accustomed to being psychologically abused that we don't even know we are being abused.

It is similar to asking the question, does a fish know he's wet? The answer is no, because his personal environment has never been dry. For me, identifying psychological abuse was so difficult because my personal environment never knew anything except shaming, guilting, and unloving experiences. Let me share with you a few personal examples of each of the previously mentioned unloving environments.

Someone who is shaming you is someone whose conversation with you is always belittling or degrading. For instance, if someone is always saying to you, "You should have known better," or "You should not be that way," they are shaming you and invalidating your own personal sense of well-being.

Internal shame is a feeling you have that something is wrong with you. So if any individual in your world is continually "shouldering" you, they are feeding your internal shame as if there is something wrong with you!

I remember one spring day I was watching a young boy, seven years old, who was painting his skateboard with spray paint. He was having a great time spraying his board, but the over- spraying of the paint missed the board and ended up on the driveway. This child was young and had no idea that spray painting his skateboard would damage the concrete driveway. In his innocence, he only knew that he was having fun painting! When his mother saw the damage to the concrete, she yelled at him over and over, "You should have known better!"

The child was devastated. All he knew consciously was that he had been having fun, but was now being yelled at by his mother; and could not figure out why. The feelings of confusion and not being good enough were all over this boy's face as a consequence of his mother's choice to shame him. Nowhere in his young mind could he connect having fun with the damage done to the concrete. A child that age has no understanding of value or harm done to his environment around him. Inside his innocence, all he knows is that he was having fun and now his mother is shaming him. Growing up in this type of external shaming environment, the natural consequence for this child will be to develop the internal illusion that says there is something wrong with him. This is another example of how when we shame people by "shouldering" them, we're being very hurtful to them as well as to ourselves.

We can also shame people by making fun of them. "You're too fat," or "You're too skinny," are very shaming comments for the person receiving them. "You're so stupid," or "You're so ugly," also invalidate someone's real truth. We shame others any time we choose to make comments that purposely hurt them by attacking their deep-rooted not good enough issues.

It is often difficult to identify our external environment as being hurtful to ourselves because our own internal voices are so big and shaming. Think about this for a moment. How many times have you said to yourself, "I should have known better," after you've made a personal mistake? This voice inside our heads is our ego shaming us into believing that there is something wrong with us because we aren't perfect. The truth is, we are human and we are going to make mistakes.

Our unloving ego, however, which was developed as a natural consequence of living our lives in a shame-filled environment, says that we have to be perfect to be okay. The consequence of this false illusion of perfection is that we continually set ourselves up to fail, which falsely proves to us that there is something wrong with us because perfection is impossible. The truth is, there is nothing wrong with you or me. Life is about progress, not perfection.

My need for perfection was created in me many years ago as a consequence of growing up in shame-filled environments. Rather than feeling the grief and helplessness associated with the unloving reality of my parents' unconscious inability to give me the emotional love I needed, I took on the false belief that said, "If I were perfect, I would receive the love and approval I naturally need from my mommy and daddy." I believed something was wrong with me and that to be okay, I had to be perfect.

It was during the insanity of this vicious circle that my toxic shame was created, and my obsessive life of trying to achieve impossible perfection was born. The choice to protect myself from external shaming environments allowed me to hear my own unloving voices more clearly. Eventually, I was able to reconnect with the actual source of these voices, which was always a wounded inner child underneath.

For me, understanding that a wounded child within me created the illusion of my perfection helped me become more aware of my unloving behaviors to myself and to my environment. As a consequence of this new awareness, I eventually changed my personal behaviors, which ultimately allowed my inner child to feel safer and more loved by me. This additional personal love enabled my inner child to feel and express the suppressed emotions from living in a shame-filled environment over the years. Allowing these emotions to be expressed has helped me create a new world in which love and recognition is my primary outside source. Identifying my own shaming choices toward other people allowed me to change my behaviors toward myself, which in turn, allowed me to heal all of my deep inner wounds.

An environment consisting of guilt-filled behaviors is also very hurtful to you and your inner child. Guilt is a feeling that says we have done something wrong. People who try to control others by using guilt say things like, "If you really loved me, you would do this for me," or "You only think of yourself; you never think of me," or "If you don't do this for me, I will find someone else who will." All of these phrases are controlling sentences of people trying to manipulate their world through guilt.

A friend of mine once confided in me that his wife was always telling him how self-centered and selfish he was whenever he went through a difficult personal issue from which he was trying to heal. She said this because he was taking extra time to nurture himself and not taking care of her. She was trying to make him feel guilty for loving himself so he would stop self-caring and see to her needs.

The way my friend stopped his wife's behavior was by sitting down with her and stating his truth. He told her that he needed her to lovingly support him as he self-loved himself through his own issues. He also shared with her that she needed to learn how to take care of herself, and he would lovingly support her own personal growth. My friend protected his little kid from his wife by setting this new boundary. Because of this new self-loving behavior, his inner child now feels safe enough to continue to grow, and as a consequence of his new growth, the old guilt-filled voices in his head are starting to go away.

The idea of allowing self-loving behaviors into their lives is so foreign to most people that to act upon them literally feels as if they are doing something wrong, which naturally pushes their own guilt buttons inside. Ironically, many people discover the depth of their suppressed guilt when they first start taking care of themselves by setting healthy boundaries. This is because the self-loving behavior is so new and different.

So if you are feeling guilty because you are choosing to take care of yourself, know that this is a very healthy and normal feeling. Over time it will shift and grow.

Another very hurtful environment in which many people live is when their spouse or partner can't or won't listen to them. I have a friend who is questing very hard to heal her little girl inside. She is in a personal relationship where she cannot be heard; not necessarily because her boyfriend doesn't want to hear her, but because he can't.

Now in my opinion, the idea of inner child growth is for everyone, although not everyone chooses to grow. As a natural consequence of her boyfriend choosing not to grow, my friend is continually being hurt because he cannot hear her. The insanity of her wound says, "If I just ask my partner in another way, maybe he will be able to hear me." The truth is, if he can't consciously hear her, he can't hear her!

It's important to understand that to continually try to change someone else so they can hear you is an impossible task and very hurtful for you. My suggestion is to find someone who can hear and support your quest to heal, and stop trying to change the people who can't.

Remember also, I am not talking about creating a personal relationship with someone who will rescue you I'm talking about finding a person who can and will listen while supporting you. The difference between supporting someone and rescuing someone is very simple. The support person is there for you while you are feeling all of your emotions: anger, sorrow, joy, or fear. The rescuer, or enabler, is a person who tries to take you out of your emotions by distracting you. The rescuer will try to keep you from experiencing your feelings by saying things like, "Please don't cry," or "You will be okay," or "I hate it when you cry."

My counselor, Sandy, is an incredible support person for me. She always just listens and guides me as I express any of my emotions. She never robs me of my integrity by telling me my internal answers or by keeping me from expressing my feelings. She is there only to hold my head when I cry and to celebrate with me during my times of joy. I have a deep sense of gratitude for her because her support has allowed me to feel and heal all of my deep inner holes.

If you are in an intimate experience with a partner who cannot hear you, don't force it. Just let it go and create a new environment with people who can hear you so you will learn and grow with them.

Finding someone who can hear you is probably much easier than you might think. There are certainly all sorts of therapists you can pay who will listen to you. I am a huge supporter of therapy because it helped me so much. For me, having an unbiased person to sit and listen to me changed my life forever.

Of course, money can be a deterring issue in this choice if you allow it to be. Ask yourself how much you are truly worth and how much you are willing to pay to stop your unloving voices. For me, I would have paid any price to accomplish this goal. I did not care about the money because I put my personal growth and my inner child's needs first. I will share with you a simple truth: If your intentions are clear and your desire to heal your inner child is big enough, you will find a way to seek help.

Another way to create a healthy support system is to look in your local paper for any type of support group. There is a world of people out there willing to support you if you are willing to seek them out. If your intentions are clear to heal yourself, you can find a healthy support system of people who can and will nurture you as you grow.

Once you find your new support system, you'll need to have the courage not just to seek them out, but to join in. Support systems will do you absolutely no good if you don't have the courage to participate.

I want to caution you that after you visit a support group, your ego voice might be saying, "I'm not as wounded as the people in those meetings, so how could they possibly help me?" or "Those support groups are just bitching sessions," or "Those people are just a bunch of low lifes and losers. My life is so much better than theirs. I don't belong there."

The truth, my friend, is that you do belong there, especially if you are hearing these voices. The reality of support groups is that each individual will see, feel, and hear exactly what he/she is supposed to in order to heal through that day. So if your personal, critical voice starts spouting off, judging and criticizing the other members of any group, remember that you are not actually judging them, you are merely describing yourself.

Don't make the same mistake I made by allowing your unloving ego voices to guide you away from the healthy support you need. I learned a long time ago that wherever two or more people gather to love and support each other, the presence of God is found. After walking through my own isolation issues, I've found each support group I've ever visited to be a warm, loving place where like-minded people are all supporting each other as they grow closer to the God of their own understanding.

The first step is knowing that support is out there. The second step is knowing how to find it. The third step is joining. It's just that simple!

As you learn what real love and support is, you might choose to re-evaluate your current primary relationship. To me, a principal source of love in any relationship is the ability of both people to communicate with each other by listening and talking openly. Communication is the key to a truly loving experience between two people.

In my own case, the lack of communication between my lover and me was difficult to identify as unloving because I was so accustomed to not listening to myself and having people in my world who could not hear me, either.

Eventually I learned that the ebb and flow of communication between my inner child and myself was a key element to my personal growth. As I learned how to listen to the needs of my inner child and act on them lovingly, my internal feelings of not being good enough went away—along with all abandonment issues. As a natural consequence of healing these internal issues, I began to understand the important role of communication in loving ourselves and receiving love from others. As my internal connection grew through internal conversations, my external desire to create an intimate relationship also grew.

Now you may be saying, "Yes, I do want to heal my inner child, and I do have some dysfunction in my external relationships, but I am not willing to divorce my spouse. So what do I do now?" The answer really comes from within you. The reason for creating a safe environment is to allow your inner child to feel safe enough to heal. Let me share with you what action steps I chose in my own dysfunctional world that allowed my inner child to feel safe enough to heal.

The primary loving behavior you must learn when creating a safe environment is your ability to set healthy boundaries. Healthy boundaries are personal action steps or behaviors in which you are consciously able to stop someone from abusing you or coming into your personal space. For example, if someone is shaming you or projecting their guilt onto you, it is appropriate, self-loving behavior to put your hand up and say, "Stop it! That doesn't feel good!" As the consequence of developing the courage to practice this self-protecting behavior, your inner child will feel safer with you because he/she will know you're there to protect him/her.

I once dated a girl, Sharon, who constantly projected her rage onto me, and I would just sit there and take it. My rationalizing voices would to say to me, "She is really not mad at me, even though she is yelling at me." I never associated her behavior as being unloving or abusive toward me.

One day Sandy asked me, "Joe, if Sharon is not yelling at you, then who is she yelling at?" I replied, "It is her old anger coming up, and she is just taking it out on me."

Sandy responded with, "Yes, and how does that feel for your little kid?"

I thought for a moment and asked my little kid that question. He said to me, "I was scared, and I wondered why you did not stop her from hurting us."

In that moment, I realized that by not setting healthy boundaries and stopping her from yelling at me, I was hurting myself. The next time Sharon yelled, I said, "Sharon, stop that! It does not feel good to me!" From that day on, she stopped taking her anger out on me, so my little kid felt safer and was able to heal more issues.

Another situation where healthy boundaries need to be set happened with a friend of mine. John was in a situation where a family member would continually shame him and use him as a verbal whipping pole. For years John's ego said to him, "I am worthless anyway, so what does it matter if someone treats me poorly?" He never knew that allowing someone to verbally shame him was abusive to both himself and his little kid. Over time, though, as John connected with his inner child more and more, he realized that to allow this type of aggressive, unloving behavior in his external world, was to continually abuse his inner child.

Then one day John mustered the courage to set his first healthy boundary. On this magical day, my friend put his hand up and said to his perpetrator, "Stop talking to me like that. That does not feel good!" In that moment, his relative was totally dumbfounded and completely shocked. In retaliation, the relative tried to strike back with more abusive talk. To his credit, John stayed in his power, and after a couple of strong boundaries were set, his relative never spoke to him like that again.

John's little kid felt very safe after that new display of healthy boundary setting. As a natural consequence of this new level of safeness, John's inner child opened up more and more, allowing his healing process to continue. So you can see that setting strong, protective boundaries is very important in the creation of a safe and secure environment for you and your inner child.

The second loving behavior needed in securing a safe environment is setting aside private, alone time to nurture ourselves as well as to connect with our inner child. One loving technique I used to nurture my little kid was to take long baths where I could be alone and just allow the warm water to nurture me. I also allowed my little kid inside to choose a stuffed animal he loved, so he could feel safer and more loved during his vulnerable times. Another thing I did was sit and listen to soothing music, which seemed to warm the heart and soul of my inner child. I'm sure that your ego is probably saying the same things mine did, "I don't have time to take long baths or listen to soft music; I'm way too busy," or "I'll be damned if at thirty years old I'm going to sleep with a teddy bear!" Well the truth is, your time is your own and what you choose to do with your time is your own choice. So if you are serious about healing your inner child, you will choose to take the time to nurture yourself with long baths and soothing music.

As far as a stuffed animal is concerned, I want you to picture the following scenario. I was thirty years old, 220 pounds, and mean as hell. I looked and acted macho in every way. So believe me, it was extremely humbling for me the very first time I chose to go to a toy store and purchase a stuffed animal for my little kid.

All I can tell you is that I had the attitude, "I don't care what I have to do to heal myself. I will do it!" Quite honestly, if I would have been told I had to stand on my head naked in the middle of the interstate to heal my inner wounds, I would have done it. By viewing the importance of my process in this way, buying a stuffed animal for my inner child was not that big a deal. Actually, the first night I slept with my new teddy bear, I knew deep inside I had made the right decision. Today, six years later, I still sleep with the same bear plus many, many more.

The third loving behavior is giving attention to yourself. A boundary you might need to work through is your own personal privacy when it comes to your actual children, if you have any. Small children demand a tremendous amount of personal attention from their caregivers. If you do not have a spouse to give you the break you need from your children in order to nurture yourself, then you might need to hire a babysitter or send the children to the neighbor.

A friend of mine, Joyce, who is a single mom with a five-year-old girl and a seven-year-old boy, taught her children that for thirty minutes each afternoon she needed space for herself. Joyce took the time to sit down with her children to explain why she was choosing time alone. She explained that her choice for alone time had nothing to do with them, and she reassured her children that she loved them very much. She also chose to explain to each of them individually that she needed to nurture and love herself so she could love them even more.

It took her several weeks to teach her children about her need for personal, private time, and with constant perseverance, the new behavior was eventually accepted. Today, Joyce's choice to nurture herself daily is second nature to the members of her family. This new self-loving choice has made her internal child very happy, too. Her little kid now feels loved and important because she chooses to take this time with herself on a daily basis. And of course, by now we all know that by loving ourselves, we can love someone else. Because of Joyce's additional self-love, her children also feel much more love.

The fourth loving behavior is time spent alone, in conversation with your inner child. Children spell love, T-I-M-E. The more time you spend communicating with your children, the more love they will feel from you. Your inner child feels the same way.

My life has been changed forever by taking a small amount of time each day to check with myself and see how my little kid is doing. I suggest people take fifteen minutes in the morning and fifteen minutes at night on a daily basis to check in with their inner child. If you choose this new loving behavior of checking in on a daily basis, you will be amazed at how your life will change. (I will explain in more detail a little further on in the book exactly what to do during those fifteen minutes.)

Remember, the first step in creating a safe environment is to identify and describe to yourself your own personal environment. If there is any external abuse in your personal world, you need to become consciously aware of it and then admit to the abuse out loud to someone else. The second step is to learn how to set healthy boundaries for yourself, so your inner child will feel safer and more loved by you. The third step in creating a safe environment is to learn how to integrate into your daily routine nurturing private time for yourself.

I assure you, if you choose to do the combination of all of these new self-loving behaviors, you will see how your life will be changed forever. Remember, too, that as you change and grow in love, the environment you create in your outside world will also grow with love.

Another friend, Tom, has shared with me that the more open and safe his little kid feels with him, the more open and safe he feels with his own wife. He tells me that after eighteen years of marriage, he and his wife have never been so close and loving with each other. This new closeness is definitely a natural consequence of Tom's inner child growth.

As he is learning how to love himself, he is naturally able to love his wife more openly. They both are looking inward toward their own inner child to heal their pain, and are connecting with their new sense of inner love. Tom and his wife are willing to support each other while they are healing their inner child wounds.

As an example of this, Tom shared a story with me about a dear friend of his, a young girl in her early twenties, who was killed in an auto accident. Her life was seemingly taken away for no real cause. During the course of this shockingly tragic event, no one shed many tears for the first few days. Then as reality set in, all the true emotions started to flow.

Tom said that his first emotion was to be very angry with God, and he shared this anger with both his wife and me. We both were very loving and supportive as he vented his rage. Neither one of us criticized nor judged his choice of expression. (Yes, even when someone is damning God, it is loving behavior to just listen and support.)

The next emotion he felt was grief. He felt expressed grief

over losing a good friend, and he felt suppressed grief from his inner child associated with the death of a family member many years ago. When Tom cried with me, I just sat there holding his hand, allowing him to feel all of his feelings. When he cried with his wife, she just held him like a small child until he was finished. The next night his wife needed support, so Tom held her for hours as she reached the depths of her own personal pain. Each of us needs to allow others to do, say, and be who they need to be—no judgment, just love!

Through this tragic experience they each grew individually as well as together. Their relationship and marriage has never been stronger because of their choice to individually grow and support each other's growth. In my experience, it is very obvious to say that safe and loving environments promote a tremendous amount of personal and spiritual growth in ourselves and the world around us.

My friend, I will tell you that sometimes creating a safe environment in our personal world is not easy, although I promise you the consequence of your diligence will be spectacular. A safe environment will allow you to create a life of love that only your imagination can grasp now. The degree to which you love yourself is the degree to which you can love others; and this is why creating a safe environment is one of the key aspects of healing your inner child wounds and the world around you.

Love of Two

As we develop our own personal sense of who we are And where
we
are going
We develop a feeling of great love from within ourselves.
This love is a connection to the "all that is" And the spirit of
who we really are.
Knowing that the degree to which we love ourselves Is the
degree to which we can love others
Is a great motivator in seeking this source of internal love.

Our personal quest to know all our real truth Is also a key to
remembering this love.
Our questing for love so very often allows our path to cross The
path of another who is also seeking the same truth.
The love of two happens as two people, Seeking inner love,
connect with each other.
The love of two is based on openness, Honesty, and
communication with each other.

The love of two, is a feeling of endless abundance, With no
boundaries or attachments.
The love of two is a symbol of two spiritual lights Coming
together to make one light of love.
The love of two knows no fear
Because both people know this love is a gift from God.
The love of two is a fulfillment of a promise That destiny
automatically makes true.

The love of two is the open quest of
Two spirits, which grow hand-in-hand, with God as their bond.
The love of two is a glorious reflection of Each other and for
each other's inner love. The love of two is two spirits becoming
one In life,
in trust, and in love.

Love of Two

CHAPTER 8

Creating a Dialogue with Your Inner Child

As our environment becomes safe and our intention to heal our inner child grows, the next real step in healing our inner wounds is to learn how to communicate with our little kid. Remembering that loving communication is a two-sided reality, we need to learn how to talk with our inner child as well as listen to his/her needs. For me, talking to my inner self came very easily, but my listening skills were extremely weak.

I asked myself, "How do I actually communicate with my inner child?" For me, the first step toward inner communication was to learn how to converse with my inner child through writing. This came easily to me because I was willing to do anything I was taught to stop my pain. Let me explain how and what I did to start this dialogue process.

The first thing I did was to set clear in my mind the image of the actual age of the child within me. He was approximately seven to nine years old, with long, curly hair and a sad face. He also was wearing a Little League baseball uniform and cap. This discernment was a consequence of the following meditation.

The technique I am about to describe is a self-loving tool I used frequently during my quest to reconnect with my inner child. The first step of this meditation is to sit or lie in a comfortable spot. I always made sure I was in an environment where I felt very safe, and where I knew I would not be interrupted. During most of my experiences in the beginning, I had a friend or a therapist guide me through this meditation so I could feel totally relaxed. My suggestion to you is to definitely find someone who is willing to support you through this experience, especially if you are new at using this type of tool.

Once I was comfortable in this safe environment, I would start breathing deeply. Understanding that breath is the source of all life, I learned that deep breathing helped me reconnect with the real life of my inner child. As I sat there, my partner would encourage me to breathe deeply into my stomach and then to exaggerate my breath as I blew out. I would continue with this process over and over, paying close attention to how my breath felt as I inhaled and then exhaled.

I was told to feel the sensation of my stomach expanding with each breath, as well as to pay attention to what my stomach felt like with no breath at all. Most of the time it felt more comfortable to cross my hands over my stomach so I could feel with my hands the expansion and contraction of my stomach as my breath of life entered and exited.

As my breathing continued, my partner would then ask me to start relaxing all of my body parts. I began by relaxing my feet, then my legs, then my stomach, then my chest, arms, and head. Throughout this process, I would keep breathing deeper and deeper into my stomach. At first it was very difficult for me to breathe into my stomach because my normal pattern of breath was only to my chest. So I had to make a conscious effort to learn how to breathe deeply into my stomach.

As I began to feel safe, comfortable, and relaxed, my partner would ask me to call for my little kid. What I would say to myself in my own head was, "Little Joe, please come to me." At first nothing happened. Then my partner asked me to remember a time as a child when I felt very safe and joyous. My partner told me not to force this memory, but to allow whichever memory was supposed to surface to come forward.

I remembered playing as a child in my backyard in a bunch of old apple trees. My young friend, Brad, and I would play in those trees for hours and hours. We felt as though we were the only people on the planet when we were in those trees. Interestingly, until I did this meditation for the first time, I had not remembered this childhood scene in many, many years.

This scene was my inner child coming out to me for the first time. My partner told me to trust that my little kid remembered this because it was where he felt safe. As I was asked by my partner to continue breathing into my stomach, this original scene changed into a vision of me as a little boy wearing a baseball uniform.

The reason I chose to use this image when I first began to communicate with my inner child is because during the next several minutes of this deep breathing exercise, no other image appeared. In subsequent sessions of meditation, I would ask for my little kid to come to me, and this same vision would surface.

In the beginning I could see my inner child, but he would not or could not talk with me. So to conclude my meditations, my partner would ask me to walk up to my little kid, hold his hand, and allow him to take me to a safe place of his choice. The next image I always saw was the two of us sitting at a waterfall and watching the water cascade to the bottom. My final instruction was to say to my inner child, "Little Joe, I love you, and I will always be here for you." With those words I was guided out of my meditation.

Now whether you do this meditation with a partner or by yourself, don't be discouraged if you don't see your inner child the first couple of times. Remember, the little kid part of you has been buried for many, many years. It's also important to know that I am a very visual person. Some people can't see their inner child; they can only feel his/her presence. Other people can only hear their little kid. There is no right or wrong way to reconnect with your inner child. Whatever way seems to be most comfortable for you is your God-given method of connection.

Once I regained some type of contact with my inner child, the next step was to learn how to communicate with him. I started this communication by committing to myself to allow at least fifteen minutes each day to stop my life and communicate with my inner child. Writing with my inner child was easy once I got started in the routine, but creating this habit in the beginning was a tough venture for me.

I realized very quickly that I knew nothing about this aspect of myself, so consequently, I had no idea how to start my communications with him. Then I read in a book that the easiest way to start communications with my inner child was to write a letter introducing myself to him. In this letter I needed to tell him about my adult self and what my intentions were in regard to him. So a letter addressed to my little kid is how I started my internal communication process.

When I wrote this letter to my little kid for the first time, it actually seemed as though he heard me. Words can't explain that original sensation, but I just know in my heart, he heard me.

After this experience it was very clear that I could write to my little kid. The question now was how to get him to communicate with me. I needed to get to know my little kid—his likes and dislikes, his fears, and his joy. The key here was to be able to ask my little kid the appropriate questions, and then allow him to answer me in a way that was comfortable for him.

The technique I used to accomplish this goal is called dominate/non-dominate hand dialogue. What this means is that I would write down a question for my little kid with my dominate hand, then I would switch hands and allow my inner child to answer me with my non-dominate hand. This technique is used to force you to take the time to write your answers out slowly and deliberately with your non-dominate hand. It may feel uncomfortable, and you might have to accept, on faith alone, that your non-dominant handwriting represents your inner child's perception.

The following is a list of questions I asked my little kid in the beginning to discover additional information about him:

How old are you?
What is your favorite color?
What is your favorite food?
What is your favorite game?
How many brothers and sisters do you have?
What hobbies do you like?
Do you like to play sports?
Do you like to climb trees?
Do you like to swim?
Do you like to play make believe?
Do you like to run?
Do you like to wrestle?
Do you like to sing?
Do you like to dance?
Do you like to hike?
Do you like to hunt frogs?
Do you like girls?
Do you like to play hide and seek?
Do you like to go outside for recess at school?
Do you like school?
Do you like to draw?
Do you like math?
Do you like homework?
Do you like vacations?
Do you like to fish?
Do you like to color?
Do you like the cold weather?
Do you like Christmas?
Do you like going to church?
Who is your best friend? etc.

The list can go on and on. In the beginning I gave my little kid easy questions he could answer with a yes or no response. Since I allowed my non-dominate hand to answer the questions, I knew each reply was that of my inner child. Doing this exercise taught me remarkable things about my little kid.

In a comparable exercise, I asked the same questions of the adult aspect of myself and received totally different answers.

I realized that over the years, my little kid's likes and dislikes had been totally ignored because this aspect of myself was so completely buried. Of course, I had no idea I was burying this part of myself because I was doing it unconsciously.

One thing I learned very quickly when working with my inner child and the rediscovery of his needs and his pain, was not to beat myself up for being so unconscious to his needs. A fundamental question of unconsciousness is: How can we help something we don't even know exists? The truth is, I did not even know that I did not know the child within me existed. So with this in mind, I will remind you to be very gentle with yourself as your little kid reveals himself/herself to you.

As time went on, and my inner child became more apparent in my life, I was able to ask him more loving and supportive questions. These questions and statements would allow this aspect of me to start sharing more and more of himself with me. My intention was to allow enough communication to happen between the two of us so that my inner child would feel safe enough to open up with me and really share how he was feeling.

I want to remind you again that the reason I had all of the crazy and unloving voices in my head was because I had holes and wounds in my emotional self and soul. The key I found to healing these holes was to allow my inner child to express his feelings to me regardless of what those feelings represented. The source of my hole was my wounded little kid inside me. The source of my little kid's wounds was my lack of a safe emotional environment throughout my entire life, and my inability to share and express my true inner feelings. I was not allowed to be mad, sad, or scared as a child because society and my family structure would not allow it.

In learning how to be a nurturing, loving adult to my inner self, I also had to learn how to listen and accept all of the things my inner child had to share with me. I say this to you because

---

Dear Little Joe,

I am writing this letter to you in hopes of introducing myself to you. I am thirty years old, lost, and alone; and I hurt every day. I own my own catering company now and I have several employees. My dream is to be very wealthy someday, but to tell you the truth, most of the time I can't even pay my own bills.

I work all the time, so I don't really have any hobbies. I drink alcohol and smoke marijuana every day. I don't know why I drink and drug. I guess until this letter, I've never really thought about it.

Little Joe, the reason I am writing this letter to you is to help you get to know me. It has only been a few months since I even learned you exist, so a lot of this stuff is very new for me.

I hope you will learn to trust me enough to let me get to know you. I am here for you, too.

Luv, Joe

---

when my little kid started to open up with me and share his true feelings, I was extremely surprised at what he had to say. (I will give you some examples of my own personal dialogue later on in this chapter.)

After I found out more about my inner child's likes and dislikes, I wanted to discover more about how he was truly feeling. To accomplish this, I started asking him more and more questions about his emotional well-being. I also started asking my inner child how I could love and support him even more. I had no idea how to be a loving, sensitive adult to my inner self, so I asked him to help me.

I mentioned earlier that if you just take fifteen minutes twice a day to be with your little kid, it will change your life forever. This is why! When I first started asking my inner child about what he was feeling or how he was feeling, his answers always blew my mind. He would tell me how angry he was at my father for never being there with him, and how much he hated his sisters for picking on him all of the time. He would also tell me how glad he was that my mother was always around, although he hated it when she said, "You should have known better."

My inner child was filled with rage, terror, and hatred, and I was so surprised to find all of this out about my inner self. I had no idea all of this suppressed emotion was in me—I mean, absolutely NO IDEA! So I remind you again not to be too shocked at what you hear and write as your little kid starts to open up to you. My guess is that you, too, will probably be amazed.

Here are some of the additional questions I asked my little kid on a daily basis during our fifteen minutes together. I chose to start my dialogue sessions with two simple questions:

"How are you doing, Little Joe?"

"How are you feeling, Little Joe?"

I chose to keep a legal-sized pad of paper with me at all times. I would write one or both of these questions on a piece of paper with my dominate hand, and then I would allow my left-hand, or my non-dominate hand, to reply. The following is an example of some of my first conversations:

Adult Joe: Good morning, Little Joe

How are you doing today?

Little Joe: Okay.

AJ: How do you feel today?

LJ: I'm very angry with Angel for leaving us. I hate her. I also hate my daddy for never being there at my baseball games. I remember the first time I wrote down on paper that I hated my father. I felt a tremendous amount of guilt. The idea of hating anyone went totally against my good-boy nature. Owning my hatred for my father was a very difficult reality for me to face. This is where I learned very profoundly about the internal reality of living as a multidimensional being.

I learned that just because my inner child did not get his needs met, it did not mean that as an adult I did not love my dad; even though it caused feelings of anger and hate toward my father. The truth is, I love him very much. As I learned more about this concept of being a multidimensional being, it allowed me to validate and own all aspects of myself. I then was able to nurture and accept the little kid parts that were very angry and needed to be heard in order to heal, as well as my adult aspects that understood intellectually my parents did the best they could do.

It's important to explain in more detail the concept of intellectually understanding something. Intellectual understanding is a reality and a concept of the adult aspect of self. This concept is a belief system of acceptance and perception rolled into one thought or idea. Yes, intellectual understandings are fine and good, but they do not stop the unloving ego voices in our head. Remember, the unloving voices are a consequence of a wounded little kid, and all our inner child knows and feels is that his daddy was not at his baseball games. As a young child, I did not have the capacity to intellectually figure anything out, since the development of intellectual capacity usually does not begin until eleven or twelve years of age.

It's okay to intellectually understand that our parents did the best they could; but for a small, emotionally needy child, this is not usually enough. So in my inner child's quest for healing, I acknowledged, listened, and allowed him to express everything he needed to say or feel. At least twice each day I would ask my little kid those two simple questions, and then I would allow him to express his true answers to me. Over the next couple of months, I literally filled at least twenty legal-sized pads of paper with my inner child's expressions.

Other examples of questions I would ask my little kid during these sessions were:

Adult Joe: Good morning, Little Joe. How can I help you today?

Little Joe: By listening to me and not shaming me for being so angry. I can't help it. I hate him!

AJ: How else can I help you today, Little Joe?

LJ: By being here for me and listening to me. AJ: Little Joe, how can I nurture you today

LJ: I need a hug. I need to be loved. I am scared I won't be loved if I'm angry.
AJ: Little Joe, it's okay to be angry. I will love you and accept you regardless of what you are feeling.
LJ: I'm glad. I'm scared to be me. I'm angry.
AJ: Little Joe, I hear your anger. It's okay. I am here for you and I will never leave you, because I love you!

It is important to remember that when replying to your inner child, you should nurture him/her as much as possible through validation. Let your inner child know it is okay to have feelings. Make a special effort to share over and over that you love him/her regardless of those feelings. Explain that your love is unconditional.

In the beginning, your inner child may be afraid to share or even feel his real feelings because most of us experienced severe consequences in the past when we expressed those feelings. For example, if I had yelled in anger at my father when I was a child, I seriously would have put my own life in jeopardy. My father did not allow anger to be expressed at all, especially anger pointed toward him. So consequently, I had to suppress my anger year after year just to survive.

Another reason our inner child might be afraid to express his/her real feelings is because of our inherent fear of love being taken away by our primary caregivers. A child is born with only two basic fears. One is of loud noises; the other is that our primary caregivers will take their love away from us.

Think about the second example logically for a moment. A child is at the total mercy of his primary caregivers. The caregiver's choice to love and to take care of their own child is literally the child's only lifeline to survival. So naturally, in the eyes and perception of a child, if a parent does not love him, the parent won't take care of him; and obviously if a child is not being taken care of, he believes he will die. I understand that as an adult this statement might seem a little extreme, but for most children, what I've just shared is exactly how they process this reality. Children will instinctively do whatever it takes to get love and approval from their parents. So if a parent says, "Don't you get angry with me or I will punish you," the child hears, "I will take my love from you." Rather than risk fear of death, the child will naturally suppress the rage.

I hope you can see why it might take some time for the little kid in you to feel and express his real feelings. A lifetime of conditioning has made this new reality of expression very scary for him. This is also why I suggest a tremendous amount of love, validation, and encouragement during the personal nurturing process of your little kid.

As time went on, additional questions came to mind to ask my own little kid. These were directly related to the environment in which I lived.

As I mentioned in Chapter 7, one of the primary necessities for healing our inner child is a totally safe environment. I realized over time that my wounded little kid had a totally different idea of a safe environment than my adult did. So little by little, I would ask my inner self about different friends and different social and work settings in which I found myself. For example:

AJ: Little Joe, how do you feel about going to bars?

LJ: I hate it! It's very scary for me and I don't like it! It is too loud and the people are not nice to me. I don't like the way you get when you drink. Drinking hurts me.

AJ: It's okay, Little Joe. I will to my best to change. I love you.

I remember when I first realized that drinking alcohol was hurting my inner child. I was in total shock and disbelief. Being a practicing alcoholic and drug addict, I really did not know what I was going to do about this newly found reality. So for the longest time, I purposely avoided asking my little kid this question again. Later in the book, I will explain in detail what happened for me regarding drugs and alcohol as the time became right for me to confront this dilemma.

Other questions I would ask my little kid were about my personal relationships:

AJ: Little Joe, how do you feel about Katie, the woman we are living with?

LJ: I like her, but she drinks; and when she gets mad, she yells at us. That scares me. I am scared of her anger. I don't feel safe living here.

Of course, when I heard this for the very first time, it was a very challenging truth for me to accept. Katie drank and smoked like me, and she was sweet as pie until she got pissed. She was so full of rage that when she exploded, she could literally bring the house down.

At first, I really did not know what I was going to do about this new truth. So as before, I just stopped asking my little kid the question until I was at a personal place where I could deal with his answer.

The other questions I asked my inner child were about my career.

AJ: Little Joe, how do you feel about our work situation?
LJ: I like owning our own business, but I hate working with our family. I don't feel safe working with my dad.
I am mad at him and
I want to quit!

I was again stunned when I learned how my inner child felt about the family business I had built and worked in for many years. In fact, I was totally stunned and amazed at all of his replies when it came to my personal life. My adult self had no idea that my inner child was so uncomfortable in each of these environments.

Needless to say, my world was my reality. So I was unable and unwilling to change any of these situations right away. Over time, however, because of the love I had for my little kid and my huge desire to stop the voices and heal my wounds, I chose to change each of these personal realities. (Later in the book I will share in detail how each of these lifetime changes transpired.)

Since I did not like what I was hearing concerning how my little kid did not feel safe, I started asking him what he did enjoy. This is what I would ask:

AJ: Little Joe, where do you feel safe?
LJ: I like going outside and being in nature. I like the lake. I like the mountains. I like sitting by a waterfall.
I like going to Sandy's house and getting a massage.

These were all desires of my little kid that I could integrate into my daily routine little by little. I found a beautiful secluded lake up in the Georgia mountains, which also had a waterfall. My little kid loved it there and he loved me for taking him.

These past dialogue sessions I've shared are just a few examples of the hundreds of possibilities from which I could have chosen. I decided on these three examples because they illustrate the extreme difference of opinion between my adult self and my inner child regarding the three most important relationships in my life.

My social settings, my career, and my personal committed relationships are without question three of the most influential experiences that affect the safety in my personal environment.

As you can see by these examples, my adult's desires of reality were totally different from what my inner child needed to feel safe and heal.

In my quest to know and understand my inner child's needs, I used the following questions as nurturing tools which allowed my inner self to communicate with me more clearly:

AJ: Little Joe, are you angry with me? If you are, it's okay because I want to hear more about your pain.

AJ: Little Joe, I can hear that you are sad. It's okay to be sad. I'm here for you today.

AJ: Little Joe, I can feel your fear. Can you share more with me about it so I can understand you better?

For me these were great questions to ask my inner child during each of my fifteen-minute sessions with him.

The next loving action I integrated into my daily routine was to stay consciously aware of whatever my little kid was feeling throughout the day. I now understood that I had no personal experience of what lifestyle environments my inner child felt safe with. So throughout my daily routine, whenever I became aware that my little kid was feeling mad, glad, sad, scared, anxious, or any feeling I was uncomfortable with, I always found it helpful to stop whatever I was doing and communicate with him. I would ask him things like this:

AJ: Little Joe, am I doing something that is hurting you?

AJ: Little Joe, am I not doing something that is hurting you?

AJ: Little Joe, am I ignoring you, or have I discounted you today in any way?

AJ: Little Joe, what can I do to make you feel safe right now?

AJ: Little Joe, what do you need from me right now?

These are all questions I would ask during any moment of the day when I felt the emotions of my inner child jump either up or down. It was through the conscious choice of listening to his replies to these questions that I learned, one day at a time, which environments he felt safe with and which environments he did not. Eventually, by listening to my inner child's needs, I changed the choice of environments I visited daily, and I changed my personal relationships with different friends.

Another loving act I chose to integrate into my life with my little kid was stopping my world for just five or ten seconds several times during the day and telling him that I loved him and that I was here for him. Over time, I could feel how much he liked this. Another thing I did to remind myself of my little kid was to put notes all over my house saying, "I love you, Little Joe." I put these notes on my bathroom mirror, on my TV, next to my bed, on my front door, and on my refrigerator. I put these notes everywhere—even in my car and on top of my bottle of whiskey. I intuitively knew if I did not remind myself of my little kid all the time, I would forget him. This technique helped me remember my wounded little kid inside on a daily basis, which in turn truly inspired my quest to heal his wounds.

Extremely important when I communicated with my inner child was the loving affirmation that he was okay, and that I loved him unconditionally. These are some of the statements I would say to my little kid during my conversations with him:

AJ: Little Joe, it's okay to be angry. I'm here for you. I love you very much and will never leave you. I promise I will stay consciously aware of your needs and will never leave you again!

AJ: Little Joe, I am very proud of you. Your courage amazes me!

AJ: Little Joe, it's okay to be sad and to cry because I will be here for you, to hug you and hold you as long as you need me.

AJ: Little Joe, it's okay to make mistakes. We are human.

AJ: Little Joe, Great Spirit loves you unconditionally and has always been there with you—even though we did not know it.

AJ: Little Joe, it's okay to be who you are. You are a perfect child of God and I love you very much.

AJ: Little Joe, if you don't feel like saying anything today, that's okay, too.

These are the validating statements of encouragement I used to nurture my inner child on a daily basis. I want to remind you it is impossible to give your inner child too much love and attention. This is a perfect example of where more is definitely better!

In the beginning, your inner child probably won't trust you because this type of loving behavior is all new to him/her. So remember, consistent nurturing is the key to healing. Anyone can choose to act on these exercises for a couple of days or even a couple of months, but the true spiritual warriors are those who integrate this type of internal communication for the rest of their lives.

Internal trust is earned! It can't be bought and it can't be manipulated! It is something I had to work to acquire. The internal communication between my adult self and my inner child has created a bond of internal trust that words cannot describe. For me, internal trust was the first real step my inner child needed to develop with me so he could feel safe enough to really come out and heal.

Let's recap the steps I took in creating and developing my internal communication with my inner child:

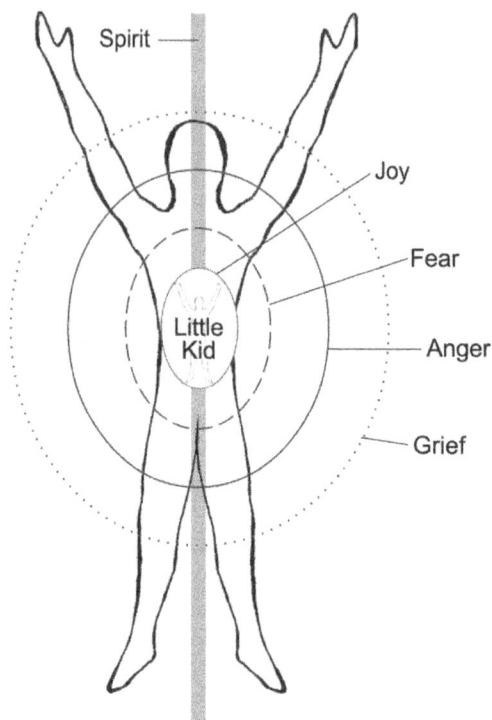

1. I took myself to a safe place and used the meditation technique I explained earlier to help me focus my conscious attention inward.
2. I wrote an introduction to my inner child, explaining to him in detail about myself and my intention regarding my quest to heal him.
3. I asked my inner child questions about him. I used my dominant hand to ask the questions and my non-dominant hand to answer them.
4. I committed fifteen minutes twice a day to a dialogue with my inner child, earning his trust by listening to him regardless of what he was saying during my inquiries of how he was feeling.
5. I affirmed and validated my little kid as much as possible, saying to him, "Little Joe, I love you." I also told him I would stay as consciously aware of him as possible and would never leave him again.

6. I learned that trust between myself and my inner child took time to earn and grow. I also learned that as this internal trust continued to build, it allowed my inner child to feel safe enough to truly feel and express what he needed to heal.

As a natural consequence of this new internal trust, my personal ability to trust myself and Great Spirit has grown substantially. My internal connection of trust and love with my inner child has transformed me into a loving, spiritual being. Remember, trust is earned; and the action step of creating internal communication is where it all begins. Fifteen minutes twice a day changed my life forever. My hope is that you, too, will choose to take your fifteen minutes and watch your own life lovingly transform as never before.

A Day of Trust

As life's process takes us down a road of change;
As we embrace the aspects of life in which we are unfamiliar;
As we love the parts of us we can not see—
This is living in trust.
To know that we don't always know;
To understand that the glass must be empty
Before it can be refilled;
To allow life to happen as it's supposed to happen—
This is life, and love, and living in the blind faith of trust.
As each challenge takes us to another bridge to cross;
As each experience allows us another lesson to learn;
As each crossroads requires another expression to be felt,
Knowing that this is the purest experience life requires of us—
This is living in the trust of God and the
Abundance of the universe.
Today my heart is empty, my life confused,
My world turned upside down,
So tomorrow my glory can shine with the love of God.
Today I know I am okay, even though I may feel differently.
Today I embrace my fears, even though this truth
Takes me into new territories.
Today I trust that the love of God is there,
Even though I can't always see it.
Today I choose trust, because to live in trust
Is to embrace the love of God.

A Day of Trust

CHAPTER 9

The Courage to Feel Again

Mustering the courage and willingness to feel my emotions one layer at a time was an absolutely amazing phenomenon for me. Let me begin with why I needed to feel all of my suppressed grief, anger, fear, and joy.

It was much easier for me to develop the willingness to move forward if I intellectually understood why I had to accomplish a particular task. The reason I chose to feel all of these old feelings was because I learned that the only true way I could actually heal something inside of myself was to feel the intensity of the unreleased emotion. Now remember, the reason I chose to heal my wounds is because of my deep desire to stop the unloving voices in my head. So when I realized it was a choice I was making to feel what I needed to heal, this new understanding seemed to make my reality of deep expression more bearable.

I wondered how my deep emotions had become so suppressed in the first place. Along my life's path there were tremendous numbers of occasions when my environment was not safe enough for me to truly feel what I needed at the exact moment I needed to feel it. What happened to this emotional energy that couldn't be expressed outwardly? I found that I had stuffed this energy back inside my emotional self somewhere. Living in a world of non-expression, stuffing my emotions seemed to be safer and more natural than to actually express them. Therefore, the more I stuffed my emotions, the deeper and more neglected my little kid felt; and since he is my true connection to my emotional self, each time I stuffed my emotions, I neglected his needs in the process.

My inner child, along with his emotional self, is also my connection to my own personal love for myself and for others. So the degree to which I neglected my emotions was in proportion to the degree to which I neglected myself. Neglecting myself is where the self-hatred, self-doubt, and low self-esteem were born. I also found that my ability to feel love for my emotional self was directly related to the love I could feel from Great Spirit in my heart.

These are just a few of the reasons why I chose to feel the deep emotions of my inner child as they came to the surface to be healed. Each suppressed feeling I felt brought me one step closer, one layer closer, to uncovering and remembering the true loving experience of Great Spirit in my heart. It was through experiencing this reality that I came to understand that God is love; love is emotion; emotions are in your heart. So when you heal your emotional heart, you will naturally feel the love of God which resides in us all!

The key to feeling all we need to feel in order to heal is to have the desire to learn how to feel again. This expression of emotions was so totally foreign to me, I honestly had no idea what people meant when they said to me, "I feel sad," or "I feel smothered." My addictions and compulsions were so big that all sensations regarding feelings were numbed out. The only physical sensations I ever truly felt inside myself were during sex or when I got stoned. So needless to say, I craved both of these activities all of the time.

The first real step I took in feeling my emotions was to stop the addictive behaviors in my life that caused my emotions to be numbed. A simple definition of an addiction is any substance, activity, or belief system that takes us out of our true feelings of the moment. The first time I saw this definition, I was amazed to realize I was personally addicted to drugs, alcohol, sex, relationships, love, sugar, food, exercise, wealth, work, and failure. Obviously, when it came to feeling my feelings, I needed a lot of help.

Now I wish I could say that as soon as I saw my unhealthy behaviors, I was able to stop them and move on. The truth was, I was totally powerless in all of these unloving behaviors so I chose to not even try and stop them. I just kept writing in my journal every day with my inner child, and listening to how angry and sad he was. Although I could hear his truth, I honestly could not feel anything. I personally lived in my head, completely out of my body. What I mean by this is that my personal internal attention was in my mind. My thoughts ran my life. My thoughts dominated everything.

Remember when I explained about the four aspects of each human being: mental, emotional, physical, and spiritual? My life's path had led me down a road to where I had totally closed down my feminine aspects of self, which were my emotional/ spiritual selves. I discovered later in my journey the reason I chose to close down so completely was for pure survival. I had accepted the reality of my past choices and now it was time for me to re-open these aspects of myself.

In my quest to experience my feelings again, a key activity was body massage. This self-loving technique literally taught me, through physical touch, how to bring my internal focus back into my body from my head.

My counselor, Sandy, was also a massage therapist. Each week when I visited her, although I would share what troubles were going on in my life, the most important aspect of our sessions was the actual massage. Week after week, I could sense myself having more internal focus in my body. She would have me breathe deeply during our work together, bringing my attention back into my body. She would also have me internally follow her hands with my mind's eye as she massaged my arms, back, feet and legs. All of these techniques were used to bring my personal, internal attention back into my body.

During those years, my obsessive thoughts of drugs, sex, alcohol, or people kept my internal attention focused outside of myself, preventing me from feeling anything. Because my feelings were inside of me, the main job of my protector parts, or addictions, was to keep me out of my feelings and into my head. That is why my protector parts worked so hard to numb me, distract me, or lie to me by keeping me in denial.

The only reason I was able to work through all of my addictions was because I developed an internal personal quest to heal my inner child. I was in a lot of emotional pain because of the wounds of my little kid, and this was the pain that motivated me to continually look inside myself to find my answers so I could heal.

Now obviously, I am writing this book after the fact. During the actual time of each of these personal discoveries of my addictive behaviors, I truly did not believe I was addicted to anything. My denial system was so strong that even though I drank and smoked at least six days a week for over fifteen years, I'd never once thought I was addicted. I never even considered the possibility that these behaviors were hurting me. Looking back now, it is easy to show how insane my life truly was. I wanted to explain in detail the extreme nature of my addictive behaviors to give you hope. Trust me, if I can work through my addictions and heal my inner child, so can you!

I have a friend right now who is not addicted to drugs, alcohol, sex, or work, so her connection to her little girl is coming much faster for her than my connection ever did. The truth is, it does not matter where you emotionally live right now. You may be like me, at the very bottom with nothing; or you might be like my friend, a fully functioning person. At either place, you can choose to reconnect with your own inner child and change your life forever.

Now what happened for me was that I could hear my little kid describing to me what he was feeling, although for the longest time I could not actually experience these emotions. My counselor encouraged me over and over again by saying in a very loving voice, "Joe, it is okay to feel what you need to heal."

With consistency and internal determination, little by little, I did regain my ability to feel again. For me, regaining my God-given ability to feel my feelings was the natural consequence of acting upon everything I have described to you thus far.

My life's focus became very clear as I developed an internal passion that expressed itself to me over and over by telling me my little kid deserves to be healed. I had been hurting for many years and now it was time for my pain to stop; to take whatever action steps were necessary to allow this little part of me to heal. I developed the attitude in which I would go to any length to heal the child within me. He deserved it!

Every day I communicated with my little kid through writing as if it were the first day of the rest of our lives together. I loved him, I listened to him, and I encouraged him to feel whatever he needed to heal. Then one day, as if by an act of God, I actually felt anger for the very first time in my adult life. This newly found expression was almost orgasmic. At first I really did not know what this experience was. I felt hot around my neck and head. I felt an extremely powerful energy in my heart and my belly. It was coming out whether I wanted it to or not.

My first anger release happened for me in my car. I realized later that the reason for this experience was because in my car I was all alone, so I felt very safe. What actually happened for me was that I started to scream and yell at the top of my lungs. At first the words I was saying were very scary for me to hear. Then I experienced this extreme feeling of guilt because the anger I was expressing was about my father.

Even though my personal fear and guilt were tremendous, there was no stopping this release from happening. Once I started to express myself, I yelled and yelled until my voice could yell no longer. The energy was so powerful that screaming was the only choice I had. I yelled things about my dad like:

I . . . f–ing hate you for never being there for me. f–ing hate you for never talking with me. f–ing hate you for ever being born.
f–ing hate you for never coming to my baseball games.
f–ing hate you!

I actually yelled many more things that day, but I think you get the picture. The bottom line was, I yelled whatever my inner child felt like yelling. I chose the most crude and vulgar adjectives I could possibly think of. I yelled that day till my voice literally gave out. It was my first anger release, and what set me off was watching my father, who was very rough and tough, turn the light switch on with his little finger. For whatever reason, this action set me off. I don't know why; I just know it pushed every anger button I had.

Now I want to remind you that my anger was and is my own. So when I reached a place of actually being able to express this anger, I chose to release it in the privacy of my own safe space. Releasing anger in a healthy way does not mean going up to the person you're angry with and actually yelling at them face-to- face. (That unloving behavior is taking your stuff out on someone else.) Releasing healthy anger means allowing the energy that has been stuffed inside for many years to start being expressed little by little. Emotions (E-Motions) are energy in motion. Some healthy ways to allow this energy of anger to be expressed include yelling and screaming profanities, punching a pillow, taking a plastic bat and beating the bed, tearing up phone books, or writing out your anger over and over. Any activity that allows your stuffed energy of anger to move through you, that is done in your own private space, is both healthy and self-loving.

During my first release of anger, there were several things that really scared me. First, the feeling of anger was so new for me that it was very uncomfortable to feel and express. Second, the energy surge was so huge and powerful I really did not know this type of experience even existed, let alone existed inside of me. Third, there just seemed to be so much anger stuffed inside of me I never thought I could feel it all. This final sensation was the personal reality that scared me the most.

My thoughts raced that night with the fear of how I would ever get all of this suppressed anger out of me. I knew I had no idea what tomorrow was going to bring for me, but I did know my world would never be the same.

◆ ◆ ◆

It was not until much later in my process that I learned about the multidimensional concept of emotional layers; however, to keep things in perspective, I want to share with you in more detail about this reality.

Emotional layers are like the layers of an onion. Each time we have an emotional release, we shed one layer of our own internal onion. One layer at a time, over time, is how we heal. I remember a very wise man asked me one day, "Joe, how do you eat an elephant?" The answer was, "One bite at a time."

So I ask you, "How do you heal twenty-five years of stuffed anger, grief, and fear?" The answer is one layer at a time.

Learning this internal concept helped me keep my journey much more in perspective. You see, my ego would say to me over and over, "There's just too much anger to work through. We can never release it all, so let's just give up and not feel any of it." However, by looking at emotional release work as a process that happens one layer at a time, my unloving ego voices began to quiet down so I could continue my healing process one layer at a time.

The following diagram may help you acquire a visual idea of what I mean by emotional layers. As you can see, my inner child was buried deep inside me under layer after layer of suppressed anger, grief, and fear. The only way I was able to experience the feeling of true internal joy was to release the feelings of anger, grief, and fear, which were in the way.

◆ ◆ ◆

For most men in our society, suppressed anger comes up first and is very strong. Internal grief, on the other hand, is very hard and very scary for me to feel. Before I could express any of my tears of grief, I had to process through the illusional paradigms that say big boys don't cry; tough guys don't cry; only wimps cry. My experience has been that for most women, the exact opposite seems to be the case. They seem to be able to connect with their suppressed grief first because of such false paradigms as, if a woman gets angry, she is being a bitch; it's not nice for little girls to be angry because it's not lady-like; etc.

Well ladies, I'm here to tell you, probably for the first time in your life, those statements are bull shit! We are all mental, physical, spiritual, and emotional beings. So to validate all of our self we have to validate all of our emotions: anger, joy, sadness, and fear.

I am here to remind you that it is okay to feel whatever you need to feel. Any emotion expressed is just energy in motion. So as long as you express your energy in the privacy of your own safe environment, my experience tells me that you will probably feel a sense of relief after each release.

After my first emotional release, I went home and got stoned out of my mind. This new experience was so mind-boggling for me that my addiction itself couldn't handle it. My old patterns of doing whatever I needed so I would not feel anything were so big and so programmed in my mind that getting stoned and stopping the expression of these feelings was my only option. So that is what I did. I got stoned, and as a consequence of this choice, the next day I felt horrible. I felt lonely. I felt abandoned.

I felt betrayed. It took me many months to realize why I felt all of these horrible things, but in looking back it's no wonder.

Think about it logically for a moment. Here I am, working together with my little kid so he can feel safe enough to experience whatever emotion he needs to express, when finally, after a tremendous amount of time and trust, he actually feels safe enough to express some of his deep, dark secrets. This choice took a tremendous amount of courage and trust on my little kid's part. And how did I choose to reward his efforts? I ignored his needs and completely closed down his feelings with my addiction to marijuana.

As a natural consequence of my inner child feeling betrayed, what happened to me? I experienced loneliness, abandonment, and betrayal. All true emotions are consequences of our inner soul's true reality. So when I betrayed the trust of my inner child, I felt the experience of betrayal in my world.

My addictive self was so big and powerful that it made it very difficult for me to build and grow a trusting relationship with my little kid inside. An example, which reflects the other side of the story when it comes to addictions, has to do with my friend, Rose.

Rose had no active addiction to drugs, alcohol, or sex, so she had the natural ability to feel her inner child's emotions almost immediately. Rose knew from the beginning that if her little girl was sad, she needed to sit and cry. If her little girl was scared, she intuitively knew that she needed to nurture herself and embrace her fear. If her inner child was angry, she automatically allowed herself to express this anger by screaming and yelling.

So now, each time an inner child issue comes up for Rose, she feels what she needs to heal, and then moves on. Her trust with her inner child continues to grow daily because she very rarely betrays her inner self with a hard-core addiction. Through her ability to release her inner grief, anger, and fear, Rose continues to experience a new magical reality called true joy! She has felt a new sense of peace and completeness almost from the very beginning of her internal quest to reclaim her inner child. I am not saying she has not worked hard, because she has. I am saying, though, that her personal reward of experiencing days filled with inner joy came much earlier in her process than it did for me. My addictions and protector parts were huge; so these aspects of myself were bound and determined to keep me in misery for as long as possible. However, regardless of our particular personality or our unloving behaviors, it is only a matter of time before we will feel the blessings of internal peace and joy that are created as a consequence of inner child expression.

It was many weeks before I felt any more true emotions or had any other type of emotional release. The only experiences I had at this point were those of self-hatred and self-doubt. I was still smoking and drinking almost every day. I was dating a woman who drank like me, so of course neither one of us thought anything of our behaviors. Drinking and smoking daily seemed as natural for me as brushing my teeth, so I continued on like normal.

I also continued to see my counselor, Sandy, as often as possible. At this point on my path I also was thinking about leaving my family business of catering food because I found a new and exciting career opportunity in the world of network marketing. I stumbled upon a nutritional company that markets patented food products that are changing people's lives. I started using this product and even with my inebriated lifestyle, I still felt a tangible difference with an internal increase in energy. Being a stony, I craved sugar every day, all day. After twelve weeks on this product, however, I had lost twenty pounds and my physical sugar craving was gone. I knew from my personal health changes that this product truly worked. So over the following several weeks, I pursued this new opportunity and learned more about the exciting industry of network marketing. I learned I could build a multi-million dollar business with no employees and no overhead. I also learned that the industry was projected to be over $200 billion strong by the year 2000. As I investigated the company, I found it to be very solid, publicly traded, with goals to be around a very long time. The more I looked at it, the more I liked it.

As time when on, I had a very important business decision to make regarding my future. I loved my new business and was having a lot fun helping people with both their health and their wealth. The best way to describe my family-operated catering company was "un-fun." So this is how I made my decision for my personal financial future: "New business = fun; catering = un-fun." I said to myself over and over, "Which do I choose: fun... un-fun, fun...un-fun?" I then followed my guts and chose fun as the direction in which my life needed to head.

Now try to picture the look on the faces of my family when I told them I was closing down our catering company because I wanted to have more fun. Four of my family members had worked with me for over ten years, but for the first time in my life I had to do what was right for me. Looking back, I can see how my inner child growth had obviously been working because

I made this life-altering decision based on a feeling—fun vs. un-fun. At this point in my life, I had no idea what was going to happen for me, but I did know my life was changing.

Over the next eight months, I kept selling the nutritional products and proceeded to close down our catering company. Now remember, my inner child did not feel comfortable with the idea of working in a totally enmeshed family business. So choosing to leave this personally unhealthy business environment was a huge step of growth for my little kid and me.

Looking back, I now know that my decision of fun vs. un-fun was the true internal connection with my inner child. It was God doing for me what I could not do for myself. This first action step of leaving my family business was truly God supporting me like the wind beneath my wings.

As time went on, and I was no longer working seven days a week, my quest to heal my inner child grew even more intense. For the first time in my adult life, my workdays were free and my time was my own. In my new venture, I was asked to write a list of all of the people I knew. It was during this process that I became extremely aware of how isolated and sheltered my life had become.

I had lived in Atlanta for over eight years and could only apply seventeen names to my original list of friends. Ten of those people were drug addicts like myself, and the other seven were family members. At that moment, the picture of my life's insanity was starting to become very clear to me. I could see my problem of isolation even though I never considered my addiction to marijuana as the source of this lifetime challenge.

I continued with my inner child exercises on a daily basis, though somehow I could tell I was not personally moving forward at all. Looking back, I now can see that each time I would really start to feel something I needed to heal, some unloving protector part would numb me out of my feelings.

Then one morning, I woke from a very graphic dream of my inner child and me. I realized during this dream that every time I drank alcohol, I was literally pouring this substance on the head of my little kid. I could visually see my inner child fighting and struggling to get away from the constant stream of alcohol being poured onto him. Obviously, his struggles were for naught because he is part of me. I realized in that dream that every time I drank alcohol, I was actually giving my little kid an alcoholic hair wash.

I woke from that nightmare terrified and shaking. I was covered with sweat and my sheets were drenched. I know now that this dream was Great Spirit telling me that it was time I stopped drinking alcohol. I shook off the dream, but those graphic visions never left my head.

For the next couple of weeks, every time I drank alcohol, I saw my inner child struggling and pulling, trying to get away from the constant stream on his head. This vision literally broke my heart. I thank God that my love for my inner child was great enough for me to make the decision to stop drinking. Consciously, I always said, "I will do anything it takes to heal my little kid."

After this dream, I knew it was time to put the cork in old Mr. John Barley Corn. I never regretted that decision, and from that point on, I never drank again.

It was obvious to me, as I put down the alcohol and stopped going to bars all of the time, that my inner child was much happier. I was totally amazed with myself because I was able to face and change another unloving behavior that my little kid really hated. Honestly, looking back at this experience, I now can see how it was God working through me.

Because of this new choice, the love for my inner child just kept growing. My desire to do whatever it took to allow my inner self to heal also began to grow again. I finally understood that God is love, and I knew that the massive gift of love I was feeling toward my little kid was the only reason I was able to stop drinking on my own.

I do not recommend that alcoholics like me try to stop drinking on their own, even though that is exactly what happened for me! My personal recommendation for people with an alcoholic challenge in their life is to visit a twelve-step program like Alcoholics Anonymous. This program is a loving support system of other recovering alcoholics who are ready and willing to support anyone who chooses to change their alcoholic behaviors. Through my own experience over the years, I have found that the choice to change an alcoholic attitude could quite possibly be the largest life change any person ever experiences. I believe that a loving support of other alcoholics is mandatory for most people to succeed during this major life change.

My life continued to lead me down a road of isolation, but I knew all of my answers were inside, so I had to just keep looking inward to heal. It was recommended to me to visit a support group, even though the idea of attending a group setting and telling my problems to total strangers was absolutely impossible for me to grasp at that point. In addition, I really did not believe I was an alcoholic since I was able to stop drinking at will. It is also apparent now that I did not know what the word denial meant. Even though I had drunk heavily for years and smoked marijuana several times each day, I still could not admit that I was addicted to anything. This, my friend, is called denial.

For me, denial is when your rationalizers are so big they keep you from seeing the truth of a problem that has a major influence on your life by saying there is nothing wrong. Being stoned twenty four hours a day, seven days a week seemed very normal to me, and I had a total lack of awareness regarding this problem. I also created an environment that surrounded me with people who acted the same way I did. So I looked into my world and said, "Well, everybody I know drinks and gets stoned every day, so it must be okay." This was definitely denial.

Now the amazing thing about my counselor, Sandy, was that she recognized my denial from the very beginning, even though she never pushed the truth of my addictions onto me. I learned, through her behavior, that addiction to any substance is something individuals have to discover for themselves. No one can tell you if you are addicted to something. Only you know your truth! Even though a codependent person will say, "I can make an addict see their addictions," in my experience, this is not true.

For those who might be living with an active alcoholic or addict, there is a twelve-step program called Alanon for you. This is a spiritual program for nonalcoholics whose lives are affected by alcohol on a daily basis. Sandy was a black belt in Alanon, so she gave the tough love I needed and watched as my addictions took me to new depths in my life.

With alcohol finally gone from my life, I did start to feel a few more emotions. I was very uncomfortable at first with the powerful emotion of grief. It just did not seem right at all for me to feel this sensation. The first time I had an emotional release of grief, I had no idea what was going on. It felt very strange for me. In fact, I really thought something was wrong with me. My personal programming was so strong in the illusion that big boys don't cry, that when the tears started to flow, I truly believed they would never end.

My first grief release came around the issue of abandonment. In my mind's eye, I saw myself as a little boy walking around, looking for someone to listen to me, someone to hear me, and someone to just hold me. As a child, I wanted someone to look me in the eye and say to me, "Joe, I love you, and everything is going to be okay. I am here for you and will never leave you." When I realized that as an adult I never got those emotional needs met, the sadness was overwhelming. I felt so sad for my little boy because he was cute and lovable, but no one ever connected with him the way he needed. The actual connection of this old truth is what made me cry.

This emotional release of grief lasted approximately fifteen minutes. The experience was absolutely amazing for me. I remember calling Sandy and telling her what had happened. I explained the whole experience and asked her very sincerely what it meant, since grieving was so foreign to me. Sandy explained that I had just had a release of old grief. I remember thinking what an amazing concept this was, to actually be able to see a memory of something I was sad about in my life, and then to be able to cry about it. "Wow!" was my only reply. "Wow!"

♦ ♦ ♦

Before I continue, I want to take a minute to explain what grief really is for me. Grief is an emotion that is felt and expressed during a time of need or a time of loss. Grief sometimes feels like someone is literally stabbing you in the heart or the stomach with a knife. Grief is an energy that when suppressed, can make your body feel very heavy and thick. Grief is an experience normally associated with tears; but tears are not always present. Grief is an emotion that when stuffed, keeps you from allowing your heart to be opened to your true personal love.

Grief is suppressed throughout the years for many reasons. I've talked several times about social paradigms that say, "Big boys don't cry," or "Only wimps cry." These illusions are simply not true. God gave us the four basic feelings of mad, glad, sad, and scared, and each of these personal gifts was designed to be experienced and expressed by all. However, our unconscious lifestyles allow unsafe environments to become key factors in why so many people have suppressed their grief year after year.

For example, you may have heard, "If you don't stop crying, I will give you something to cry about." Or how about this, "If you are going to cry, just go to your room so I don't have to hear you." Statements like these by parents are shaming and teach children that to express their God-given gift of grief is wrong. So in turn, children who cry too much create a false belief that says there's something wrong with them.

Another great example of how we are taught to stuff our grief is, "Honey, if you stop crying, I will give you an ice cream cone." In other words, we bribe our children into thinking and believing that grief is not okay.

The spiritual truth is, grief revitalizes our soul. To have a great big "Boo Hoo" every once in awhile is extremely self loving and very healthy. This experience allows us to truly validate who we are as an emotional human being. Grief also allows us to experience the internal sensations of vulnerability and humility as a consequence of this process. Both of these spiritual aspects of self are mandatory elements as we are remembering how to reconnect with the spiritual being that resides in us all. To grieve is to validate yourself and who you really are.

As I was teaching my inner child about grief, I let him know that it was okay to release his tears. I reassured him over and over again that I would be there for him when he needed to cry. Also, I reassured him that it is a false belief that says, "If I start crying, I will never stop." At this point, I just intuitively knew that I would be able to stop because I trusted that God would never give me more than I could handle.

The feeling of grief can also take us into a place of deep darkness and aloneness. I understand that this experience is very uncomfortable, even though it is very normal. As I connected with my inner child more and more, I was able to experience all of his true feelings, including his deep feelings of loneliness and aloneness.

Think about it conceptually for a moment. If you, as a young child, never really connected emotionally with anyone, don't you think the natural consequence of this reality would be a feeling of loneliness and aloneness? So if during your grieving process, deep experiences of loneliness and aloneness come up, know in your heart that you are okay. And yes, my friend, I know that these sensations do add to the intensity of an already uncomfortable situation. During my own process, it was necessary for me to experience these sensations because it was only through my aloneness that I was actually able to remember my oneness; the internal experience of connection between the conscious self and the spiritual self.

The last experience of grief I want to share with you is about the personal sensation of an internal death. During my own grieving process, I often felt as though I were grieving the death of my best friend. The truth is, as a consequence of my personal transformation, I was truly grieving the internal death of the old me. So if you are experiencing these dying sensations during your grieving process, please know that you are okay. My process over the years has taken me through this circle of life hundreds of times. The death/rebirth cycle is all part of my spiritual growth and is actually a gift from Great Spirit, because my life is always more loving and more enlightened as a consequence of this cycle.

I will admit that these grieving experiences were difficult for me in the beginning, but over time, with practice, they have integrated into my world as a normal part of my life. So if you are having a challenging time with your grieving process, know that you are okay.

I totally understand what you are going through, and want to commend you and recognize you for your courage as you walk your spiritual path through the layers of your own grief. My highest knowings say to me that if you were not supposed to be feeling these feelings, you would not. Since you have made the choice to read this book about connecting to your feelings, obviously some higher part of you also knows that you can feel what you need to heal. So even if your grief is uncomfortable for you at first, remember and trust that the joy you will experience as a consequence of your choices to heal your wounds will be considerably grander than the depths to which your grief can ever take you.

To stop the unloving voices, you need to heal your inner child wounds that created the voices in the first place. So allow yourself to feel; allow yourself to grieve; allow yourself to heal. The natural consequence of this process will take you to a feeling of wholeness that is beyond what many people can even begin to imagine.

I am very proud of you for having the courage to feel what you need to heal. Congratulations!

Dark Before Dawn

Each step of this mysterious path
Leads us closer to the light of who we truly are,
Even though at times we seem to be very much in the dark.
Faith allows the strength and courage needed to continue on,
Deep into the depths of our own inner mysteries.
Dawn appears as we recognize
And own each part of our self unconditionally. Dark before
dawn is a true sense of aloneness
Needed to feel the total sense of oneness we all share.
Life and all its mysteries are locked inside us, so close yet so
far. In walking into the dark, we truly experience all sides of
life.
Deep in the dark is the key to our true light.
To experience the dark before dawn takes the courage of a wolf
And all the attributes of Spirit.
Our soul must empty before it can fill. Our life is confused
before it can clear.
So we must accept the dark before we can see the light.

Dark Before Dawn

CHAPTER 10

The Miracle Happens

Over the following months, my ability to grieve became much easier; although each time it happened, it still surprised me. One tool I used in reconnecting to my emotional grief was music. When I felt sad, I would play a sad song; and like magic, my tears would appear. At this point in my life, my grief seemed to be centered around the same things over and over, and though I was grieving often, I really did not feel I was moving forward.

As a consequence of not drinking, my marijuana consumption was continual. I smoked reefer like most people smoked cigarettes. My connection with my inner child was there, but I seemed not to be growing. I could see my inner child, but I really could not physically connect with him. He seemed separate from me, and although the grief I felt seemed real, I intuitively knew I was not grieving from my little kid. I later labeled this type of grief surface grief because the origin of this energy seemed to be right under my skin. Each time I cried, I never actually felt better.

My addictions continued with the badgering voice that said, "Inner child stuff doesn't work. Let's just get stoned." I felt power- less to these voices, so I did just that! The struggle for me, though, was that my internal desire to reconnect with my inner child was also growing very strong. The stronger my desire to reconnect became, the stronger my addictive voices of denial became.

◆◆◆

Your addiction, or protector parts, might be wearing a different face from mine, which was marijuana; however, all addictions are very powerful. It does not matter what face it wears. It could be sex, alcohol, drugs, work, relationships, sugar, TV, food, failure, exercise, diet, etc. It will do whatever it possibly can to keep you from reconnecting with
your inner child and feeling his feelings.

◆◆◆

A turning point in the denial of my addictions happened one day during a therapy session. Normally, my time to receive a massage was late in the afternoon or early evening. Then one day, Sandy asked me to promise her I would not get stoned prior to our session. She explained to me thoroughly that her work is very powerful and that being stoned was keeping me from actually feeling the true effects of the session.

I remember thinking it was no big deal. I could go easily through the entire day without a smoke. When the next week came and the day of my session arrived, low and behold, I could not do it. I tried to wait, but I could not go six hours without getting high.

At my next appointment, I was filled with a sense of shame and guilt for not keeping my promise. She never said anything to me, but I know she knew what I had done. My need to get high was so strong it was impossible for me to wait even six hours.

I left my session that day never admitting to her that I had lied, but deep inside I started to think that possibly I had a problem. In fact, I started to think it might be time to stop smoking marijuana. At this point my ego really started to fight this idea. It would continually say things like, "If we stop smoking, we will die. If we stop smoking, we will have no friends. If we stop smoking, basically we will stop existing."

◆ ◆ ◆

Let me explain what exactly was going on in my world at this point in my life. My path was step-by-step, day-by-day, leading me to experience deeper feelings and issues. As a consequence of my commitment to growth and healing my internal life, or inner child, my external life was just naturally changing. As I look back and write about everything that happened in me, it seems as if I were clear and confident about each move I chose; but the truth is, during each shift or change in my life I was very confused, frustrated, and lost. I never acquired clarity until after the fact. My ego parts were so big and so powerful that they would fight hard to hold on to my internal struggle every day.

So as your own process of self-discovery happens for you, don't be alarmed if confusion and chaos seem to be a common state of mind. It was for me for many years. Our ego/protector parts hold on so tightly, but they are just doing their job. These protector parts were developed years ago inside of us to consciously protect us from the pain and loneliness of our younger years. Basically, our ego protects us from our unconscious pain stemming from the real wounds of our inner child. The ego acts like a bandage over our wounds. It does not allow the wound to heal, but hopefully, it will not allow the wound to get any worse.

In the unconscious state of life, which is always looking outside ourselves for love and comfort, the ego has to guard the unprotected, wounded little kid in us. As our process of self-discovery becomes more and more grand, and our internal choice to heal our inner child becomes our reality, a new aspect of self will be developed. This new aspect is called our loving adult.

For me, the longer I did this work, the stronger my new loving adult became. So little by little, my loving adult started to learn how to comfort and nurture my inner child so my ego could stop protecting him and let go. I use the phrase "little by little" to help you realize that this transformation process takes time. It took me time and internal motivation to truly learn how to nurture myself. It also took time to allow my internal changes to happen and develop in such a way for me to actually notice their effects.

I have a friend who is rapidly growing on this path day after day. As an outsider, it is very easy for me to see her personal growth. However, she does not always feel her shifts or see her own differences from day to day. I told her that this is where faith grows. In this case, the faith that is growing is in her individual process.

It is easy to have faith in the process when everything is peachy keen and things in your life are going great. However, faith really grows during times of confusion and chaos. So if your intention is to heal your little kid, and you keep looking inside for your answers, you may be assured you are personally growing.

Trust + Action + Time = Faith. **Trust** that by looking inside you will discover all of your answers. Once you have found your new answers, take **action** steps and know that these self-loving action steps, over **time**, will allow you to feel safe and comfortable with your questing process. This feeling of safeness with your higher path and your self is called **faith**.

Just because you cannot personally see your own growth sometimes does not mean that you are not spiritually growing. It is like the young blind boy who cannot see that the sky is blue. Just because he can't personally see it, doesn't mean that the sky isn't blue.

As my loving adult integrated into my life more and more, my ego parts had to move over and then eventually transform. The primary reason my ego held on so tightly was because it felt as though it were going to die. My ego was afraid of dying and was also afraid that my wounded little kid would not be protected anymore.

Remember that my ego's job was to protect me from my inner wounds; therefore, I needed to explain lovingly to this protector aspect that it had done a great job of protecting me from my painful feelings, but now I was at a conscious enough place to love and reconnect to my inner child. In turn, he could safely feel what he needed to heal.

Sometimes my protector parts let go quickly; other times it took awhile. Then there were situations where asking for help from my Higher Power was the only way my protector parts could transform. I never knew how my ego would respond. I would always remember the statement, "Sometimes quickly, sometimes slowly; it will always happen if I just keep nurturing and loving myself."

I remember the first time my ego part let go easily. When I decided it was time to stop drinking, I did. Much to my surprise, even after drinking for all of those years, I connected easily with how much this ego part (my drinker) was hurting my little kid. So I spoke with this drinker part and shared honestly how it was time for this aspect to transform; and it did. My desire for alcohol transformed easily with no real struggle. As this loving experience happened, my little kid was filled with joy and happiness.

I will share with you, though, that as this ego part truly let go and transformed, I went through a deep grieving process called psychic death. I felt such grief, it was as though my best friend had just died. In the beginning, I would get this type of grieving process confused with the grieving release of my little kid. In my experience, the grieving process of the transformation of ego is accompanied by a huge sense of gratitude. Grief and gratitude releases were very amazing for me because I did not know whether to laugh or cry.

The feeling of gratitude is there because during any letting-go process, or transformation of ego, there is a true feeling of internal freedom. When my ego shifted, it allowed me to feel a new connection to the openhearted feeling of love that is in us all.

The feeling of grief was present because an old part of myself, a part that didn't fit anymore, was dying. It's important to understand, however, that with any death there is also rebirth. With each winter there is always spring. Sometimes during this letting-go transformation, I would grieve and grieve with no sense of joy. In fact, after many of these releases I experienced feelings of emptiness and aloneness

The best way to explain this experience is that a glass must be empty before it can be filled again. These feelings of emptiness and aloneness were the natural consequence of an ego part which is fear-based, whose energy just shifted out of my emotional self during a release. The result of this process was an empty sensation where the fear-based energy had once filled the space. The lonely feeling was because these old parts of me protected and served me well for many years. They were like old internal friends. When these parts transformed, naturally I was going to feel alone, as if a good friend had moved away.

The awesome part of this entire process was that there was more empty space to be filled with the love of Great Spirit. So each time my glass filled back up inside, it filled with the love energy of Great Spirit. This experience of love was the most honest feeling of self-love I could ever imagine. However, rarely did my ego parts voluntarily transform with no struggle. Most of the time these aspects fought till the very end. I can remember spinning and spiraling in my own shame, feeling that something was really wrong with me all the time. I had this shame because of the false belief system that the letting-go process is like turning on a light switch. I thought all I had to do was make the decision to let go and my ego would automatically obey. This was not my truth. In fact, I learned that letting go was more than a natural consequence of trust, love, and faith. The more I practiced these principles of abundance on any given internal issue, the more my ego would transform.

Once my ego finally let go, I would fight with the idea of why, on Monday, my ego would hold on; but on Tuesday, it would let go. I could never figure out what the difference was between the two days. What I learned was that there was no difference between the days, so I just had to trust the divine mystery. As a consequence, I learned to accept that everything, including my ego parts letting go, happened exactly when they were supposed to.

Acceptance has always been the key to all of my struggles. During this process, I learned that I did not need to know why it was for my highest good to let go on Tuesday, and not Monday. God knew this answer, so I did not have to. Later in this process, I would ask myself, "Do I think that I know what is better for me, or do I think that God, the Creator of all that is, knows better?" Of course, I always answered, "God."

Be patient with yourself if you are trying to let go of something, and it does not happen in the time frame you desire. Trust that you are not necessarily doing anything wrong, and there is certainly nothing wrong with you. Letting go takes time, and the amount of time is determined by the great mystery, not you.

◆ ◆ ◆

Now back to when I left my session with Sandy. I was thinking it might be time to start looking at my marijuana issues. Never before had I ever even considered looking at my issues, let alone giving up marijuana. So naturally, with this new consideration, my addictive voices went crazy. After that day, I moved my therapy appointments to early in the morning so I could keep my promise to Sandy and not smoke prior to seeing her. I figured I was fooling the whole system because I could get up, get dressed, and go see her early in the morning. Then as soon as I would leave her house, I would literally get stoned pulling out of her driveway.

I chose this behavior for many weeks, all the while trying to work and survive monetarily. I also had an external relationship with a woman I was trying to live with; however, at this point in my life, nothing seemed to be working very well. My inner child connection had seemed to reach another plateau, and my outside world started to become dark and gloomy.

Then out of nowhere, as I did with my alcohol consumption, I could see that each time I got stoned, I was gassing my inner child with the smoke. The difference this time was that I really did not care. I consciously knew I was hurting my little kid each time I lit a joint, but I honestly did not want to stop smoking.

My business had almost closed because I was making no money. I drove a car that did not work, had no real friends, I dated a woman who drank, used drugs all the time, and was a stripper. I was living in the unfinished basement of a man's home, next to his furnace. My self-esteem and self-worth were so low that I truly believed everything was okay. Back then I honestly looked at my life and said, "Nothing is wrong here." That, my friend, is the perfect description of a true emotional bottom; but because my denial was so great, I never knew it.

A couple of weeks passed, and even though I had no real money for food, I always had money for drugs. I remember thinking, "Life isn't that bad, even though it really seems to be going nowhere." This internal feeling of being lost and going nowhere continued for many weeks. My drug use had become a constant experience, consuming my entire life. Every day I would wake up, do the same thing I did the day before, and wonder why my life was so miserable.

Then one day everything changed. As I shared in the beginning of my story, my friend and I were sitting in the basement where I lived, talking about how he couldn't go ninety days without any drugs or alcohol. As I sat there that morning and contemplated my personal reality, I realized I was probably fifteen years old the last time I had gone ninety days without any mind-altering substance in my body.

For whatever God-given reason, I realized that day that I had been inebriated for over sixteen years! The impact of this new awareness of myself felt like being hit on the head with a stick. Before that moment on February 13, 1994, I never clearly saw the results of my choices. The effect this new realization had on me was absolutely magical. I knew it was time for me to stop all types of mind-altering substance use.

For the first time, my connection and love with my inner child was actually strong enough for me to decide to stop smoking marijuana. I remember saying at first, "I'm not going to stop forever, just for ninety days," and that is exactly what I set out to do.

That day ended as many had before, except for one feeling; I knew deep in my soul that the next day was going to be the first day of the rest of my life. Never before had I dreamed of being totally substance free, but on that day, I did start to dream again.

To Dream Again

As we walk our life's path,
And are not being guided by inner vision, Many times we are
beaten down
And stopped by the obstacles in our way.
To grow in life is to have courage; Courage to face our fears,
To overcome our obstacles,
And to allow ourselves to dream again.
Most times this is our biggest fear of all, Because to dream, we
have to face the fear of failure.
We have to be vulnerable, Yet wise at the same time.
To dream big dreams is a process of growth that few take on,
Though the universe is moved by it.
To dream again takes courage of heart and soul, Which most
are afraid to challenge.
To dream is a natural path of joy and love, Which rewards the
Spirit ten fold.
To dream again—what a concept. To dream again—what a goal.
To dream big dreams
Is the faith that moves mountains.
My friend, have the courage to dream again Of love, peace,
joy, and abundance.

To Dream Again

The next day began much like any other day, but for the first time, I was internally motivated to be substance free. I had no idea if this was going to be possible. It was a new experience for me, and I was excited about my potential success. I remember trying to connect with my little kid that day to let him know I was truly going to stop smoking. I expected him to be totally excited and joyful, but he was skeptical. It was as if he really did not believe I had it in me to stop smoking reefer.

I was disappointed with my little kid's reaction, although looking back now, I can't blame him for his skepticism. This was a quintessential representation of how trust from my inner child was going to be earned. In this experience, only true abstinence from any mind-altering substance was going to gain the trust of my little kid. Even though I did not know it in that moment, the decision to stop smoking was the grandest experience of self-love I had ever created.

The first couple of days were surprisingly easy for me. I found myself trying to connect with my little kid more and more. I could see him, but I did not feel as though we were getting any closer to each other. All I kept hearing in my mind was that trust is earned. I also intuitively knew that sooner or later I would probably start to experience a few more emotions because of my new decision not to numb my feelings anymore.

◆◆◆

You don't have to be a full-blown alcoholic or drug addict like I was to use these substances as numbing tools for your feelings. I challenge you right now to ask yourself this simple question, "When was the last time I went ninety days without drinking, using drugs, overeating, working too much, having sex, etc.?" If you can't answer this question comfortably, then some part of you can relate to my story of how I used these substances to keep me out of my feelings. Granted my story is extreme, but the reason I tell it in such detail is because if my inner child connection and love can bring me out of the depths of my emotional world, think about what these techniques can do for you!

I want to illustrate how powerful this inner child process really was for me. The growth and willingness I acquired over these previous couple of years was absolutely a miracle. If you remember earlier in the book, I had absolutely no desire, no willingness, and no intention at all to stop my substance use. Then little by little, the more I looked inside and connected with the love of my inner child, the more my willingness naturally grew. This willingness to change was unquestionably the natural consequence of my inner child's love and connection. So if you have an issue or circumstance in your life that is hurting you, even though you are not willing to change, understand it is okay. Our willingness to change grows as our internal connection with our inner child grows.

My willingness to change took a lot of courage, and I had to have faith in order to gain this courage. To gain faith I had to have trust; and for me, real trust came from my little kid, and had to be earned, over time, by looking inside and loving him.

The longer I loved my inner child, my ability to trust, have faith, feel courage, and have the willingness to change just effortlessly developed. The reason I share all of this is because I used to shame myself for not having the immediate courage to change unloving behaviors in my life. This strong shaming belief kept me spiraling in my head for a long time. My false need to do this process perfectly also kept me spiraling out of my feelings. My ego voices would say, "You know what you need to change, so why don't you just do it now?" I was very hard on myself because my self-loving changes took a long time.

I have a friend who is in the process of letting go of a three-year relationship which meant the world to her at one point on her path. Over time, though, she grew spiritually and he did not. As she sees their differences, she knows he is not the ultimate partner for her. She knows in her heart that total closure on this relationship is inevitable, but she cannot muster the courage to finish it by saying good-bye. Each time she realizes she can't close this relationship, she shames herself into submission. She calls herself a wimp or a sissy. She shames herself because the process is taking longer than her personal ego expectations would have liked for it to take.

Willingness to change takes time. Change is the single largest fear we will ever experience in a human society. So please remember, if you don't have the willingness to make self loving changes immediately in your life, know that you are okay. Just keep looking inside for a deeper connection Time is a major variable in the growth of your own personal courage and self-love. In time, your ability to change your choices will be consciously available to you.

The other variable I want to talk about in regard to willingness to change is faith. Faith is our ability to trust a power greater than our- selves. I choose to call this power, God or Great Spirit. If you are having a challenging time overcoming your own fear of change, my suggestion is to pray and ask for the courage and strength you need from a power greater than yourself. Over time, I learned to say, "Great Spirit, give me the courage to feel what I need to heal."

There were times I had to make the loving decision to change on pure faith alone. I was often uncomfortable, scared, and confused during these decisions, but I did it anyway. This is called blind faith. It feels as though you're walking on a tight rope without a net underneath you. Sometimes it even feels as though the tight rope itself is taken from you. Believe me, I know this experience is uncomfortable. It's easy to have faith when things are going smoothly. It's when things get a little tougher that faith grows.

As my own internal connection grew through loving my inner child, so did my internal trust. As my little kid's ability to trust me grew, so did my faith. And as my ability to have faith grew, so did my internal courage. As a natural consequence of my ability to feel courage, my willingness to lovingly change was inevitable.

◆ ◆ ◆

Now back to my story. After seven days of no drugs or alcohol, I really thought I was doing very well. On the seventh day, I had an appointment on the south side of Atlanta. It was pouring rain and very cold. I got lost during this trip, so I actually missed my appointment time.

Suddenly I realized I was very close to an old drug buddy's home. It literally felt as if my car took on a mind of its own. The next thing I knew, I was pulling into my friend's driveway. I knew there were plenty of drugs and alcohol inside that would tempt me, but I did not care. My friend was not home, so I conveniently broke into his house telling myself I just wanted to rest and get out of the cold rain.

The truth is, my addictions wanted drugs, even though I went inside telling myself over and over I was not going to smoke any reefer. As time went on, my insane compulsions grew. The more I said no, the more my addictions said yes. The louder I said no, the stronger my addictions said yes. I intuitively knew that I needed to get out of there, but my natural ability to leave was gone. I literally felt paralyzed by my disease. I knew my newly-found sobriety was in trouble. I then lovingly said to myself, "If I can just sit here for thirty minutes, I will be able to get up and leave." And that is what I did.

I sat down in an old leather rocking chair and started to rock. I was in total disbelief of what was happening to me. My ability to think straight was gone. My ability to move disappeared. All I could do was sit there, minute by minute, watching the clock tick.

I swear, each minute felt like an hour. I tried to sleep, but I was not tired. I try to sing, but no words came from my mouth. I was literally white-knuckling this chair for over thirty minutes. Every cell in my body cried out for drugs, and I fought this desire with all my strength. Every unloving voice I had shamed me and blamed me, trying to get me to smoke. My internal struggle was so large that my heart was racing and I could barely breathe. After thirty minutes of absolute torture, I knew I was finished. I could hold on no longer. My fight was gone!

It had been fifteen years since I had prayed. I always thought it would be very hypocritical for me to ask for some power called God to get me out of a tough spot, especially when I knew damned well I was going out the next day to act in the same way. (It's important to point out that anytime I have mentioned God or Great Spirit thus far, it is in hindsight. Everything I had done, and even the personal growth I had experienced up until this particular point in my life, was accomplished despite my false belief that I wanted nothing to do with some unseen force called God—until now!)

With desperation in my heart and fear in my soul, I stood up from the chair with both arms extended outward and said humbly, "God, if I am not supposed to drink or drug today, I need your help." The next sensation I felt was a rush of energy running from my head to my toes, with a little tear sliding down my left cheek; and with that, my paralyzing compulsions for drugs and alcohol were gone.

I left my friend's house that day having no idea of what had happened to me. It took me over two years to consciously connect with what had transpired.

Instantaneously, like a burning bush, Great Spirit removed my fifteen-year addiction to drugs and alcohol. To this day, except for one small experience, I have had no type of numbing substance in my body. Each day of my life I thank Great Spirit for this incredible gift.

I was truly blessed that day—February 20, 1994—with the gift of love and life. This is a day I will never forget, and will never stop talking about. I humbly asked for help from God for the first time in my adult life, and in receiving this help, my life was instantly changed forever. The more we look inside for our answers, the more answers we find. As I said earlier, when your intentions are to heal your inner child's wounds, the annoying voices in your head will naturally go away. Creating a safe environment for yourself is a critical element in allowing your inner child to experience the safeness he/she requires to feel what he/she needs to heal.

Eyes That Fly

As we walk our path of life,
We naturally look for our eyes that fly.
Our need to discover all of our hidden desires of love And peace
becomes strong.
Our life will lead us to lessons that will show us the way; The
way of our internal will.
To find our true self is to find our eyes that fly. To find our
purpose on earth is also a way to fly.
To find the courage to live the life we were meant to live, To
have what we were meant to have,
To be who we were meant to be; This is to live with eyes that
fly. Sometimes life's path leads us
Through thick and very confusing times Where we see nothing.
Though always remember that our eyes that fly are within.
If times are tough and lonely, And you feel like you want to
stop, Look to that vision of freedom—
Freedom of our soul; Freedom of our heart.
To live with eyes that fly takes a lot of courage. To live and
learn that we can fly takes time.
To be willing to fly takes the soul to a whole new place.
Eyes that fly; what a glorious place. Eyes that fly; what a
courageous path. Eyes that fly; our purpose on earth.

Eyes That Fly

I've given you numerous examples of what it sounds like to be manipulated by shame or guilt. I've taught you exactly what techniques I used to reconnect with my little kid; first by visualization, second by communication, third by listening. Last, but not least, I've shared from my heart how this powerful technique of reconnection has taken me from a totally spiritually bankrupted, drug addicted life, to having all my compulsions removed in one divine instant.

I hope my experiences have shed some internal personal light on where you are right now. I will say once again, if my inner child reconnection can help create such a deep and powerful inner love for me, then just imagine what it can create for you.

In the next part of this book I'm going to share with you the strength I gained as a consequence of putting no numbing substances in my body, and my great desire to feel what I needed to heal. I will be as open and as honest as I possibly can. I applaud you for having the courage to seek and feel what you need to heal.

PART TWO

I am going to share how stuffing the four basic feelings of mad, glad, sad, and scared affected my life. I also will share my personal experience of how learning simple self-loving techniques allowed me to release my suppressed emotions and heal my deep inner wounds. My hope is that you will be able to take any or all parts of my story and use it to enhance the quality of your own life.

Learning the truth surrounding my emotional being has totally set me free, and it is in this freedom that I am able to live my life of love and conscious connection to Great Spirit. I tell you honestly that the depth of my past pain has allowed a greater height to which I can experience joy today. My suggestion is to read and reread this portion of the book to learn how to release your own inner emotions. I commend you for your courage as you journey deeper on your path of self-discovery.

Always remember that God will never give you more than you can handle, so choosing to feel what you need to heal is part of your own personal destiny. Trust this truth, my friend, and Spirit will be your reward!

CHAPTER 11

Denial

The next several days passed very quickly for me. I slowly began to realize that my desire for any type of drug or alcohol was gone. I remember thinking, "Now that I've stopped smoking and drinking, my life will be so much better." The truth is, I went through painful physical withdrawals from both of these substances for many months. At this point on my path, though, I truly felt that I, myself, was the only reason my addictive behaviors were gone. I had no concept of how a Higher Power actually worked in my life.

The first noticeable difference was an attraction to the outdoors. With my new drug-free lifestyle, I decided to change all of my old playmates and playgrounds. Every friend I had did drugs, so I eliminated them from my life almost overnight. The only real acquaintance in my life at this time was my girlfriend, Summer; and even though she still drank and drugged, for some reason her choices did not seem to bother me.

I found that my connection with my little kid seemed to grow deeper almost every day. I started thinking about my inner child more and more. I returned to communicating with him through writing in my journal every day instead of just every once in awhile. My ability to visualize my little kid more clearly also grew because he was not covered by the cloud of smoke anymore.

I remember the first time I went all day without feeling guilty because I had not consciously hurt my inner child at all that day. This was a new experience for me because prior to this time, I smoked or acted on some other addictive behavior every day, and I consciously knew I was hurting my child within. Being aware of this internal abuse, I always felt guilty. Now that I was not consciously hurting myself any longer, I acquired a sense of personal freedom in my life for the first time.

The next several days passed very quickly for me. I slowly began to realize that my desire for any type of drug or alcohol was gone. I remember thinking, "Now that I've stopped smoking and drinking, my life will be so much better." The truth is, I went through painful physical withdrawals from both of these substances for many months. At this point on my path, though, I truly felt that I, myself, was the only reason my addictive behaviors were gone. I had no concept of how a Higher Power actually worked in my life.

The first noticeable difference was an attraction to the

outdoors. With my new drug-free lifestyle, I decided to change all of my old playmates and playgrounds. Every friend I had did drugs, so I eliminated them from my life almost overnight. The only real acquaintance in my life at this time was my girlfriend, Summer; and even though she still drank and drugged, for some reason her choices did not seem to bother me.

I found that my connection with my little kid seemed to grow deeper almost every day. I started thinking about my inner child more and more. I returned to communicating with him through writing in my journal every day instead of just every once in awhile. My ability to visualize my little kid more clearly also grew because he was not covered by the cloud of smoke anymore.

I remember the first time I went all day without feeling guilty because I had not consciously hurt my inner child at all that day. This was a new experience for me because prior to this time, I smoked or acted on some other addictive behavior every day, and I consciously knew I was hurting my child within. Being aware of this internal abuse, I always felt guilty. Now that I was not consciously hurting myself any longer, I acquired a sense of personal freedom in my life for the first time.

Now before I go on, I want to take a minute and explain what I mean when I say I wasn't consciously hurting my inner child anymore. Consciously hurting ourselves is miles apart from unconsciously hurting ourselves. For me, to consciously hurt myself is to have an awareness that my personal behavior is being detrimental to my inner child and myself.

I was consciously hurting myself by choosing not to change the unloving behavior to a loving behavior, or being powerless to make this change. For example, I knew in my heart that smoking reefer every day was hurting my little kid; although for the longest time, I felt power- less to change this choice.

I have a friend whose little kid told her over and over that she did not feel safe or loved by her boyfriend; however, for six months she chose not to do anything about this situation. I have another friend who runs his own small business with an abusive family member. His little kid told him on numerous occasions that he did not feel comfortable or safe in this work environment. After four years, he finally was able to do something about this unloving partnership.

I share different examples of how we consciously hurt ourselves for a specific reason. When we first start this emotional path of growth, we will naturally see many types of situations or environments that are hurting our inner child and us.

By walking this conscious path with our newly-found ability to see unloving situations more clearly, we will begin to make some conscious changes.

If you are currently in an unhealthy situation and you know you are hurting yourself, it is okay if you can't immediately change. Understand that changes, even for the greater good of your inner child, take time; sometimes quickly, sometimes slowly. For me, the only way these non-loving external changes happened was as a direct reflection of my internal ability to love myself. The more I looked inside and learned how to love my little kid, the deeper my connection was with him. As a consequence of this newly found love connection, my ability to change my outside world grew effortlessly. With these internal changes integrating into my life, it became increasingly not okay with me to allow activities where I consciously knew I was hurting my inner child.

Now if you are wondering how I knew if something was not comfortable for my inner child, all I did was ask him! Every time I asked my little kid about some situation and what his level of comfort was, he would always answer me honestly. It was difficult at first to accept his honesty, especially when his answer did not agree with mine. As a consequence, it took time to change the unhealthy situations in my life.

Sometimes even if a situation was extremely unhealthy for me, it felt safer for me to stay in the misery rather than face my fear of change. Also I had many ego parts that would try to interfere with any type of self-loving change. My rationalizer would say things like, "Well, maybe I just won't smoke reefer all of the time," when my little kid knew we needed to quit completely. My doubter would come in and say, "What does my inner child know anyway? I can't let him run my entire life. I don't trust his judgment or his answers."

My addictions would say, "If I end this unhealthy relationship with my girlfriend, I will never find someone else who will want to be with me—ever!" I also had a codependent voice that would say I couldn't leave my unhealthy situation because I didn't want to hurt my partner's feelings. The truth is, I was afraid to be alone and feel my own grief of abandonment. This ego aspect would try to keep me paralyzed in fear, so that I would not change my unloving behaviors or move forward out of unhealthy environments.

Of course, none of these fear-based responses were true. My loving inner child is connected to the wisdom of the universe. It took a little time, especially in the beginning, to learn how to trust my inner child over these powerful ego voices. I also had to remember that throughout my entire life, these voices of fear had been the only voices to guide and control my life. Naturally, it took me time to shift my awareness and response to a different loving aspect.

In the beginning, my biggest challenge was to learn which voices were ego and which voices were my inner child, Higher Power, or loving adult. The technique I learned was easy for me to follow. I learned that any voice speaking in absolutes such as, can't, never, don't, all or nothing, it has to be my way or no way, it's final, I know that I know, it is always, or any other fear-based response, was my ego. In turn, any voice I heard speaking from a place of love, such as I am here for you, I will support you, I'm proud of you, I can hear you, it's okay to be sad, was my little kid, my Higher Power, or my loving adult.

I eventually learned to distinguish between the different voices by writing on a piece of paper what they were saying to me. Then as I was able to hear things more clearly, my life's direction came down to a simple choice. Do I choose to be guided by fear or faith, doubt or trust, cants or coulds? In the beginning, it was very scary for me to trust myself and follow my loving voices. Over time, though, these loving voices have become who I am.

This transformation of consciousness is very simple. If you follow love, you will feel loved. If you feel internal love, you naturally become love. And as you become love, you will effortlessly remember who you truly are. This feeling of love is the grandest experience of Spirit that a human being can ever imagine.

To hurt ourselves unconsciously is something totally different. This is when our behavior is unloving to others and ourselves, and we are not even aware of it. In this unconscious state of awareness, we can't see our own self-abuse until it is time to see it. A perfect example of this for me is that I never saw my alcoholism as a problem until the day I decided to stop drinking. I never saw any unloving behaviors until the moment I recognized them. I was blinded by my own denial.

The hardest thing for me regarding my unconsciousness was that I had a very difficult time not shaming myself with my own remorse. I always felt as though I should have been able to see my unconscious behaviors as unloving, even though I did not realize I was hurting myself. I understand this sounds insane, but this is how confused I was about my entire process of transformation until I heard the phrase, "We don't beat a baby for touching a hot stove." What this means is that a baby who has never seen or felt a hot stove has no idea of the harm that can come from touching it. So this baby, who is not aware of the natural consequence of touching a hot stove, does not deserve to be shamed for this unloving act.

The same is true of human transformation of consciousness. On any given day, we have the ability to only connect consciously with as much as our awareness will allow. So in turn, as we become more and more internally aware of our love and trust, we become more and more externally aware of love and trust issues.

It used to amaze me how on a Monday I could perceive a particular behavior as okay, but on Tuesday I would wake up and perceive the exact same behavior as unloving. My biggest ego spiral would happen for me when I would try to figure out why I did not see this situation on Monday instead of Tuesday. The answer, I found, is that there is no answer. Trusting the mystery, or divine flow, is the only way I established any type of peace surrounding this unloving behavior. I learned that some things have no answers; they just are.

As we walk this spiritual path of unconsciousness to enlightenment, we will begin to recognize in our day-to-day lives the different aspects that we choose to change. The basic definition of unconsciousness is to be asleep or unaware. So naturally, in a state of unconsciousness, we are going to do, be, and say things that are not very loving to ourselves and others. The key to growth, however, is that as you become consciously aware of your unloving behaviors, hopefully you will choose to change them. For me, choosing these changes, regardless of how big or small, allowed me to grow spiritually every day.

Please understand we cannot change yesterday; we can only grieve the effect it has on us today. We also cannot predict tomorrow, but we can be prepared to change each moment as we choose a more self-loving approach to life. Remember, you can only love others to the degree in which you love yourself. So allow yourself to change and allow yourself to grow with love as each new awareness enters your life, knowing that your love for others will naturally blossom.

◆◆◆

I wish I could share with you that as time went on my life magically seemed to get better. That was not my truth. In fact, as my sober days started to add up, my ability to feel more emotions became much more apparent to me. I began to realize that with no external numbing substances in my body, I could experience what I needed to feel when I needed to feel it. In the beginning of sobriety, as a consequence of my deeper connection with my inner child, my feelings started to come back a little more each day.

It took me awhile to stop shaming myself about experiencing all of these new feelings. I thought I must be doing something wrong or I would not be feeling so horrible every day. The truth is, in the beginning, the more love I gave to my inner child, the more open he became with me. The natural consequence of him opening up and trusting me was the awareness of my true inner pain.

I also started remembering aspects of my childhood I had totally forgotten. I remembered things like how lonely and sad I felt each night when my father would leave for work, because I always wished he had stayed home with me. I remembered how sad and confused I felt when I was nine years old and my oldest sister went off to college. I remembered how confused I was about sex at twelve years old because no one had ever sat with me and explained how it worked. My list of old childhood memories went on and on, and as I made a deeper connection with my inner child, those suppressed memories surfaced.

I began to feel the anger and resentment I had toward people and friends who had treated me badly. If you become confused about why you are feeling and remembering so much old stuff during this initial process, a deeper connection with your inner child is the reason.

Emotions in a healthy environment are energy in motion. Most of us, however, have lived in less than perfect environments when it comes to realizing and expressing our true emotions. During my own childhood, each time I was not able to experience my emotions in the moment, this energy had to go somewhere. In fact, my unexpressed emotions had to be stuffed back inside. As my internal connection grew with my inner child, I stopped stuffing my emotions, so naturally they had to come out. I had stuffed my feelings of being mad, glad, sad, and scared for over thirty years, so when it was finally time for me to release them, that is exactly what happened.

The first two months of sobriety were not too bad. I had a few emotional releases, but not very many. In these first days of sobriety, my cravings for any mind-altering substance had gone away for the most part. Each time I did have any type of cravings, I used this sensation as a red flag to alert me that my inner child was getting ready to feel something he needed in order to heal. A couple of times during these cravings I would go outside, lie on the ground, and ask Mother Earth to remove the energy of the craving so I could feel my little kid's wound. Several times this technique of asking for external support from Mother Nature helped me through the craving, and allowed me to actually feel what I needed to heal.

Then on April 15, 1994, my craving for drugs hit me like a ton of bricks. I was on my way to Florida on a business trip. With each mile I traveled, my cravings got stronger. I consciously knew my inner child was hurting, although I could not connect with his pain. My cravings became so strong that I had no chance to stop them. Once I reached my destination, the first thing I did was get stoned. The quantity of marijuana I smoked that night was very small, but its effect was horrible. I spent the entire night feeling extremely paranoid and totally disconnected. My remorse and guilt also flooded in because of my unloving behavior. I kept saying to myself over and over, "How could I have been so weak?" The truth is, I was totally powerless over what happened that night, which was my 59th day of sobriety.

Later that evening, I realized my craving for more drugs was gone, and I realized the quantity I smoked was less than one- fourth of a joint. At 3:00 in the morning, I intuitively knew that something was up with my inner child. I had no idea what it was, but I knew it had to be big.

The next day I woke up early. I felt very peaceful, regardless of the prior evening's events. I decided to take advantage of the Florida beach and go enjoy a long walk by myself. As I completed my walk, I sat for awhile to enjoy the awesome power of Spirit in the ocean. As I sat there that morning, I started to have full-blown visual and emotional memories of being sexually molested as a child.

I saw in total detail, as if someone had plugged in a movie projector, what had happened to me twenty-four years before. I was seven years old when two sixteen-year-old boys sexually abused me very badly. I went into total shock, knowing without a shadow of a doubt that everything I had just seen in my mind's eye was totally true. On that day, my little kid had the courage and trust to open up and show me our old severe abuse, which had been totally buried in denial for so many years. I suddenly knew why my cravings to protect myself were so great the night before. I also knew that my life would never be the same again.

I left Florida with a new awareness of a past trauma to my inner child, which put a lot of old pieces together for me. It blew my mind to realize that not only was I trying to recover from multiple addictions, but I was a survivor of sexual abuse.

I remember thinking, "My God, what could possibly be next?"

On my drive home, I truly wondered if I would ever tell anyone what I had just experienced. My first thought was to keep this a secret forever. Then as the hours went by and my feelings of being lost and alone overwhelmed me, I knew I needed to share this trauma with someone. That drive home to Atlanta from Florida was the longest six hours of my life. Every possible emotion came up for me. Shame and guilt raced through every cell of my body. The thoughts of how I could let them do that to me started to become very loud in my head. I also wondered why I never fought back or yelled. Self-hatred was oozing out of every pore of me. I could not accept that big, bad, 220-pound Joe could have had this type of abuse in my life. Then my greatest feeling of shame came forth, saying that there really was something wrong with me because I was molested as a child.

It took me many years, and a lot of work, to heal from this new awareness of severe abuse. Thankfully, the more I looked at and connected with my inner child's truth, the more I healed.

◆◆◆

Let me explain how I nurtured my inner child enough to heal these deep, dark wounds. I do want to say that if you were also sexually abused as a child, know that you are okay! I'm here to tell you there is hope, and you can heal these wounds just like I did. You are not alone. Experts guess that as many as seven out of ten little girls experience some type of sexual abuse during their pre-adult life, and three out of ten boys experience the same type of abuse. So if sexual abuse happened to you, please seek support. There are groups and therapists who support this type of abuse almost exclusively. I know that the primary feelings around any type of sexual abuse are shame, guilt, sexual addiction, and isolation. These experiences all stem from the consequence of this severe trauma.

As a child, it is impossible, without proper support, to digest or process such a hurtful event. Being extremely resilient, a child will do or believe anything he/she needs to for survival. My own little kid just shut down completely and totally forgot the event. Other people have dramatic memories, but deny that it ever happened or that it has ever affected them. Some people protect themselves from the real pain of this event by blaming themselves for their own abuse.

As a sexual abuse survivor, you are not to blame for the actions that happened to you as a child. You were powerless.

By thinking that sexual abuse has not affected your entire life, you are lying to yourself. Sexual abuse affects all facets of our being—the emotional, spiritual, mental, and physical. So stop blaming yourself, and move through the shame and isolation to seek help.

I understand, my friend, that it will take a lot of courage to do this; but if I can do it, so can you. I understand that at first your shame and humiliation might be great; however, in healing these issues, your freedom and joy will far surpass any depth of pain you might be feeling right now. Remember, if I can do it, so can you! Please seek support as you heal your wounds, and watch how your world will be changed forever.

◆◆◆

I lived the next five months in total shock. I would process this newly-found issue just about every day. My life was a living hell. I still lived with Summer, but our activities together were about nil. I felt so vulnerable that I never wanted to leave the house. My business activities were almost obsolete, so my fear of lack of money haunted me every day. I remember day after day sitting on the couch, thinking about what had happened to me; just waiting for my inner child to cry some more.

I had grieving feelings surrounding my self-pity and confusion. I would continually spiral with the same shame-based questions, "Why me? What did I do that was so wrong to be punished like this?"

During the beginning years of this new awareness about my personal abuse, I realized I had taken on the belief that God was punishing me because he let this type of experience happen in my world. Eventually, I learned that God has nothing to do with people's free will. God did not make these boys hurt me like they did; it was their choice based on their own abuse. I will tell you, though, this concept may have been easily said, but honestly, it took me a long time to actually believe it. Looking back now, it's easy for me to see why I took on the belief that God was punishing me.

As a child, the only exposure I had to God was through the Catholic church. My perception of this organization was simple: I was taught to believe that if I did anything wrong, then I had sinned, and God punishes sinners by sending them to hell. I personally never understood this whole false belief system of hell, particularly as I got older; but as a child, I took everything at face value. So because my abuse felt so wrong as a little kid,

I took on the false belief that God was punishing me because in some way I must have done something wrong. It took me a couple of years to heal this skewed belief of Great Spirit.

It's important to elaborate on this ego belief that God created a horrible place called hell where he sends all sinners. First of all, I think most people believe that God is all powerful and all love. I believe that if I stated that God is pure unconditional love, most people would agree with me. So if God is pure unconditional love, and unconditional love has no conditions attached to it, then God's love for us must be totally accepting of all aspects of self. Therefore, if God's love for us is in total acceptance of us, there can be no judgment because total acceptance means no judgment. As a consequence of no judgment, the idea of a judging God is totally ridiculous.

If God is all love, with total acceptance, producing no judgment, then the concept of right and wrong, or sins, cannot come from God. In turn, the concept of punishing people by sending them to hell because they have supposedly done something wrong, cannot come from God. In fact, the whole false concept of hell was produced by our egos years ago to keep us in fear of God.

Think about it logically for a moment. To fear pure love, or God, makes no sense at all because fear cannot exist where love resides. I choose to love a God with no judgment. As a result, I have gained the courage to let go of the judging and criticizing of myself, allowing love and acceptance to enter. Keep in mind that the degree to which we love ourselves is truly the degree to which we can love others.

In my experience, I have found that many organizations try to motivate their followers to love God through the fear of the consequence called hell. To me, this type of manipulation is extremely abusive and has nothing to do with the love of Great Spirit.

CHAPTER 12

The Magic of Anger

After about five months of processing my self-hatred and feelings of not being good enough, something happened that made a huge impact on my life. My girlfriend, Summer, called me late one night at our home to ask me to come pick her up from a bar where she was drinking. Of course, being a good boy, I went to pick her up—no questions asked—sober as a judge. Everything about that evening seemed normal except for one thing; for the first time in my life, I felt very angry.

One reason for my anger was that I was not able to drink and party anymore like she was. I was also angry that she asked me to come pick her up because she was drunk. Most of all, I was angry with myself because I actually went and did it.

I will never forget how great it felt for me that night to own my anger with Summer, face to face. For the first time in my life, I was not projecting my anger; I owned it. I told her I was angry she was drunk and had called me to pick her up. I told her I was angry about having to do this when I did not want to. I also told her I felt the environment in which we lived together was not safe anymore for me. I shared my truth and told her I was going to move because my little kid was not feeling safe living with her.

Now of course, because of where Summer was back then, she could not hear or understand anything I was saying, but it didn't matter to me. At that particular point in my life, I was processing my self-hatred every day; therefore, I had no money, no real job, and no ability to get off the couch. Regardless of my reality, however, in my heart I knew I had to leave.

Summer and I spoke about my decision in more detail the next day. We decided I would leave by the end of the month. I had no idea where I was going, but I knew I had to go. As the end of the month neared, I finally realized what had truly happened for me on the night I picked up Summer from the bar. I had been so angry I could not see straight, and for the first time, I actually knew this feeling of anger was all mine. I consciously became aware that my personal anger was a part of me; it was my stuff and my responsibility. With this new place of personal ownership, I intuitively knew it was time to do something about it.

Two days before I actually had to leave, I remembered my father had created a one-room area in our old catering warehouse. I realized this would be the perfect place for me to stay. This warehouse was in the business district of a small Georgia town, about fifty miles north of Atlanta. I knew I wouldn't know anyone in this city, but I decided it was okay because, in my new world of sobriety, I didn't know anyone in Atlanta, either.

On the last day of August, 1994, I walked out of my one-and-a-half-year relationship with Summer into a total void. It felt strange for me to leave her because we were great friends, we rarely fought, and we had a great sex life together. On the surface, except for the fact that she still drank, our relationship seemed perfect to my adult self. The truth for my little kid, however, was that he did not feel safe with her anymore. So I had to go.

I left her apartment that day while she was still at work. I never even said goodbye because my pain was too great. I just knew it was time to go, and that is what I did. In that moment, I felt as though I were walking into a total black hole of the unknown. As I pulled out of her driveway, I remember crying because I was leaving a close friend, and because I was scared to death. Looking back on that day, even though I did not know it at the time, God was totally driving my car because emotionally I was a total wreck.

I was living on pure blind faith. I was leaving my old world with no money, no job, no friends, and with a car that barely ran, heading toward my new world in the mountains of northern Georgia. To tell you the truth, I was in such an emotional state, I don't remember the drive at all. I just remember driving into nowhere land, with only my inner child to guide me.

On the surface, I acted very confident about my decision, but the entire time I questioned whether or not I was making the right choice. I had no idea where my path was leading me; I just knew that my life's choices had to change. I felt I was looking for something, but I had no idea what it was. I knew intuitively something inside of me was changing, although I could not connect it to my new truth at all. I did know that where I was living in that moment was not okay, and I hoped where I was going would be better.

Honestly, I was absolutely terrified with my life during those days. Most of the time I felt totally crazy and extremely alone. The only voice that kept me moving forward was my quester voice saying, "My little kid deserves to heal. He deserves it." In response to this voice, I continued to drive out of my old life in Atlanta and into the darkness of my own mystery. I realized on this drive north, as my courage to continue moving forward grew, the main reason my inner child did not feel safe around Summer was because she was so angry and not yet on her conscious path of enlightenment. Summer's life was taking her one way, and my life was taking me another. Neither of us was right nor wrong – just different. As this new awareness came to me, I knew I was making the right decision. I was still terrified of what lay ahead, but I knew my choice to move forward was right for me and my little kid.

I arrived in Gainesville, Georgia late that afternoon with only two pairs of pants, three shirts, and a pair of tennis shoes to my name. I had moved so often over the years that moving was very easy for me. The difficult part was settling in. I walked into this big, cold warehouse and then into a two-room area.

It was cold and dirty, but it did feel safe. I immediately got started cleaning the place and putting my clothes away. I realized then what a vagabond I had become. I owned almost nothing. I guess when you can't work and you live on almost nothing, you end up with nothing. To be honest, though, I really didn't care. At this point in my life, the only thing that mattered for me was to stay dry, eat once a day, and heal my inner child. The room had high vaulted ceilings filled with cobwebs. The floors were bare concrete with some small areas covered with extremely dirty carpet. My new dwelling did have a bathroom that was clean and a kitchen with a working sink and stove. I remember feeling extremely grateful for these simple necessities. I sat there that night, all alone, wondering what had happened to my life. I remember being grateful because I had a CD radio player to keep me company. I had no TV and no heat, but I did have a telephone. My first call from my new home was to my counselor, Sandy; although on that particular weekend she had actually gone out-of-town. As I hung up the phone, I sat down and felt the depths of how lonely and alone my life had become. I was in a strange town with no money and no friends, and I started to wonder how things could possibly get any worse.

For the next couple of hours I sat with my journal, writing to my little kid, trying to get him settled in. This was our conversation:

Adult Joe: How are you doing?

Little Joe: I am very scared.

AJ: Why are you scared?

LJ: Because it is the first time in our lives that we are completely alone together.

AJ: Are you okay with this?

LJ: I am, if you are.

With this I tried to sleep the rest of the night away.

My anxiety from this huge move made me very sleepy, but I remember waking up in the middle of the night shaking with terror. As my eyes opened, I could not remember or figure out where I was. It took me a good hour to calm down enough to fall back to sleep. At that moment I felt I was in a living hell. The funny thing was, though, I knew in my heart that I was exactly where I was supposed to be.

The next morning I woke up in a pretty good mood. It was very early, but the sun was already out. I remember feeling every muscle in my body aching. It was not unusual for me to feel like this because of all of the emotional releases I had every day. Sandy explained my muscle soreness. She said that when the body stuffs emotions, it stores the energy in the cells and muscles. When we have an emotional release, these violent energy surges cause the body to be extremely sore.

Most days, I woke up feeling as though my body had just been run over by a truck. I don't tell you this to scare you, but to educate you on the physical effects of emotional release. It's important to remember that if your body gets really sore and sluggish, know that you are okay. The only relief I have found for this soreness is long, hot salts baths combined with a lot of rest and time.

As the rest of my day progressed, I realized very quickly why I needed to be totally alone for awhile. The answer was rage! As usual, I communicated with my inner child through journal writing, and he thanked me for leaving the unhealthy environments of my old girlfriend's home. He also said to me,

I am angry. I am angry at everything...
I am angry that we are alone.
I am angry with all of my old girlfriends who left us.
I am angry with my father for never being there for me.
I am angry with my sister for going away from us.
I am angry with my grandmother for dying.
I am angry with God for not rescuing me.
I am angry at everything and everybody I have ever known.
I am angry at the world.

When my little kid made this last statement, "I am angry at the world," I experienced a tremendous amount of feeling surrounding this reality. I jumped up and looked for something to hit. I found a shovel, broke off the handle, and began hitting everything in sight. This was the first time in all of these years of releasing that I actually felt and knew that my anger was coming from my inner child. He was so angry, I thought I was going to explode.

I swung the handle over my head and slammed it down onto my bed with extreme intensity. I had released anger before, but it was nothing like this. I yelled and screamed every profanity I knew for at least three hours. My hands actually got blisters on them from swinging that handle over and over. I was very grateful for the high ceilings because I was not hindered at all in my swings. I released so much energy that day it is hard to describe.

I remember every time I thought I was done, I would stand and start all over again. Time and time again I beat that bed. Finally, after three hours, I had just totally run out of gas. With that I dropped the handle, lay down, and fell asleep.

When I woke up, I literally felt as though I had just lost my mind. The rage I expressed that day had come from a very deep place without any restrictions, and my ego asked the question, "Is this normal behavior or is there something really wrong with me?"

The following day I called Sandy, and she helped me clarify what had happened. She explained to me that my little kid finally was feeling totally safe with me, so he would start to release his deepest, darkest emotions. My decision to follow his internal guidance was a huge step in allowing my little kid to begin to trust me. As a natural consequence of this deeper level of internal trust, his ability and desire to open up to me grew tremendously overnight.

The sensations I experienced the previous day were absolutely, without question, the single most intense moments of my life. I hung up the phone that evening with Sandy thinking, "Wow! If my little kid is really opening up to me, I wonder what else he has to share."

◆◆◆

Let's break from the story for a moment so that I may explain what it feels like to release the kind of rage I just described. To be honest with you, the feeling of power is absolutely awesome. The anger energy being released is happening in a completely safe environment, so no one, including you, is being hurt. This type of expression is a pure form of energy release and there is nothing to be afraid of. Personally, I chose to have this type of release by myself because it felt safer for me this way. Some people choose to release anger with someone else present because they are afraid of its end results. Whichever way your inner child feels comfortable is okay.

Remember to give yourself permission to say anything you need to say about anyone during these experiences. I chose to say every vulgar thing possible to allow all of the anger energy to be released. Also, know that just because you have one day of anger release doesn't mean you are finished. For me, the next four months of my life proved to be filled with similar anger experiences.

Other ways to release anger are through writing, or tearing up phone books. I used these techniques when my body was too sore to swing the handle, or when my throat was too sore to yell. Sometimes when my little kid was angry with any particular person, I would get a photo of that person, put it on my bed, and beat the picture into a million pieces. I remember beating into a thousand pieces the photos of old friends who had left me. Then I would pick up the pieces off the floor and beat them again.

The absolute key is to do whatever it takes to allow your anger energy to come up and out. Personally, I have released anger now for over six years; however, without a doubt, those first four months were my most intense times because it happened every day, at least three hours a day.

So remember, if you feel like you have a lot of anger to release, you probably do. Understand, though, that it will only come out a little at a time; so in turn, it takes time for it all to be released. If your anger seems to last a long time, this is okay. Also, if your anger seems to overwhelm you, or you think there's too much to express, always remember God will never give you more than you can handle. So again, please know that you are okay.

In my opinion, the first day an individual truly has the ability to feel the emotion of anger in a healthy environment needs to be a day of celebration. Our false belief systems around anger are deeply rooted. In fact, ninety nine percent of society still unknowingly judge anger as bad or negative. Most people also label this emotion as hurtful or hateful. The truth is, none of these false paradigms is true.

The emotion of anger itself is not the problem. The problem comes when people choose to take their anger out on society. This God-given emotion was not originally designed to cross someone's boundaries; for example, by yelling, hitting, or manipulating someone. The healthy emotion of anger is designed to allow an individual to feel when someone has crossed his or her own boundaries. So, my friend, it is very loving to feel healthy anger when someone is hurting you in any way.

Another key for allowing anger to flow is to not label it as bad or negative. These are confining labels of the ego, because to label anything is to judge it. For me, when I was judging something, there was no way I could fully accept it; and lack of acceptance is where my resistance to any emotion grew. I also learned the hard way that my internal pain comes from resisting an emotion, not from the emotion itself.

All emotions are God-given gifts. When I learned to look at them like this, my resistance to their expression lessened. I know this seems much easier said than done, especially in the beginning. Anger, fear, and grief were all such new expressions of life for me that in the beginning, they were extremely uncomfortable to feel. With time and practice, though, I found that all emotions have a wonderful consequence to their expression.

It takes a lot of courage to actually own and uncover our lost, self-called anger. It is truly a day to celebrate when we are able to feel and express anger in a healthy environment. It takes the courage of a true spiritual warrior to work through all of the false fears and actually feel this awesome God-given gift called anger.

I also want to remind you, one last time, that the expression of suppressed anger is done in the privacy of your own private space, using the techniques already discussed. Anger is never healthy if you are projecting it on society in any way. So to truly heal the deep suppressed layers of rage, the key is to lovingly allow this emotion to flow through you using techniques like those mentioned. Just because some aspect of you is angry with someone does not mean that you don't love them, too. From the beginning of this journey, I have released suppressed anger concerning every living being in my life, but I never stopped loving any one of them.

If you find yourself in the middle of a rage-filled portion of your path, I know you will probably think that you can't possibly have any- thing to celebrate. All I can say to you, my friend, is trust me. Under these layers of rage I found the real spiritual me. Most people cannot comprehend the experience of living as our true Spirit; but again I say, just trust yourself, because it is awesome. If I can do it, so can you. Find the courage to feel what you need to heal, and the consequence will be spiritual and magical.

◆◆◆

I realize my story is very extreme, so if you're thinking you really don't have three hours every day to release anger, I understand. Let me offer hope to you by sharing a friend's experience with anger.

When Sally first started communicating with her little girl, she really thought she had no stuffed anger at all. Her ego continually told her she had nothing to be angry about. Over time, though, with the intention to connect deeper and deeper with her inner child, Sally eventually started to ask her little girl if she was angry.

In the beginning, the only feeling Sally experienced in response to this question was fear. It took time, and continual nurturing and communication, before her little girl shared that she was terrified of anger.

Her little girl does not always speak to her in words. Most of the time, Sally's clarity comes to her in her knowing. One day she remembered how scared she used to feel every time her mother would take her anger out on her by yelling and screaming. Sally's little girl only experienced the emotion of anger as something hurtful, and something to be afraid of. So once this old belief was discovered, Sally was able to talk to her little girl and explain the truth about healthy anger. She told her inner child over and over that it was okay to be angry. She explained to her little girl that it was okay to express her anger because she was in a safe environment, and no one would ever shame her again for this feeling. Sally was very patient and loving with her inner child until she actually felt safe enough to start expressing her suppressed rage. Unlike me, Sally has a full-time job, a nice apartment, and a new car. Her path obviously does not allow her to release three hours a day, day after day. So she chooses to release her anger whenever time is available. She uses the technique of screaming in her car on the way to work to release her anger. She spends time on the weekends alone with her inner child, allowing her to feel and express her feelings. She also writes in her journal a lot, which allows her little girl to express herself by writing some of her anger down on paper.

In my opinion, the key to Sally's success in her anger release is that she does not judge her little girl for being angry. She gives her little girl permission to feel and say anything she needs about anyone she knows. She never shames her inner child for expressing herself; in fact, she encourages her to feel what she needs to heal. As a natural consequence of these loving choices, her inner child now has become much more comfortable with the healthy expression of this deep emotion called anger. Sally's little girl trusts her more now, too, because she is allowed to feel what she needs to heal and is never shamed for it.

The primary reason for not shaming our inner child for his/her anger is because as an actual child, very few young people are allowed or encouraged to express their anger. In fact, most children are shamed or hit if they express any anger at all. The consequence of this type of shaming behavior is a deep wound in our inner child surrounding anger issues.

Think about it logically for a minute. Anger is a God-given emotional gift, so of course, each child has the natural ability to feel it. However, because most children are never validated or encouraged to express their anger, they start believing there is something wrong with them because they have angry feelings. As we grow up in a society that perpetuates shame around anger issues, we feel there is something wrong with us because we feel anger. Over time, we internalize this sensation, and toxic shame is created. The more this vicious cycle happens, the deeper our sense of personal shame grows.

As we start the process of becoming aware of our stuffed anger, and start the re-education process for our inner child that it is okay to have this feeling, we also have to start breaking the old spiral of toxic shame associated with anger. So remember, if by chance it takes you a long time to actually feel suppressed anger, know that this is okay. It took a long time for my inner child to feel safe enough to actually trust me, and to know that it is okay to express anger.

If you are someone who has been hurt by someone else's anger by constantly being yelled at, by physical abuse, or by sexual abuse, it might take your little kid even longer to work through his/her fears and reconnect to his/her own anger sensations. So please be patient and loving with your inner child, continually reassuring him/her that it is okay to express rage; and trust that time is the only variable for your own personal celebration of the magical experience of releasing stuffed rage.

Personally, I experienced the creation of a deeper sense of internal peace by being able to release my suppressed anger. I will admit that this internal peace was certainly not there every day, but had a strong presence on certain days. I guess the best way for me to describe this new sensation of peace is that even though I was processing and releasing every day, and my life seemed to be one big raw emotion, I still knew deep in my heart that I was doing the right thing. Some deep part of me kept growing and saying, "We need to get these emotions out of ourselves. Better out than in."

I listened to this voice and continually allowed my emotions to flow out of myself in a safe environment. This was the foundation of my newly-found sense of peace. Peace, to me, is a feeling of safeness and trust, and by continually following my path, I realized I had both.

An external consequence of allowing my stuffed anger to flow out of me was my tolerance for the rest of the world. I could actually drive in traffic, and not feel like I was going to explode. I could see and speak with my parents, and not want to bite off their heads. I could actually sit down and read a book, and not feel like I always needed to be moving around. For me, the process of releasing this pent-up volcano of anger energy allowed me to see the world through a totally new pair of eyes.

My friend, it is hard to explain the concept of human transformation of consciousness if you have never experienced it. However, this phenomenon just naturally happens for us as we choose to release our stuffed emotions. The experience is similar to that of a blind man who has been blind all of his life. Then one day, with some miracle surgery, his sight is regained little by little.

I used to wake up on the mornings after a big emotional release, and perceive the entire world in totally different way. The color of the trees and the sky would be brighter. The way I looked at everything would be different. My personal need for any type of mind-altering substance was gone, so my personal feeling toward life in general got better every day. I finally was able to wake up and want to live, instead of wanting to die. My entire outlook on life changed. One day I would feel like I was living in a black cloud, and then after a big release I would live as the sun itself.

As these experiences were happening for me, I had no conscious idea of what was going on throughout the day. I describe this phenomenon as human transformation of consciousness. My vibration of consciousness literally raised itself from day to day. Over time, the self-hatred voices inside of me, which used to shame and persecute me, effortlessly went away. The experience of always feeling as though I had done something wrong also transformed. My self-hatred and low self-esteem diminished naturally and effortlessly, because of my choice to allow my suppressed anger to be expressed outwardly instead of holding on to it inwardly.

My anger-turned-inward was responsible for my self-hatred and low self-esteem; so as I helped my inner child point this suppressed anger in the appropriate outward direction, the natural consequence was the growth of my self-love instead of self-hatred. Naturally, the more self-love I felt, the more my inner child's wounds were able to heal from the inside out. Of course, as I have mentioned many times, the consequence of the healing of my inner child's wounds was the unloving voices in my head effortlessly being transformed.

Naturally, all of this has taken time to manifest. This healing process did not happen for me overnight. Day by day, though, with my intention to heal in place, it did happen for me. No more wounds! No more voices!

Today it is hard to describe to you how great it feels not to be badgered by my old unloving voices. The freedom I feel as a consequence of this new realty is absolutely magical. I am so grateful to Sandy and to Great Spirit for allowing me the strength and courage I needed to feel and express my deep suppressed rage. The greatest single day of my life was probably when I learned how to allow my suppressed rage to flow out of me instead of holding it inside.

My friend, please trust me; I know expressing anger at first is very scary, but as you walk through this fear, you will be walking through a veil into a life of self-love and glory. If I can do it, so can you. Please ask Great Spirit for the support you need to feel what you need to heal and watch your life change forever.

In Search of Our Light

As we observe with an honest eye The reality of humanity,
We find that the greatest sense of separation Is a life of light,
or a life in the dark.
This is not a judgment of good or bad, right or wrong;
It is a discernment of different spiritual paths.
So often our paths are changed by life's actions, Creating
pain from within,
Or a simple voice that says something needs to be different.
Even though change is very difficult for most, It sometimes
is truly necessary.
As we develop a willingness to learn, Change also becomes
very empowering.
The sense of living in the light
Is a spiritual path that is seeking the truth; The path of
a warrior who has the courage to accept
A life of love and service to others, And a sense of an
enlightened Spirit
With an awareness that all feelings start from within.
As we muster the courage to live our light, We are a beacon
to a society of hope.
Hope allows all paths to search for the truth.
A simple helping hand or a word of encouragement Can change
others' lives forever.
The higher purpose of life is to learn life's lessons, To grow with
love, and to help others do the same.
As we live with love for ourselves and others,
We suddenly realize the light we have been searching for
Has been there all along.
This light is the love and compassion of the Spirit Of which
we truly are.
The search for our light is an inner voyage seeking truth,
Seeking abundance, seeking love.
The search for our light is a path that reaches a place
No one has gone before.
The search for our light is the quest to live The life
of our true Spirit.

In Search of Our Light

CHAPTER 13

Loneliness vs. Aloneness

Other experiences that happened for me a lot during the beginning years of my process were the feelings of loneliness and the fear of aloneness. They sound similar, but in reality they're very different. Loneliness is a feeling that often is associated with fear and grief. It is an experience associated with needing or a longing for someone or something else in our lives.

For me, loneliness was felt more during this process because of my new awareness of my wounded little kid. I realized during this process that as a child I was lonely all of the time, so I continually sought some type of connection with anyone who was around me. Naturally, since I lived in an unconscious environment, everyone I knew was emotionally closed down and seemed to be very distant, which was very sad, very scary, and very lonely for me.

As a child, the creation of activities in my life was healthy because they were all done in moderation. As I got a little older, I started to do more things so I would not feel so lonely; and all of these old behaviors turned into avenues for keeping me out of my true feelings. As life continued for me, these behaviors eventually turned into addictions. By transforming my addictive behaviors, I began to slow down and experience my emotions again; consequently, the old feeling of loneliness was inevitable.

Aloneness is an experience that happens as we understand more fully that we can embrace our solitude and heal ourselves. It is an expression of self that, when validated, will reconnect an individual to the oneness that resides in us all. Aloneness is very scary, though, because it feels like you are on a rowboat in the middle of the ocean with no land in sight. It feels like you are the only person on this planet.

The biggest difference between aloneness and loneliness is that aloneness normally has no externally connected desire to be with someone else to fix us. Aloneness is associated also with the spiritual phrase, in the world, though not of it.

Extreme feelings of aloneness normally happen in the beginning of the emotional growth process. This happens because as we grow and change consciously, and our environment does not, we become aware on a very deep level that we are uniquely different from our environment and are, therefore, very alone.

I supported myself through deep feelings of aloneness in two ways. First, I created a new external environment with like-minded people who, at least to some degree, were looking at life the same way I was. I sought out people who emotionally were trying to grow in twelve-step programs or through inner child awareness. I looked at opened-hearted churches I could attend to find an external support system. I also used my counselor, Sandy, every day as a support person and a loving guide of light through my very dark and scary times of aloneness.

The second thing I did to feel my aloneness was to teach the inner child aspect of myself that spiritually we have never been alone. The universal truth says God has always been with us, regardless of whether or not we can see or sense this presence.

Now for me, my inner child took on the belief that God abandoned me because of the extreme abuse I went through. My little kid would say, "If God is truly with me, then why did he let those boys rape me?" The answer is, God allows the choice of free will to exist in all situations. This is the greatest gift to mankind. God will not stop any action or activity of a human being, regardless if it is loving or not; however, God will provide the internal strength and courage each person needs to survive in any environment.

I explained to my inner child that God gave us the courage to live, even though we wanted to die after our abuse; that God was the source of our strength when we wanted to give up; and God is the love inside us helping to nurture us through our deepest, darkest times. Over a long period of time, this is how I educated my inner child that even though we did not know it consciously, God has always been there, supplying us with the courage, the strength, and the love we've needed to live and flourish. As my inner child healed some of his deepest wounds, he was able to reconnect to this truth and experience the oneness that resides in us all.

I healed my loneliness by developing a strong and loving nurturing adult inside of me. I realized that the reason I always felt so lonely was because I was alone so much as a child. As a consequence of my father working two jobs, and my mother basically raising four children by herself, my emotional needs of time and love could not be met. So as a child, whenever my needs weren't met, I took on the belief that there was something wrong with me.

It's important to note that it's normal for children to blame themselves for everything. Children, through their narcissism, believe they are the center of the universe. So when anything goes wrong, children will naturally take on the belief that it was their fault.

As a child, my emotional needs weren't met, so I naturally developed a lonely feeling inside and went seeking love. Living in an unconscious environment, true love was not something that was ever going to be found, and as a child, I naturally took on the insane belief that I did not deserve to be loved. Of course, looking at it logically, we know that all children deserve to be loved.

Now the question I asked myself was, "How do I heal this deep, lonely feeling?" My ego would tell me that all I had to do to not feel lonely was to have a girlfriend, or to be around a lot of people. However, neither of these choices stopped my lonely feeling inside. I could be in a group of a hundred people or more and still feel totally lost and lonely. I also could be intertwined in a totally committed and intimate relationship with the woman of my dreams and still feel lonely inside. During this process, I eventually became aware that wherever I go, there I am. So if I am experiencing a feeling of loneliness, it does not matter where I go or with whom; the feeling is still there inside.

It took me a long time to accept this statement as a truth because my ego always said, "I just have not found the right girl yet." This statement is not true! I learned that only I can heal my own feelings of loneliness. Whenever I experienced deep feelings of loneliness, I used these feelings as a red flag to warn me that my inner child needed me because some emotion was coming up for him. I learned to help him through this difficult time by using my experience of loneliness as an internal signal that he needed extra nurturing from me as a loving adult.

It was during this time on my path that I truly learned what it meant to be a loving adult. I first needed to learn how to be loving to myself. Before this time, I could love my little kid only by closing the world off from us completely and waiting for him to release his suppressed emotions. I give myself an "A" for effort, but the truth is, there is a lot more to loving our inner child than that. So I decided to learn some additional self-loving techniques to help nurture my inner child through these difficult times.

The first action I always chose was to communicate with my little kid through journal writing. Our conversations would go something like this:

Adult Joe: Little Joe, how are you feeling?

Little Joe: I am feeling very lost, and lonely, and scared.

AJ: Would you like to share with me more about that?

LJ: Yes. I remember always wanting my daddy to come to my games, and he never did. I was always the only boy whose father never came. I guess he doesn't love me. I guess I did something wrong.

AJ: Little Joe, I hear your pain and confusion. Would you like to share with me some more?

LJ: I wish my daddy had come to my ball games. I feel sad and lonely because he must not love me.

AJ: Little Joe, I hear your pain. Would you like to share more?

LJ: I just wanted someone to love me and hug me. I just wanted to be loved.

This is where I would stop writing and in my mind's eye I would hug and love my little kid. If you noticed, I never tried to convince my child that our daddy did love us. I simply allowed him to express his view of the situation, and acknowledged him for what he was feeling in the moment. I acknowledged that I heard him, and persuaded him to share more with me by leading him with a question like, "Would you like to share more with me?" Whenever I asked this question, my inner child rarely said no. Like most kids, he is a talker.

At the very end of our communication, when he would tell me what he really wanted from my father and never got, I would stop our conversation, and in my mind's eye, give him what he asked for. As a loving adult, I would literally re-parent myself by giving my little child the attention he needed.

Other times when we would have conversations together, my little kid would not be able to ask for anything. As a loving adult, I intuitively learned that if my inner child was lonely, he needed to be hugged and loved.

Numerous times during our conversations my inner child would feel lonely and afraid because he felt as though he had done something wrong. During these conversations I would acknowledge his confusion, and then I would restate the truth for him so he could see the reality more clearly. Here is an example of one of these conversations:

Adult Joe: Little Joe, how are you feeling?

Little Joe: I am lonely and scared.

AJ: I hear this, my friend. Would you like to share more with me?

LJ: One day my mommy and daddy got in a fight, and I was scared.

AJ: Little Joe, I hear your fear. Would you like to share more?

LJ: They were yelling at each other and were angry. I must have done something wrong. They must be angry with me.

AJ: Little Joe, I hear your fear. Would you like to share more?

LJ: I don't like it when they are angry. If my daddy leaves, who will take care of me? He must be mad at me.

AJ: Little Joe, I hear your fear. Why do you think our daddy is mad at you?
LJ: Because he is mad and is yelling at Mommy.
AJ: Little Joe, I hear your confusion. The truth is, sometimes adults
get angry at each other and fight, but it has nothing to do with you.
You have done nothing wrong. You are just a little boy.
You are perfect and lovable, and did nothing wrong.
he truth is, now I am here to take care of you. I love you, and will protect and take care of you.
LJ: What about my mommy? Who will take care of her?
AJ: Little Joe, Mommy has a Higher Power, too, so she can take care of herself. It is not our responsibility to take care of our mommy.
LJ: Will you help me?
AJ: Yes, Little Joe, I will love and protect you forever!

When these types of conversations arise, it is the responsibility of our loving adult to explain to our confused little kid the truth of the real situation. The situation I just shared happened for me when I was eight years old. It was very confusing for me at that age because my parents never truly fought in front of me. During that fight, though, I thought my father was going to abandon us forever, so I took on the false belief that I had to take care of my mother. That fight affected my entire life from that day on. In a normal conscious environment, the next day after a confusing situation like this everything would have been explained, and love would have been felt. However, in my situation, the next day nothing was said and everyone acted as if this fight never existed. As a natural consequence of no loving explanation, I held on to those false beliefs the rest of my life.

As I learned to re-parent my inner child, I also learned how to guide him out of my old false beliefs, enabling him to experience the real truth. I also reassured him over and over that I would be there for him to hold him and hug him as he expressed his tears of fear and confusion.
As a loving adult, we not only need to be there to listen to our inner child, we also need to explain the true loving reality to him/ her. As an actual child, many things were very confusing for me, so it felt very loving for my little kid each time I took the time to explain the truth.

Another example of being a loving adult happened to my friend, Sally. She was personally going through a very lonely and alone time in her life. She had just separated from a boyfriend of three years; and her roommate, who was a lifelong friend, had gotten married and moved away. The process of internal transformation had taken her life to a place where she had very few close friends in her world. Little by little, as her inner connection grew, she realized that her external connection with people was extremely limited. As time went on, her feelings of loneliness and aloneness became extreme. I often reminded her that this was a red flag to communicate with her inner child. As her feelings became more intense, this is what her little girl shared with her:

Adult Sally: Little Sally, how are you feeling today?

Little Sally: I feel very lost and lonely.

AS: I hear that and I feel that. Would you like to share more?

LS: I was always alone. I remember talking to my mommy and daddy, but they never heard me.

AS: I hear you, Little Sally. Would you like to share more with me?

LS: Yes. I remember listening to my mommy and sister fighting, and it would really scare me. I would go outside and sit on the grass, always hoping someone would come out and be with me, but no one ever did. I would sit out there all alone, feeling lonely, wishing someone was with me.

AS: I hear you, Little Sally. I am here with you. I will sit and be with you as long as you want me to. I love you and will always be here for you.

In this particular example, Little Sally did not need to be talked with or guided, she just needed to be sat with and embraced. Sometimes the greatest gift we can give our little kid is time. Time spent together just sitting and being with your inner child can be very nurturing. For me, when my child within needed to be hugged and held, I would get in a safe place, grab my teddy bear, and just lie there holding my bear, rocking both my inner child and myself to sleep.

I used my bear as an outside stimulus for love and support. Holding and hugging my bear gave me the physical sensation of safeness and love I needed to help nurture my little kid. In the beginning, it was very uncomfortable for me and my huge ego to hug and hold a little teddy bear. In fact, at first I refused. However, with time and practice this loving behavior became second nature. Today my bed is covered with all types of bears and dolls because it brings such incredible peace and joy to my inner child and to me.

Another example of being a nurturing adult to our little

kid happens as our inner child is experiencing the pain of severe abuse. A perfect example of this happened on a national talk show featuring a well-known author and speaker of human development. This speaker was talking with the audience about how different traumas in our childhood can create blocks that hold us back in life. He shared his knowledge of needing to re-experience these events, and releasing stuffed emotions surrounding the drama. He claimed that if you feel the suppressed emotion, the old blocks will naturally go away.

I sat home that day listening intently as this man told the world what to do and how to heal. I was initially excited because I felt as though finally someone on a national scale was talking about emotional release and its healing benefits. The longer he talked, though, the more I could tell he was coming from his mind and not his heart.

I continued to listen to the program as a young man raised his hand with a question. He asked the speaker to show him how to actually accomplish what he just talked about. The young man was invited to the stage and as he stood there, the speaker guided this young man back to a tragic event and asked him to explain what happened. The young man, in tears, proceeded to explain to the world how at eight years old he walked in his home and found his mother murdered. The man was crying hysterically as he recapped this event. The speaker then told the man to have the little boy in him walk back in to the trauma by himself, to feel these feelings alone.

I remember at this point shouting at my TV, "No! Don't send the child back alone! You idiot, you are re-abusing this man's little kid on national TV." I could not believe it.

The young man, following the direction of this so-called expert, did exactly that. The tears of grief and terror were very apparent. My heart sank. I knew right then this facilitator had not healed his own issues because to heal our inner child wounds, our nurturing adult needs to be with the child during the re-visitation of a crisis. Basically, all that had happened on this program was a repeat of the original trauma that had occurred twenty years ago. Being all alone, the little child in this man had no idea how to comprehend what he had just witnessed. Putting him back in the trauma all alone and unprotected was re-abusing him, not healing him.

When I shut the TV off that day, I cried and hoped that what I had just seen was staged for the audience. I don't know if it was, but for the sake of that man's little kid, I hope so.

To develop this entire situation into a healing, loving event, all they had to do was bring into the picture this man's loving adult and Higher Power. I would have had the man take several deep breaths to get him into his body and help him feel connected. Next, I would have him ask his little kid to join him and then ask the child how he is doing? If the little kid is okay, then we ask the child if he is ready to feel some of the grief surrounding his mommy's death. The whole time, I would have this man reassure his little kid that he is not alone, and that they will be doing it together this time. If the little kid is afraid and is not ready to experience this grief, we would stop here.

Personally, I always validated my inner child's knowings of what he could handle and when. I never pushed my little kid to experience something, because this is self-abuse. The truth is, whenever my little kid was ready to feel something, he would always let me know.

If my little kid was ready, we walked together hand-in-hand back in time to the experience, creating a new and safe place for the trauma to be felt. The addition of the loving adult to the scene does not inhibit the child's feelings; it enhances his safeness, allowing him to feel what he needs to heal. Whenever I would go through the release of deep trauma, I had my loving adult, my Higher Power, and the angels of the universe with me to help allow my inner child to feel safe as he re-experienced the deep, suppressed emotions.

For the young man in my example, I would suggest he carry his little kid back to where he found his mother dead. I would have him hold the child within as his little kid cried. I would have him tell the little boy over and over how much he loved him, and that he would always be there for him. I would teach the man how to personally embrace his little kid as he experienced the loss and felt his fear of abandonment. The child in him needs to know that he will always be there for him no matter what. This is how the child truly heals.

For twenty years, the little kid in this man wondered who was going to take care of him now that his mother was gone. For twenty years, this man went from relationship to relationship looking outside of himself for someone to take care of his wounded eight-year-old little boy.

Using this technique of integrating the internal loving adult to nurture our little kid, the true healing and empowerment begins because we learn how to nurture ourselves by loving ourselves. As we accomplish this, our abandonment and co-dependent issues will naturally transform.

Now for me, when my little boy was done crying, I always let him know how proud of him I was for his courage to feel what he needed to heal. I let him take me to a safe place in our mind's eye where he loves to rest and feel nurtured. In this safe place, I would nurture my little kid for as long as he needed. This self-loving technique is how I personally healed the extreme trauma that happened in my own life.

After having extremely deep releases, I always made sure that the next couple of days were spent nurturing myself. I was never surprised when my personal energy level was extremely low, and I felt weak and vulnerable for a few days. These were all physical signs of a deep, emotional release. To nurture myself during these times, I often took extra baths during the day, and got a lot of sleep.

Let's review the self-loving techniques I used to heal my own fears of aloneness and loneliness. I would always begin by communicating with my little kid through journal writing. I would ask him how he was feeling and what he needed from me. If he needed to be heard, I would sit and listen to him as he spoke to me through his writing. If he was confused about something, I would listen and then lead him and teach him the truth surrounding his confusion. If he was lonely and scared, and just needed to be hugged, I would get my teddy bear, go to a safe place, and hug him as I rocked myself to sleep. And last, but certainly not least, if he was ready to re-experience his deep trauma, I went with him to hold him, to reassure him of his safety, and to love him as he had the courage to feel what he needed to heal.

The introduction of a loving adult into my internal process helped me heal many different things. The grandest gift of all, however, was healing my fears of aloneness and loneliness.

CHAPTER 14

Grief

As the next couple of months passed, my dwelling in Gainesville began to feel more like home. After I cleaned up and put some pictures on the wall, I gained a whole new appreciation for it. I realized for the first time in my life that I was completely alone, and I was doing okay with it. My late-night episodes of terror had subsided, and my gut-wrenching feelings of loneliness let go little by little. The need for me to kill something or someone because of my stuffed rage had also been released. So all in all, I felt much better than I had emotionally felt in a long time. The only real thing that was bothering me now was that I always felt extremely tired, as if my body weighed a thousand pounds. Several times I asked Sandy what all of this was, and she always gave her standard answer, "You'll see."

I used to hate it when she said this to me. My ego wanted all of the answers right now. I wanted someone outside of me to come to my rescue by giving me my answers. Sandy, through her years of experience, knew what was coming, but she never robbed my personal integrity or enabled me by giving me my answers.

Then one spring day, the answer I had been seeking for so long became clear to me. The answer was grief! I mean a lot of grief. During all of this time of processing and learning how to love and communicate with my inner child, I always felt a little grief, though my primary emotion of choice was anger. It was much safer and easier for me to feel anger than it was for me to feel grief, which is very common for most men. Let me tell you, though, that time is the only variable for each of us, man or woman, to feel what is under our rage; and it is grief.

Grief is an emotion of sorrow or loss. Some grief is stuffed in our heart, some in our stomach, and some is stored in our lower chockras. Grief is an emotion that was stuffed every time we were neglected, not listened to, or abandoned as a child. Grief is a feeling that, when felt, is normally associated with tremendous amounts of tears, and a lot of moans and groans. Grief is the tool we use when we are rediscovering the dark side of who we are.

There is grief associated with feelings of remorse, guilt, or shame. There is grief associated with the false beliefs of I'm not good enough, I don't deserve, and I am not lovable. Grief allows us to express the stuffed energy surrounding traumas such as sexual, physical, or verbal abuse. It is felt as we are transforming one vibration to another—what I call experiencing a psychic death. Healthy grief is felt when someone who is shaming us, or trying to make us feel guilty, crosses our boundaries. It can be felt with the loss of a loved one or the loss of a job. Healthy grief is felt any time we go through any type of external change that allows us to grow internally.

Grief is felt in a hundred different ways if you are living in a conscious and safe environment to be able to express it. For me, as for most men, I was not taught how or why I needed to grieve. I learned how many different types of grief there are through personally experiencing each one of them.

I realized later why Sandy never told me what was in store for me. I had learned how to successfully stuff my grief for over twenty years. So when the grief started to come, it really came. I remember day after day having as many as five different releases of grief. Each release was about something different. I remember wondering many times if I had lost my mind, or if there was something really wrong with me. There were weeks when the only feeling I experienced all week was grief. When I asked Sandy about this, she always said, "Joe, you stuffed your grief for twenty years. Now you are allowing the miracle of releasing it to happen. Do you want the emotion in or out?" Of course, I was in so much pain that I wanted to say, "In," but I always said, "Out!" I actually remember numerous times crying so hard that I would literally pass out from exhaustion.

Not long after this, I moved from Gainesville into a spare bedroom in Sandy's home. I was very grateful for this because her constant love and support helped nurture me through these very difficult times. It was still very difficult for me to ask for my needs to be met back then, so asking anyone to hold me or hug me during one of these huge releases was absolutely impossible for me.

Over time, however, my self-hatred diminished, and in turn, my need to do everything alone also left. A couple of different times during that next year and a half, I was able to allow Sandy to hold me as I cried, which took my tears to a much deeper level.

Now you may be asking yourself the question, "Why do I really need to feel all of this old pain to heal?" Join the club. Every day I asked that exact question. The answer for me was relief.

Today I can say that I feel whole and free of all of the old wounds that caused such havoc in my life. For example, my wounds from abandonment would keep me addicted to relationships that were hurtful to me. My wounds of guilt and shame kept me continually feeling the empty, scary sensation of not being good enough. My wounds regarding remorse for my past actions kept me trapped in the false illusion that I didn't deserve to be loved by God or anyone else. As a consequence of having the courage to feel what I needed to heal, all of those old false beliefs went away. The natural consequence from transforming these beliefs was the release of all of my old unloving ego voices.

Now does everyone have the opportunity to feel the depth of grief I have felt, to allow him or her to experience the heights of Great Spirit in their heart? Yes! Will everyone feel it? Probably not. But that is okay. Wherever your path is leading you, that is your own personal destiny. I needed to feel my deep grief because that was the only way I knew I could share my experience, strength, and hope with others. Sharing my life story with others is my higher purpose. Yours may be different. So please don't make the mistake I did, and compare your path to anyone else's. Your destiny of healing is your own private gift from God.

The story of my friend, Kathy, is a perfect example of how people's paths are different. She is a single mom with two children. She has been on this personal path of self-discovery for over three years. Her life was changed forever the day she came in touch with her inner child.

Kathy has had memories of childhood sexual abuse all of her life. She remembers an uncle and a teacher who both totally crossed her boundaries as a child. Her most visible desires to heal were expressed through her co-dependence and her rage toward her children.

Over the past three years, she has had tremendous amounts of healing in both of these arenas. She home schools her children now, and has not taken her anger out on them in a very long time. This past year, because of her growth, she was able to take her ex-husband to court for back child support. Through all of this, she has been able to create a loving environment for her children and herself.

She feels that her inner path of self-discovery has been extremely successful during this time, and so do I. Now has Kathy felt a lot a grief? Yes. Has she released a lot of rage? Yes. Has she felt or grieved any of her deep childhood issues? No, not at all. Her life is filled with love, and her personal destiny on her path is being fulfilled; however, her internal path of self-discovery is different from mine, even though the consequence is just as wonderful for her.

Another friend of mine, Mike, has a thriving business, a

loving wife, and two beautiful children. He became aware of his little kid about two years ago when he chose to get support from a counselor during his quest for sobriety. He realized that his little kid, at age ten, totally closed down because of the sudden tragic death of his older brother. For over twenty-five years, he had held on to, and stuffed, all of those tears of loss. He never let anyone get to close to his heart because that would mean he would have to face his fears of abandonment surrounding his brother's death.

In the past two years, Mike has actually had five releases of grief around this loss. His path has led him to release and re-express this deep pain very slowly. Because he has accepted that God is in control of his rate of release, he is very pleased with his progress, and so am I. I am also extremely proud of his courage to feel what he needs to heal. When Mike had his first release of grief a year ago, it was the first tears he had shed in over twenty years.

So if you have not cried in a long, long time, know that you are okay. If you keep looking inside, time is the only variable before you will experience the magical relief of a good cry.

The techniques I used to help my little kid feel safe enough to feel his grief were the same as for all the other emotions, except for the addition of soft, loving music. I used music to help me penetrate my many layers of protection. In the beginning, music became my best friend. Over time, I learned to use its nurturing sounds and loving words to help me feel what I needed to heal.

Here is an example of what I used to do with my inner child when I felt sad:

Adult Joe: Little Joe, how are you feeling?

Little Joe: I am feeling very sad.

AJ: I hear that and feel that. Is there anything I can do for you?

LJ: I need love. I need to be held.

AJ: Is there something you would like to listen to?

LJ: Yes.

At this point he would name a song, and I would stop writing in my journal, sit down in front of my music box, and put his requested song in the player. Normally, as a consequence of listening to the music, time was the only variable for me to feel my deep feelings of grief. Many times I would sit there playing the same song over and over again. If I needed to grieve for twenty minutes or two hours, I would play the same song over and over. Listening to music took me out of my head and into my heart. The soothing sound of the rhythm kept me feeling safe and focused.

On numerous occasions, I sat with my teddy bear, rocking myself back and forth, crying my eyes out with the sound of the music. Many times as I cried, I could see in my mind's eye what my tears were about. Other times, I just intuitively knew the meaning of my grief. And still other times, I cried and had no idea why; I just knew I was sad.

In the beginning, after every release of grief, I wondered if this was my last release. My hope was that it was, but my intuition told me it wasn't. So, my friend, if you are having a difficult time getting in touch with your grief, find yourself several songs that touch your heart. Then the next time you feel sad, allow the music to help you open your heart so you can experience the awesome release called grief.

My life was designed in such a way that I could sit alone in front of that music box for hours or even days, until all of my grief around a certain issue was released. A friend of mine, Jan, has to balance her time of releasing her grief around the rest of her life's busy schedule. She has a routine of self-nurturing techniques, which allows both her and her little girl to feel safe and loved. She talks with her little girl frequently through the writing techniques

I have shown her, so her little girl feels heard. She also takes a lot of long baths to nurture herself. When she feels sad, normally she is able to feel her grief pretty quickly and release it. If she can't seem to cry alone with her Higher Power's help, she will call a friend to help support her through her grief over the phone. For some reason, her little girl feels safer to release when she hears a loving voice on the other end of a phone, so Jan feels safer expressing her grief with someone else supporting her. For me, personally, I feel safer doing my crying alone.

It's important to understand there is no right or wrong way to process through your grief. Whatever environment and at whatever rate allows you to feel safety and trust, this is for your highest good. I have shared the experiences of several different people to shed some hope on every type of process available. My process was all-consuming, very deep, and very quick. Other people lead active, full lives of love and prosperity as they go through their own healing. So however you are guided to feel what you need to heal, know that it is perfect for you.

My hope is that you have gained some insight and some hope on how you, too, can heal your deep inner child wounds. Remember, all emotions are God-given gifts. I know it is challenging to feel these emotions at first because they seem so new, and there are so many of them. Trust me, though, if you take the time to love yourself by nurturing your inner child, the life rewards as a consequence of healing your wounds are remarkable.

I will be forever thankful to my counselor and friend, Sandy, for her patience and unconditional love as she guided me back to my own light and love. The relentless pursuit of her own self- healing allowed me a living example of self-love from which to learn. The courage to heal herself and to follow her highest purpose, which is to teach people like me how to empower themselves, changed my life forever. My hope is that my ability to put my experience of healing into words will help you change your life, too.

To summarize Part Two, I will remind you that all emotions are God's gift to us. Great Spirit will never give us more than we can handle. So as your connection to your inner child grows, understand that the natural consequence will be the release of suppressed emotions.

If your inner child is angry, give him/her permission to yell, cuss, beat the bed, tear up phone books, or anything else needed to express this rage. If your little kid is scared, lonely, or confused, communicate through the writing techniques I have discussed, and be there to embrace his/her fears. When your little kid is sad, hold him/her with a teddy bear of your choice, and listen to some soft music as you rock yourself into your deep tears.

I have tried to explain, to the best of my ability, how I gained an inner strength of love and faith with Great Spirit as a consequence of feeling my feelings. For me, the degree to which my inner child trusts me is in exact proportion to the degree to which I have the inner ability to trust Great Spirit. My faith in God comes from my inner trust, and my inner trust comes from my inner child. In order for me to develop my inner child's trust, I had to earn it. Talk is cheap on this path. I earned my inner child's unconditional trust in me by doing everything I have described to you.

Today, the natural consequence of my internal trust is a limitless sense of faith in a higher power, which I call Great Spirit. When I first started the emotional release portion of my path, I had no idea that my inner connection to Spirit would be my reward. My only real desire was to heal my little kid; but what I received was much, much grander. I now live a life of internal abundance and love, and feel extremely whole and free from all of my fears. My life is guided by my heart, not my head; and my ego voices are almost gone.

There are times when I wake up in the morning so full of love, I pinch myself to see if I'm truly awake. I am happy to say that the internal strength I have gained through having the courage to feel what I needed to heal is fabulous. I look in the mirror each day and can honestly say that I love who is looking back at me. I share this with you because if I can be healed of my pain from the depths at which I started, imagine what you can do for your life.

We all have the same Spirit, although each of us has covered it up in different ways. Remember, God is love; love is an emotion; emotions are in your heart. So when you heal your heart, you will naturally feel the love of God residing in us all. Have the courage to heal your heart through the techniques described in this book, and the magical consequence you will receive will be the love of God in your heart.

Great Spirit has given me the strength and courage to feel what I needed to heal, and has always been there for me, even when I consciously had no perception of God. My path has been magical, and I hope, my friend, that your magic is just around the next bend. All of your inner dreams will come true if you don't give up.

Today

Today I moved through the confining veil of ego. I've reached a
place of self-value and self-love. Today, when I look out into the
eyes of another, I see my growth vs. my lack.
Today I feel gratitude for being one of the chosen few To walk a
conscious path with God.
Today I see the beauty in the moment; to cherish all we have,
And the abundance of all life.
Today I feel a joy for life;
To live a life filled with growth and well-being.
Today I feel love for the child within and the friends by my side.
Today I see a full life
Free from the inner bondage of self-hatred and self-denial.
Today I see life filled with love, joy, and spontaneity.
Today I live life in a place of fullness, As a beacon of light for
others to follow. Today I live life free to be who I am.
Today I live life through the eyes of my child.
Today I live life to love, to be loved, and to grow in love.
Today I am free, and that is my gift to me Today—all day.

Today

PART THREE

In Part Three of this book, I will describe the spiritual consequence that happened for me as my inner child healed and integrated. I will share how I learned the different techniques that allowed me to become more honest in my life today, and how I took responsibility for my past actions. I also will share with you how I used a twelve-step spiritual program to help me develop a loving relationship with myself, society, and a Power greater than myself.

For me, the development of different spiritual aspects of myself was very unexpected. Today these parts of me play an active role in guiding my life, along with my inner child and loving adult. If you are skeptical about the reality of the spiritual world, please know that this is okay. I, too, was very skeptical of all of this God stuff.

My intention is only to share my experience with you. Take what fits and please leave the rest. My purpose is one of pure exposure. Perhaps my explanation of my experience in some way will help to validate that your spiritual self has always been there with you, too. Regardless of your current belief system, I hope you will be able to relate to the different spiritual aspects I will discuss in this next section, allowing your mind and heart to be open to change and growth.

For me, the introduction of Great Spirit and all of my spirit guides into my world has totally healed any feelings of emptiness and aloneness. My hope is that your path leads you to the same level of fullness through a deep spiritual connection and the internal integration of your inner child.

CHAPTER 15

Integration of Great Spirit

Over the next year and a half I lived with my counselor, Sandy, and every day I felt what I needed to heal. The frequency of my emotional releases did not lessen, although my attitude about releasing did improve. With each passing day, I realized what was happening for me. I could feel that the wounds inside my inner child were healing because the voices in my head seemed to be subsiding.

The desires in my external life seemed to be changing quite drastically. My choices in self-loving behaviors grew to the point where they became second nature for me. My inner child and I had a very close and communicative relationship with each other. Writing with him in my journal seemed to lessen because my ability to feel what he needed grew more each day. I intuitively knew how to handle situations that used to baffle me in the past. My idea about life over the past couple of years had completely changed, and I was finally starting to accept my new world.

At this point on my path, I chose a very simple life with few friends, few activities, and very little work. Most of my life seemed to be in a self-loving cocoon. In this cocoon state, I was healing, grieving, and transforming each day. Even so, as my little kid healed more and more, I still felt something was missing. I had no idea what it was, but I felt empty and alone inside. To be honest, though, these feelings were so much more improved from what I had experienced for such a long time that for several months I never even talked about what was going inside of me.

I had been free of drugs and alcohol for almost two years, so my ego kept me from thinking I had an addictive personality. My mind kept telling me I was only interested in healing my little kid; nothing else. Sandy continually suggested that I might want to check out a twelve-step program. I never understood why she insisted on telling me this because I had been alcohol free for over two years. Then one day, as if through an act of God, I got the desire to visit a meeting.

The morning I chose to go was very bright and sunny. I remember feeling a tremendous amount of fear, and I had no idea what was going on inside of me. Some parts of me wanted to go; some parts of me definitely did not. It felt as if a huge tug-of-war was going on deep inside my soul.

Now for those of you who don't know, all twelve-step programs are spiritual programs. They are created around twelve spiritual principles; each principle coinciding with a descriptive step. The entire process, if done continually, is designed to help each individual create a loving, more communicative relationship with themselves, society, and a power greater than themselves.

For me, walking into this meeting for the first time, I had no idea any of this existed. All I knew was that once I walked through those doors, I felt as though I had come home. Never had I felt such a deep feeling of safeness associated with a place or any environment. As the meeting started, and the different formats were read out loud to the group, I remember thinking that all of these people just looked like normal folks. Everyone seemed very friendly and very kind. Of course, being the newcomer to the group, parts me felt very uncomfortable, but this was only because of the newness of this experience.

I remember wondering why I was actually there. To be honest, I had no idea. As the meeting progressed, I listened very cautiously. I was scared to death because I had no idea what I was going to say or how I was going to act. I don't remember what the topic was that first day; all I remember is that they said I should think about coming back the next day, and that is exactly what I did.

The process of a twelve-step program is really very simple. First you decide if the love and support of other people is something you really want in your life. If the answer is yes, then you continue to attend the functions until such time as you are ready to leave.

The first time the process was described to me, I didn't know what they were talking about; however, in time I, too, felt the miracle! The experience of a twelve-step program guided me out of the extreme isolation in which I seemed to live. Even though my little kid was healing, I still sometimes felt lost and alone. The program gave me a place to go on a daily basis where everyone who attended seemed to be spiritually heading in the same direction.

Each person there talked a different language from my approach with my inner child, but they all were looking inside themselves for their own answers. In addition, they all used a particular tool to help support their personal growth. This tool was the belief in a power greater than themselves. Some people called this power God; some people had no name at all. However, everyone seemed to have their own belief and their own relationship with whatever they called this entity.

In the beginning, the mention of the word "God" gave me the willies. The hair on the back of my neck would literally stand up with even the mention of the word. So if the word "God" bothers you, it is okay. I later named my higher support system, Spirit or Great Spirit, because it sounded more spiritual to me.

As I continued to attend my meetings, I started meeting people and making new friends. Then one day I heard a man speak who seemed to be telling my life story. This guy was sharing from his heart what he had been going through for the past couple of days. It literally felt like he was reading from my own personal diary. I could relate to everything he said. His experiences were my experiences. It was truly amazing to listen to him because I could have closed my eyes and thought I was the one doing the talking. After this meeting ended, I mustered all of my courage and walked across the room to introduce myself. My fear of rejection was so great that I almost missed my chance; but based on what happened, obviously God was doing for me what I could not do for myself.

As I introduced myself, my new friend smiled, reached out his hand, and said lovingly, "Hi, Joe. My name is Payne. Welcome." All my fear left me as he spoke. My need for a friend was extreme, and it seemed like this need had finally been fulfilled.

Payne and I sat and talked for probably an hour. He explained to me the concept of having a sponsor and working the spiritual steps. He said that a sponsor is someone in your life you can call to ask for support and love. This is someone with whom you create a trusting relationship over time, so you don't feel as though you're always walking this spiritual path by yourself. He also said he was not going to give me advice. His only role was to share his experience, strength, and hope with me as I was guided through the steps.

That sounded good to me even though I had no idea what he was talking about. I left that day on "cloud nine." I remember having a little spring in my step as I walked to my car. I had no concept of what was happening for me, but I will say that it sure felt nice.

That night as I wrote with my little kid, I could tell something happened. My inner feeling of peace and trust seemed to have grown by leaps and bounds in just a few days. My internal connection with my little kid seemed to have grown and developed to a place I'd never been before. It felt as though something deep inside of me had shifted and let go. It took me many months to truly be able put into words the experience of those few days.

My disease had taken my life to a very low bottom where I had lost everything and felt completely isolated. Early in my recovery, my wounded little kid needed to be alone in a safe place to release pain, which kept me in a lot of isolation. Both experiences, although on opposite sides of the healing path, had the same effect; I literally lived in my own internal prison.

Asking Payne to be my friend and having him accept was

like having the key to my own prison door. The creation of this relationship with Payne felt like turning the key and having my internal doors start to open. Looking back, I realize I had finally reached a place on the other side of my growth where I felt safe enough to allow another human being to love me. My friendship with Payne was really my first bridge back into the reality of the rest of the world.

The process designed to assist you in your internal quest for a Higher Power relationship is called twelve-steps. Back in the early 1930s, a man named Bill Wilson divinely inspired the steps. Please don't quote me on Bill Wilson's history or the history of the original twelve steps because I really don't know it. What I do know, though, is that over the years twelve-step programs around the world have helped millions of people recover from many different types of addictive behaviors. From alcohol to sex, and all substances in between, twelve-step programs can help.

My inner child processing had not slowed down at all; however, my world was looking a lot brighter with the introduction of a new, loving support system. As the days turned into weeks, and my relationship with the people in the program grew, I again started to feel out of place. I listened to everyone talk about how the program was the only way they could get sober, but for me this was not the case. My love for my little kid and my commitment to this healing are what started my sobriety. My compulsions were removed instantaneously by just asking. So for a long time, as I visited many meetings, I felt a little out of place because most people's compulsions for alcohol took time to be removed. In five and a half years, I have only heard one other person share a story of compulsions being removed like mine. Sometimes quickly, sometimes slowly definitely fits here.

I share this with you because I want you to understand that many people have used twelve-step programs to relieve their addictions; I did not. So wherever your path leads you, know that you are okay. I personally used the program to create a more loving adult in myself, and to create a relationship with my Higher Power, Great Spirit.

The first question is usually, "Why do I need to have my addictive behaviors removed?" The answer is because any behavior or attitude in which you are powerless is basically running your life. All addictions coincide with your ego, and ego is always a fear-based perception. So if you don't stop these behaviors or attitudes, you are choosing to live a life of fear, not love. Remember that the intention of this book is to show you how the different love-based techniques I used to heal my inner child stopped the unloving voices in my head.

When you spiritually remove fear-based behaviors or addictions, the natural consequence is a more attuned loving adult, which allows your inner child to feel safer with you. The safer your little kid feels, the more he opens up. The more he opens up, the more he releases. The more he releases, the more he heals; which takes us back to the beginning. When you remove the unloving voices in your head by healing your little kid, your quality of life will be far better than you can imagine.

The next question is, "How do I know if I have an addiction to something or someone?" The easiest way to tell is, if you think you have a problem, you probably do. Also, if there is any substance or behavior that some part of you refuses to let go, this is a big red flag that an addiction is possible.

For example, a friend of mine said to me, "I will never give up drinking my wine because I like it too much." Now I am not calling this person an alcoholic just because she gets drunk once a month. My red flag for her is the word never. Absolutes are descriptive words of the ego. Whenever the ego is strongly and boldly holding onto any substance or behavior, addiction is probable.

Another example is when someone says, "I have to have sex, or I will die," or "I can't stop working so much, or I will lose my job," or "I can't stop talking with or seeing this person because I will hurt her if I go." The words have to and can't are also words of the fear-based ego and indicate probable addictive behavior.

Another very common addiction is to food and body image. If you find yourself binging, purging, starving yourself, or continually overeating, there is also help for you. In my experience, I have seen twelve-step programs spiritually remove all of these unloving behaviors, allowing you to heal the source of your true pain, which is a wounded little kid.

So if you hear yourself using the above expressions or something similar, I hope you take a good look in the mirror and be honest with yourself. The process of self-discovery truly starts with self-honesty. If you hear these voices attached to any situation, at least consider the possibility that a red flag of an addiction is being presented to you.

Another possible way to discover if you have an addiction to something is to try to go ninety days without this substance or behavior. When you make this decision of abstinence, listen to your internal voices. If there are voices that are really fighting your choice, this is another possible red flag. And if you can't go ninety days without drugs, alcohol, sex, overeating, sugar, codependent behaviors, or whatever challenge you face, this could be another red flag for your addictive discoveries.

My friend, I want to reassure you that if you have an addiction to something, you are still okay. There is nothing wrong with you. We live in such an addictive society that so many of our addictive behaviors are learned behaviors. Our challenge today, though, is to break this paradigm, have the courage to change our fear-based behaviors, and grow spiritually. I also want to explain to you that under every addictive behavior or attitude there is a wounded little kid just waiting to be heard, waiting to be felt, and wanting to be loved. So my suggestion is to at least consider the possibility of different addictive red flags for the healing sake of your inner child.

Now if you are clear on a particular addiction or a series of addictions like I had, this is where twelve-step work comes into play. For our purposes, let's use the twelve steps from Alcoholics Anonymous which are the basis for many other twelve-step programs:

We...

1. We admitted we were powerless over alcohol, that our lives had become unmanageable.
2. Came to believe that a Power greater than ourselves could restore us to sanity.
3. Made a decision to turn our will and our lives over to the care of God as we understood Him.
4. Made a fearless moral inventory of ourselves.
5. Admitted to God, to ourselves, and to another human being the exact nature of our wrongs.
6. Were entirely ready to have God remove all these defects of character.
7. Humbly asked Him to remove our shortcomings.
8. Made a list of all persons we had harmed and became willing to make amends to them all.
9. Made direct amends to such people whenever possible, except when to do so would injure them or others.
10. Continued to take personal inventory and when we were wrong promptly admitted it.
11. Sought through prayer and meditation to improve conscious contact with God as we understood Him, praying only for his will for us and the power to carry that out.
12. Having had a spiritual awakening as the result of these steps, we tried to carry this message to alcoholics, and practice these principles in all of our affairs.

The first time I saw these steps, I had no idea what they meant. That is why it is very important to have someone else guide us through them. I'm going to take a little time to explain my experience with each of the steps, and how I interpreted and integrated these spiritual principles into my life, which helped me and my little kid heal on even deeper levels.

Step 1: *We admitted we were powerless over (fill in the blank), and that our lives had become unmanageable.*

This step is naturally the hardest step for most people to take. I know it was for me. It was very difficult for me to admit I was powerless to anything because my ego continually told me that I had control of everything and I didn't need any help. It was also difficult for me because of the shame-based false belief system that if I have an addiction to something, there must be something terribly wrong with me.

This belief is just not true. I personally believe that most people have some type of addiction to something in their lives. I encourage you to have the courage to walk out of the shame and admit to yourself your own addiction. As I said before, the list of possible addictions is huge, so before you read further, please take a moment and evaluate yourself in regard to the following list of possible addictions:

Alcohol	Work
Marijuana	Money
Cocaine	Relationships
Cigarettes	Sex
Sugar	Love
Exercise	Television
Weight loss	The Internet
Weight gain	Pornography
Running	Food
Sleep	Trying to fix someone else
Failure	Letting someone control your life
Success	

The list goes on and on. This first step of admitting our issues is so powerful because it is the first step out of the fear of denial and into the light and love of recovery. For me, as I started to see and admit my different addictions, my inner child immediately felt safer with me. The trust between my loving adult and my little kid grew stronger each day.

The hurtful consequence of addictive behavior is the denial and neglect of your own wounded little kid underneath it.

So naturally, as your inner child sees that you are able to be more honest about your behavior, his hope arises that someday, with the addiction arrested, his wounds can finally be healed. The day I was able to admit that I was an alcoholic and drug addict was truly a day of celebration for me. Naturally, though, if you are still at a point where admission of any addiction brings up a lot of shame for you, celebration is probably the last thing on your mind. I want to explain the meaning of, "We admitted..." For me the "we" in this statement is a representation of you, your inner child, and God as an internal support system. The only way I was able to make this new assessment of my life's behavior was because God was with me. One day I did not see my problems, the next day I did. I was able to have this type of awareness shift only because of the presence of a Higher Power in my life.

So if the "we" stands for you and God, obviously God has a plan for you to change your behaviors, or you would not be able to see your behaviors as unloving and needing to be changed. Also if the "we" stands for you and God, remember that God will never give you more than you can handle. Whatever new changes of perceptions happen for you, God is with you all the way.

The second word is "admitted," not accepted, because there is a long way between these two spiritual truths. In the beginning, I admitted that I possibly had a little challenge with my alcohol and drug consumption. I admitted to just possibly having a problem. It took almost two years of intense introspection to be able to actually accept my disease. I learned that acceptance of anything is not a light-switch concept in spiritual growth.

It always angers me when I read these so-called spiritual books that suggest all you have to do is accept an issue and it will go away. This is true, of course, but no one ever tells you how to go through the process to get to the acceptance. Anyone who describes acceptance as a light-switch approach to spirituality is describing an intellectual technique to a heartfelt sensation. Acceptance is an experience, not a thought. So if you can't yet accept any particular situation in your life, please stop shaming yourself, and know this is okay. Acceptance is a process that happens as the internal healing around your issue occurs. To start this process, you must go through different phases.

Acceptance of any internal challenge comes from first admitting the challenge exists. Then comes experiencing all of the feelings around this challenge; i.e., mad, glad, sad, scared. Next comes allowing time to pass so that your new awareness surrounding this particular challenge will have time to enter into your consciousness to be heard and healed. Finally, as your inner child heals his/her wounds, and your ego has time to transform from fear to love, then and only then are you able to feel the natural consequence of healing an issue, which is called true acceptance.

How do we know when we've healed or accepted a particular situation? For me, it is when I am able to rethink an issue, and the only feelings are those of love and compassion. This is how I know I have truly accepted something. So in the beginning of our quest to discover all of our old non-loving behaviors, the first step in a time-variable process is to admit these issues exist. This will eventually lead to the self-loving feeling of acceptance.

My friend, it takes courage to do whatever is needed to heal your little kid. I know admitting you are powerless to anything goes against your very own nature; but trust me, the consequence of this inner courage will change your life forever.

The third word I want to talk about in Step 1 is the word "powerless." Powerless, for me, is something I had no idea ever existed before I started this process. My ego said, "I am not powerless over anything. Just ask me! I have complete control. I can stop drinking or overeating anytime I want to; I just don't want to."

My ego also said, "Why would I ever want to stop having sex? It's natural for a young Italian man to want sex all the time." My ego said a lot of other unloving things to me for a very long time. Since I allowed my fear-based ego to run my life, I never knew I was powerless to stop these unloving behaviors because I never tried to stop.

You see, I mistakenly identified with my ego my entire life. The more I acted in ego, the bigger it got; and the bigger my ego got, the larger my false sense of worth became. It wasn't until I discovered my inner child, and the loving needs he desired for me, that I realized my addictive behaviors were harmful to me.

To be totally honest, I had no idea I was hurting myself. I was unconscious to the truth that addictive behaviors are designed and perpetuated for the sole reason of suppressing our emotions. I was totally unaware that every time I drank alcohol, it was as if I were pouring the bottle of whiskey on the head of my inner child; or when I worked too much, that my little kid felt abandoned and ignored. I had no idea that overeating or my obsession to exercise were all behaviors that kept me from feeling and fulfilling my little kid's needs. The truth is, I didn't understand that my behaviors were hurting me and the people around me every day.

So if you fit into any category of unconsciousness about your behaviors, know that it is okay. I, too, never knew I was hurting myself until my path led me to a place of learning about self-love. It was when I chose to do whatever it took to allow my inner child to heal, and I decided to move from ego behaviors to love behaviors, that I felt the feeling of powerlessness to my self-defeating behaviors for the first time.

The inner battle I felt between my ego and my loving adult was tremendous. In the beginning, my ego parts were terrified to let go and be transformed because throughout my entire life, these aspects protected me from all of my deep inner feelings of rage, grief, and fear. In order to let go, my addictive ego had to feel safe. For me, this is where Great Spirit came into play on a daily basis. By admitting I was powerless to alcohol, drugs, or any old unloving behavior, I felt my first sense of inner humility which cracked my ego just enough to allow Great Spirit to consciously enter my heart and help me.

My first admission of powerlessness was basically my first admission that I needed help. Step 1 worked for me with a little humility and willingness to ask for help. This step was the beginning of numerous miracles that have happened for me and millions of people around the world associated with twelve-step programs. Taking this step and actively admitting to myself I was powerless was very difficult, but extremely necessary on my road to spiritual enlightenment.

Admitting to the powerlessness of my ego is the only thing I feel I can do one hundred percent of the time, and from this is a place of honesty where the rest of my spiritual process has developed in my life. The spiritual principle for Step 1 is honesty, so as I looked at the rest of what this step said, I found that this ability to be honest with myself brought a clearer light to my life, allowing me to give myself love.

The second part of Step 1 says that "our lives had become unmanageable." For me, when I first was directed to look at this part of the step, I was totally confused. I looked at my life and said, "My life is not unmanageable."

I was willing, though, to be honest with myself about the question of my life being unmanageable, and I started looking outside of myself to find this answer. I looked at my work, which I enjoyed, and my roommate situation, which was better than it had been in years. I saw that I wasn't drinking, smoking, working too much, or overeating anymore, which felt great. In fact, I wasn't doing anything in my outside world that was hurting me, so I was extremely confused when it came to saying that my life was unmanageable–because externally, it wasn't.

Then one day it hit me. My unmanageability was not in my outside world; it was in my inside world. The unloving, shame-based, fear-driven thoughts that were in my head every day was where my life was totally unmanageable. Once I discovered where to look for the answers to the question of unmanageability in my life, a light bulb turned on for me. I could finally hear myself thinking crazy, fear-based thoughts all the time. So at the suggestion of my sponsor, I started to transfer these thoughts to paper.

When I first started, I thought that I would be done in ten minutes. Well, four hours and twelve legal-sized pages later, I was still writing. I just couldn't believe how many crazy thoughts I had. To help you discover some of your own unmanageable thought patterns, I will give you some examples of things I wrote:

God does not love me.
No one has ever loved me.
I have to talk to my ex-girlfriend because she has no one else to talk to. I don't deserve to be loved.
There's something wrong with me because I've never felt loved.
If I don't drink, I will die.
If I don't drink, no one will like me.
If I'm not a people pleaser, no one will like me.
If I don't work eighty hours a week, I can't make any money.
It is everyone else's fault that I feel like hell all of the time.
I have no friends.
If I get fat, no one will love me. Sex equals love.
If I eat a lot, I will feel better. Marijuana made me a nice person.
Something is wrong with me because I was molested as a child.
I don't deserve to make money.
I can't make any money until I am totally healed.
I can only be happy if I'm in a relationship.
If I wanted to, I could stop drinking at just one beer.
My dreams will never come true.
I'll never meet someone like me.
No one ever listens to me.
No one ever loves me for who I am.
I can't write a book.
I can't stay sober.
If my girlfriend hadn't left me, I would be okay. I can't let anyone get too close to me.
If I'm big and strong, I'll get more attention. I did too

many bad things for God to love me. I hate God.

I hate myself.

I hate my life.

I can't take this path anymore.

I need someone else to take care of me.

If I just lived on the beach, I would be okay. No one can hear me.

No one will ever hug me when I cry.

My list went on and on. I was actually amazed at how much stuff was racing around in my head. It wasn't until I wrote it down that I could actually put a tangible handle on my intangible thoughts.

Until this moment in my life, I thought I was a positive thinker. The truth is, part of me did see the world as a half-full glass while other aspects of me saw the world as half-empty. Can you relate to any of these thoughts? If so, I suggest that you stop right here, put down the book, and start writing your thoughts on paper. You'll be absolutely amazed at what you find out about yourself. Remember that the principle of Step 1 is honesty. So try to be as honest as you can when it comes to expressing your unloving voices through writing. I know from personal experience that it can be humiliating and even scary to see how we truly think; but if you have the courage to complete this step, you will be on the road to actual freedom.

As you find the courage to write down what you hear, please be careful not to shame yourself for what you see. Know that all fear-based thoughts are a consequence of a wounded child inside of you. Having the courage to honestly write down your thoughts is a huge step toward self-discovery in the quest to heal your own little kid. As you heal your inner wounds, the natural consequence is that all of these fear-based thoughts will effortlessly go away.

As I exposed myself and my thought patterns to paper, I had a clear, guided picture of who I truly thought I was. Today I live a life totally free of all of those old thought patterns. For me, total internal freedom has been achieved by starting with Step 1. Seek and ye shall find totally fits with this step. Courage and honesty is the beginning of a world of true bliss and total freedom for you. To recap Step 1, have the courage to admit you are powerless over people, places, and things. Find humility to ask for help, and seek the honesty to write down your unmanageable thoughts. This is as simple and as clear as I can share with you about the first step for me. Now you just have to take action and see for yourself what results happen for you.

Step 2: *We came to believe that a Power greater than ourselves could restore us to sanity.*

In reading Step 2, I had no conscious idea what any of it meant, so it took me a long time to truly get it. The principle around this step is hope, and at this point in my life, hope was exactly what I needed.

"Came to believe" is the action part of this step. It is something for me that just happened as a consequence of this internal process. Came to believe means that one day I had little or no faith in a Power grander than me, and over time I did. In other words, I moved from one belief system of God to another in a very short period of time. Each time I thought about the words, came to believe, it literally felt as though I moved from one place or vision, to a higher place or vision. Then one day I connected the whole experience together—Came to believe that a Power greater than myself could restore me to sanity—and in one instantaneous experience, it happened for me.

One evening I was sitting outside of a movie theater grieving some deep grief, when I consciously connected with the internal truth that Great Spirit, or God, has always been with me to help and support me through this process. One moment I did not see or feel God's presence, the next moment it was as clear as day. In this moment, I realized deep in my soul that the only reason I had been relieved of my powerful obsession for drugs and alcohol, was because a Power greater than me removed the obsession. Until this time, my ego continually convinced me that I stopped all of my unloving behaviors on my own. The truth is, I did none of it on my own. Great Spirit had a large part in my entire transformational process.

That night I made the deeper connection that I was being helped and supported daily by a Power greater than myself, and my feelings of deep aloneness started to shift out of me. I truly started to experience the feeling of safeness I needed to change. In that moment, for the first time in my life, I experienced a sensation of deep hope, and felt consciously safer in the knowledge that Great Spirit was inside of me.

For me, hope is a deep sensation associated with love, trust, and change. I knew at this point on my path that I was truly going to be okay, regardless of where my path was taking me. For the first time, I had a new conscious reference point from which to observe life; and from my new perspective, I could see how healing my inner child was not just about me doing it by myself. I finally connected with the conscious truth that God had been with the me the whole time.

I cried with joy that night for several hours. My inner child immediately felt much safer in the conscious knowledge that we were connected to a Power greater than ourselves who was here to help and support us. The natural consequence of my little kid's new sense of safeness was a deep sensation of peace and serenity for me in my life. In my heart, I truly knew that I was okay.

Now if you are confused about any of this and wondering what I'm talking about, know that you are okay. If your ego keeps saying, "I don't feel anything helping me or supporting me on my path," that is okay, too. All I'm saying is for you to try and remember that even though you can't feel the presence of God in your heart yet, that does not mean that God is not there.

The poem, Footprints, is the perfect way to help describe how we live most of our unconscious lives.

Footprints

One night a man had a dream.
He dreamed he was walking along the beach with the Lord.
Across the sky flashed scenes from his life.
For each scene, he noticed two sets of footprints in the sand;
One belonging to him, and the other to the Lord.
When the last scene of his life flashed before him, He looked
back at the footprints in the sand.
He noticed that many times along the path of his life There was
only one set of footprints.
He also noticed that it happened at the very lowest and
Saddest times in his life.
This really bothered him and he questioned the Lord about it.
"Lord, You said that once I decided to follow You,
You'd walk with me all the way.
But I have noticed that during the most Troublesome times in
my life,
There is only one set of footprints.
I don't understand why when I needed You most You would
leave me."
The Lord replied, "My son, My precious child.
I love you and would never leave you. During your times of
trial and suffering, When you see only one set of footprints, It
was then that I carried you."

–Author Unknown

I felt a deeper sense of self-love in this new awareness that God truly was supporting me through each day of my life. I consciously became aware that the source of my inner strength, and desire to quest for deeper healing, came from Great Spirit. I realized that my courage to feel what I needed to heal also came from Spirit. And finally, I became aware that the love I felt for my inner child and myself also came from God. Because all of my strength, courage, and love were inside of me, I discerned that God must also be inside of me.

Connecting to the hope that a Power greater than me was supporting me daily, truly changed my life. I looked at life in a totally different way from that day on. I felt less lonely because I felt more interconnected to everything and everyone around me. For the first time in my adult life, I felt I was consciously reconnecting to my own Spirit.

My love of life grew each day because my feelings of love and safeness grew inside of me. My ego parts started to let go on deeper levels because of my new perception of spiritual support. Naturally, the deeper I let go, the more the sunshine of Great Spirit could shine through.

I began to consciously dream about how magnificent the power and love of Spirit truly is. I would sit and look at nature in a totally different way from how I had before, knowing that Great Spirit made the trees, too. I felt humility for how tiny I am vs. the awesome power of God. As my humility deepened, my sense of gratitude grew because I knew in my heart that God is all love, all giving, and all powerful. I also knew that God gives everything possible to me simply because I am alive. The feeling that God is like a loving, nurturing father started growing in me for the very first time in my life.

Step 2 was huge for me because for many years my hatred and confusion of God kept me isolated and alone. Coming to the belief that a Power greater than myself would help me regain the sanity of self-love totally brought me out of my self-absorbed isolation.

During this process, deep in my heart, I truly knew that there was a God and I was in it. My deep connection with my inner child was the sole reason I had the ability to emotionally connect to Great Spirit in my heart. It truly made sense to me: God is love, love is an emotion, emotions are in your heart; so to heal your heart by healing your inner child, you will feel God's love which resides in the hearts of us all.

Today I feel alive because I experience the love of Spirit in my heart almost every day. Whenever I ask to feel God's love inside, I experience a warm sensation of spiritual love vibrating through my body. Every day my self-love grows as I connect deeper and deeper with my inner child's journey of self-discovery and self-love. As my ability to love myself grows, my ability to love others also grows effortlessly. Always remember that any feeling of love is God; so as your ability to love grows, your ability to feel the love of God in your own heart also grows. The consequence of this is a wonderful sense of peace and love within you on daily basis.

I know, my friend, that you may be totally confused or really hurting inside, so it may be hard to imagine experiencing the feelings I just described. I, too, used to feel empty, sad, and scared all of the time. Now I don't! The hope that a Power greater than myself was supporting me increased my ability to have the courage to heal my inner self. As a consequence of healing myself, today I feel a grand sense of self-love in my heart, which I call Great Spirit.

Remember, if I can do it, so can you. Just know that God is with you as your choice to heal manifests in your life. Healing promotes love, and love is God. So heal yourself and feel the love of God in your own heart. This is the experience, strength, and hope I share with you about Step 2 as you quest to feel whole with God in your heart, as I do. Follow your quest, and the experience of God will be your reward.

Step 3: *We made the decision to turn our will and our lives over to a Power greater than ourselves.*

Just like every other spiritual concept I had learned while experiencing the twelve-step life process, I had no idea what this step was trying to tell me. For me, the concept of turning my will and my life over to something else made no sense at all. As time went on, though, a clarity around this step permeated my being. Step 3 is about learning faith. In order to learn faith, however, we first need to be able to know how to trust, because faith is the spiritual action step of trust. So in the next couple of pages, I will describe how I learned to trust myself more, and was able to have more faith in a Power greater than myself.

Let's separate this step into two parts. The first part, "Made a decision," is the key phrase to see the simple clarity in this complex step. Making a decision means we're willing to change our conscious perception from one place to another, choosing to allow this action step of spiritual growth. In my opinion, this step could be asked more simply like this, "Do I choose to allow Great Spirit to integrate into my life and help guide me?" If you answer no, stop here and return to Step 2. If you answer yes, then basically, in my opinion, you have accomplished the first part of Step 3.

The next question that comes into play is, "What have I just made a decision to do?" As we look more intently at the second part of Step 3, we can start to get some clarity on this question. The second part of Step 3 says "to turn our will and our lives over to a Power greater than us." When I first read this, I was extremely confused because all my life I was taught that my free will was a God-given gift. So if I have to turn my will over, how can I keep my freedom of free will in place?

The answer is simple. As human beings we have the choice (free will) to act any way we choose. One choice is to act out of fear, the other is to act in love.

Fear-based choices are things like:

greed	lying
dishonesty	manipulation
crossing boundaries	sloth
control issues	gluttony
projecting anger	false pride
cheating	lack
stealing	plus many, many more.

Love-based behaviors are things like:

faith	courage
integrity	willingness
humility	brotherly love
discipline	perseverance
awareness of God	helping others
living our dreams	plus many, many more.

Any choice is okay with God because he gives us free will. What Step 3 is saying for me, though, is that if I have the faith to act in loving ways, leaving the outcome of a situation to Great Spirit, then I have turned my will and my life over to a Power greater than myself, which I call God. So the essence of Step 3 is having faith that whatever happens is for my highest good as long as I am acting in loving ways.

When I first began to choose to allow this step to integrate into my life, my biggest fear was that if I changed my old behaviors I would not get what I wanted. Whenever a situation arose where I did not get what I wanted, I asked myself how could this possibly be for my highest good? What I eventually realized is that God's Will for me is to internally grow in loving ways. Looking at life like this, I learned that every situation enables me to personally grow. Now whenever a situation arises and the outcome does not happen as expected, I know that the

God-given lesson might be for me to find the courage to let this particular situation go. Other God-given lessons might be for me to have the willingness to be flexible, or the expression of deep grief as a consequence of the loss of my desired outcome.

A perfect example of this happened for me seven years ago when the woman of my dreams, Angel, left me for another man. At the time, all I could see was confusion. My anger at God and her were so great I could see no lesson. Over time, however, I realized my God-given gift around this experience was the pain itself, because it became so great I had to surrender to Great Spirit. After this surrendering process was complete, my life was never the same.

As a consequence of Angel leaving, I gained a new insight into my emotional self, which eventually led me to healing my inner child. Today I am forever thankful for this extremely painful situation which, at the time, I thought was the end of my life. In reality, though, it allowed me to gain a new life.

Turning my will (or choices) and my life (the direction of choices) over to a Power greater than myself has brought a lot of internal peace to my life. I integrate God's Will with my will each day by having the faith to live life in a conscious, loving way, and to trust that every experience I attract to me is for my highest good.

To be honest, most times it did take quite awhile for me to actually see the clarity of any unexpected outcome. However, I can say, looking back over my path, that one hundred percent of the time the natural consequence of this so-called unexpected outcome has always been grander than my original desire. To gain total clarity, however, I still needed two important questions answered surrounding Step 3. First, if Step 3 is just about choosing to live in loving principle, why doesn't everybody do it? Second, how do we know if we are acting in principle for our highest good?

The answer to the first question, in my opinion, is fear and lack of education. People don't understand that if they act in love vs. fear, their quality of life will be enhanced tremendously. Your ego, which is fear-based, has been in charge of your life for so long that to change from fear-based behaviors to love-based behaviors is sometimes very difficult and scary. The only way I was able to embrace this extreme fear of change, and learn how to act in love when it came to my outside world, was to learn how to love myself and to have faith that a Higher Power was working in my life.

By practicing self-loving principles, my original pain was healed because my inner child was shown the love he needed to heal. As he felt loved, he also felt safer with me. This enhanced his ability to trust me, which enhanced my personal ability to experience trust. Since faith is the action step of trust, the more efficient my inner self became at trusting, the easier it was for me to have faith in a Higher Power working in my life.

It was like a spiral. The longer I lived with conscious intent of inner self-love, the more my ability to trust grew. With this growth, my ability to have faith in a Higher Power also grew. As this process continued to deepen for me, my conscious connection with my Higher Power also deepened.

Today I feel as though my entire life has been turned over to these self-loving techniques of Spirit, and as a consequence, I live a very peaceful life inside and out. The longer I live in principle with myself, the more I experience the ability to integrate my internal behaviors of self-love into my external world. My choice to live in loving principle with the rest of the world has become a natural behavior as I practice loving principles with myself. Over time, my ability to have faith in my personal behaviors concerning society has also grown. In other words, today I trust myself when it comes to choosing external loving behaviors over fear-based behaviors.

As you probably can tell, the principle around Step 3 is faith. So for me to be able experience true faith in a Power greater than myself, I had to be able to trust myself first. To create a more internal trusting ability, all I had to do was go back to my inner child and treat him in a loving manner. In turn, he could allow himself to trust me even more; and again, the more my little kid trusted me, the more I could trust a Higher Power with the choices of my life.

Now remember, internal trust is earned. So sometimes it takes awhile for your new self-loving behaviors to have an actual effect on your inner child. If you continue to treat yourself with love, however, your ability to trust yourself will grow. As your internal ability to trust grows, so will your ability to have faith; and as your ability to have faith grows, your capacity to allow a Power greater than yourself to integrate into your life will also mature. Faith also takes time to grow, so if you are questioning your own capacity for faith, it's okay. When I first started this process, I had no faith at all. Now my entire life is in the hands of Great Spirit, or what I call living in pure, blind faith.

The second question is, "How do we know if we are acting in loving principle or for highest good?" Every time I personally questioned whether my behavior or decision of any type was for my highest good, this is what I would ask myself, "Is this choice of behavior taking me closer to God or farther away from Him?"

Since I was the only one who could answer this, I had to learn which red flags would help me discern my highest answer.

I used a couple of techniques to do this. First, in any situation, I would ask myself the question, "Is this situation taking me closer to God or farther away?" If I felt fear or tightness in my chest or stomach, I learned that these physical sensations were telling me intuitively not to act on this particular situation. The converse was also true. If I asked the question about something, and I felt very open and loving, this was an indication that my best choice was to move forward in this direction.

Let me give you an example of what to do for yourself so you, too, can learn what inner truth feels like. Ask yourself the question, "What is my name?" Then answer the question with your correct name. For example, "My name is Joe." Then stop a second and feel what it feels like to experience your truth. Based on hearing and experiencing the truth, you will feel a comfortable sensation of truth and openness.

Now ask yourself the same question, "What is my name?" This time, though, answer with a false name. Then stop and sense what it feels like to claim a false truth. For me, there is an uncomfortable feeling in my heart and stomach, as well as knowing that something is wrong.

This is a perfect little exercise I would suggest you do on a daily basis in the beginning to help you learn what it feels like to experience truth over non-truth. When I first stopped drinking, I often used this technique prior to going into a bar. I would ask the question, "Is going into this bar taking me closer to Spirit or farther away?" Every time I asked this question, I experienced a tight, uncomfortable feeling in my chest and heart. I came to realize that this uncomfortable feeling was Great Spirit saying to me that it was not for my highest good, for that day, to enter this establishment. The more I trusted these feelings and acted on their guidance, the more I learned to trust myself intuitively.

A red flag of higher choice discernment for me was when I was depicting old, unloving behaviors. I always knew intuitively that these behaviors were not taking me closer to God. For example, if I tried to manipulate someone by shaming them or projecting my guilt onto them, I knew this was not taking me closer to internal serenity. Another example is if I lied or cheated someone. I knew something unloving was going on inside of me, so I needed to stop and change my external choice.

Another technique I used to identify old fear-based behaviors was if I heard of a voice saying, "If you don't do it now, you'll never be able to," or "No one will know except us," or "They have plenty of money; so if I take a little, it won't ever be missed." I learned that these were my ego voices trying to rationalize non- principled activities. Whenever I heard my ego trying to get me to do something, I knew that it probably was not for my highest good to act in this manner.

So Step 3 was simply a decision to allow spiritual principles to integrate into my life. Faith came into play whenever I had to trust that whatever outcome arose, based on my self-loving behaviors and choices, was God's Will for me.

Now I actually believe that my genuine will is God's Will for me also. My ego always tries to get me to believe that I don't deserve absolute abundance. Since my definition of God is pure love and abundance, His Will for me has to be total love and abundance. I now realize that even if I don't understand the final consequence of a situation in the moment, I do feel safe because I have faith that God knows; and I trust that His Will for me is total abundance. So even though I don't always see the abundance of a situation in the moment, I trust that in time the clarity I need to feel comfortable inside will eventually happen.

As I integrated the twelve loving principles into my internal world as well as my outside world, my ability to have faith in a Power greater than myself became effortlessly grander. My desire to turn my entire will and life over to a Power greater than myself became much more focused, but I will tell you from my own experience that this spiritual concept is much easier said than done. I used to say, "I will allow God into some aspects of my life; but in other parts, I don't need any help." So if that sounds familiar to you, know that it is okay. It took me many years and a lot of practice to allow God's Will to integrate into all aspects of my life.

For me, the most difficult place to allow God's Will was in my work world. For many years I thought that selling nutritional products was the only thing I was ever going to do to create income in my life. I was terrified to allow God into this part of my life because of the fear that God would not want me to sell these products anymore, and because of this fear, I held on to my nutrition business with both hands.

I want to explain a little further what I mean by holding on to something. When it came to my business opportunity, I was totally closed down to even the possibility of allowing anything else in my life. My conscious focus was solely isolated on the business. I held onto this mental attitude so strongly because of my false belief that said, "If you let go of something or think about something else, it has to leave your life." This paradigm is simply not true. The only things that will naturally leave your life as you let go are the unloving situations or belief systems that are not allowing you to grow spiritually.

I finally realized that God's Will for me was to be happy and abundant. So with this new awareness, I was able to allow my consciousness to be open to the possibility of other potential income opportunities entering my life. As I was able to let go of the fear-based belief that my nutrition business was the only opportunity for me to create income, my mind and consciousness naturally expanded to the universal truths that the world has billions of opportunities to create income. Because we have free will, we have the capability to choose whichever opportunity causes us to feel the greatest sense of internal joy and fulfillment. I know that in order for me to experience God's Will in my job, I also have to feel joy and abundance while doing this job. A very sad reality is that so many people stay in their current job situations even though they hate them. Most stay because they're afraid they can't get another job. The fear of paying their bills is so great that they forget they have a choice of whether to stay or leave their current situation.

Personally, had I stayed in that place of fear, I would not have ventured to sell nutritional products, or write this book, or create my seminar company called Spirit Walkers. Today I have it all. I sell nutritional products that help people with their health and their wealth, and I share my love with the world through my writings and public speaking.

The way I know that I am in the spiritual flow of faith is based on how I feel. Today it feels as though my entire life just seems to move forward very freely, as though one loving thing after another seems to happen in my life very synchronously. My ability to feel the open experience of freedom in my heart is also very apparent as a consequence of living consciously in Step 3. My conscious intention of integrating God into my life's choices moment-by-moment basically has become second nature for me as my decisions to allow the integration of Step 3 happened in my life.

There are many ways we can experience an extreme feeling of freedom in our lives. Have you ever been driving down the road when you hear a familiar song, but in a totally different way? It's as if you are experiencing in your heart the same feeling the musicians feel as they're creating the music. The experience of the music seems to come from a different place than usual. Perhaps you felt so free you just wanted to sing at the top of your lungs, with the windows down, without a care in the world. This sensation is the feeling of freedom I experience in my heart every day. To be perfectly honest, my life's path has been blessed in such a way that I feel that same sensation of freedom in all aspects of my life. It is so awesome and I thank God daily for this. Another example is when you are feeling the euphoria of being in love with someone for the first time. This feeling of open- hearted euphoria is a similar experience to the feeling of the freedom associated with Step 3.

So to recap Step 3, remember that to start this step is to make a conscious decision to allow spiritual principles into your internal life as well as your external life. The natural consequence of this loving behavior is your own ability to trust yourself. Naturally, with more capacity to trust, your ability to have faith in the integration of Great Spirit into your life will also grow. For me, this integration has allowed me a life of total abundance in all areas, which is God's Will for us all.

Now as you go through this process of integration and you hear ego voices claiming different realities, remember these are red flags. Each time you hear an ego voice, check in with your little kid to see if your personal love is needed on a deeper level. My belief is that God's Will for us is total abundance, and anything less than this is ego. Keep in mind that an ego voice is normally the consequence of a wounded little kid underneath it. As you identify a deeper wounded part and allow this part to heal, your ego-based "lack" voices will naturally transform. With the absence of these voices, your life will naturally experience the total abundance of God's Will and love.

Giving your inner child love is the key to all the spiritual attributes of God. With your inner child healed, your ability to act with love rather than fear eventually becomes intuitive instead of deliberate. This takes time, though; but the reward for your determination will be magical. Allow Step 3 to integrate into your life and watch your world change forever. My world has changed magically. My hope is that you find the courage to allow yours to do the same thing as a consequence of taking Step 3.

CHAPTER 16

Self-discovery

Step 4: *We made a fearless and moral inventory of ourselves.*
Step 4 is the first stage in repairing the damaged relationships with other people, ourselves, and a Power greater than ourselves. Making a moral inventory basically means to write out the wrongful acts we have chosen in our lives that have hurt others and us.

In my situation, as I began writing down all of my chosen activities which were not actions of principle, I was totally amazed. I finally saw that my unloving behaviors of the past were truly based in fear. When I first saw this step, I thought it was going to be a lot like a Catholic confession. The truth is, Step 4 is about having the courage to really be honest with yourself. As I continued writing out my fear-based behavior, I came across long forgotten things I had done. I started to remember how I stole things from people, and how I lied and manipulated people all of the time. I realized that my behaviors of the past were always about getting something I wanted, or about keeping something I already had. It was also during these writings that I truly saw how scared I was—all of the time.

During this fourth step, I also realized that so many of my unloving behaviors were the direct result of my wounded little kid. The ego parts that were developed years ago to protect me were the exact parts that were acting out and hurting me in the present. I remember writing the context of the step down on paper and wondering how could I ever have done these behaviors. The truth is, during the actual acting out of these choices, I had no idea I was hurting myself or anyone else. In an unconscious state of mind, my ego was in total control of my life; therefore, I naturally listened to the fear-based voices because it was all I knew.

As I had the courage to write down the exact nature of my wrongs, I discovered a tremendous amount about myself. My rationalizer voice was such a huge protector part for me that I could steal something, and in that moment really believe I deserved it. Many of my unloving behaviors were also enhanced by an extreme alcohol, drug, and sex addiction. So in a state of inebriation, my choices were even more skewed than normal.

Step 4 is the first action step that starts the process of walking out of our toxic shame. Toxic shame is a feeling that there's something wrong with us. Feelings that you're the bad seed or a defective person are sensations of toxic shame. As I wrote my fourth step, I became aware of why I was the way I was. I finally understood that my unloving behaviors and choices were a natural consequence of my wounded kid. Seeing this new awareness generated a lot of hope in my life because for the first time, I felt I was living in the solution regarding my unloving behaviors. The more I wrote, the more fear I felt. I realized that I was writing down things I had never told anyone before. Putting these behaviors down on paper was very uncomfortable for me. As I wrote, I often skipped over particularly uncomfortable memories for fear of their disclosure someday. Eventually, I wrote everything I could remember. I kept thinking of the phrase, "We are only as sick as our secrets," which kept me motivated to find the courage to write down all of my old choices. Over the course of several days, I was actually able to write out several pages of old information.

I wrote down every behavior or circumstance for which I felt shame. I was astonished at my life. Most of my life's choices were based in fear, and until that moment I had no idea why. I was totally amazed when I learned how all of my unloving behaviors were actually hurting me. It was easy for me to see the hurt I caused by stealing from someone. It took me awhile, though, to understand how the same situation hurt me, also. It wasn't until I learned the concepts of self-esteem, self-worth, and personal integrity that I understood how living out-of-principle hurt me.

Self-esteem is a concept that describes how we view ourselves. Every time I stole something, I would view myself as a thief. Every time I manipulated someone to get my way, I saw myself as a con-artist. Whenever I crossed someone's boundaries, I described myself as a hard-ass. Each time I drank, I shamed myself as an active alcoholic. The list goes on and on. So in essence, whenever I acted in a fear-based manner, unconsciously my self-esteem dropped because my view of myself was lowered. Self-worth is a description of how we feel about ourselves.

With this in mind, I can use the same examples, realizing that every time I crossed someone's boundaries in any way, I experienced feelings of guilt and remorse. Choosing to continue my unloving behaviors because I knew no better only deepened this sense of guilt and remorse. Living in guilt produced the illusion that I had done something wrong, and I experienced it every day. As my old behaviors continued, the feeling that I had done something wrong changed to the feeling that something was wrong with me. This reality is called toxic shame. High self-worth and toxic shame are at opposite ends of the personal value scale. So the longer I chose to live out-of-principle, the lower my self-worth became.

Personal integrity is a personal quality that measures our own ability to trust ourselves. If I describe myself as a thief, a liar, a con-artist, a hard-ass, and an active alcoholic, where do you think my ability to trust myself really was? In this place, I had no self-trust or personal integrity. In this place, I had totally lost my real sense of self, and felt truly empty.

Another way we lose our sense of self is if we are always living for someone or something else. For example, if you identify yourself completely as just a mother to your children, or wife to your husband, eventually you'll lose a sense of who you really are. Another example is if you identify yourself totally as your job, claiming that when you become president of the company you will feel better; or if you make more money, you will be fine. Basically, this is saying that your sense of self is directly related to something outside of yourself. The consequence of directing your discernment of who you are, based on something outside of you, is that you lose the true spiritual sense of who you really are. Constant behaviors in any of these false beliefs will lead you to a feeling of emptiness or spiritual bankruptcy.

Your self-worth, self-esteem, and personal integrity will eventually be zero if you keep choosing those old behaviors as a means of survival. I like to describe this place of zero as being spiritually bankrupt. The beautiful gift that Step 4 gave me was the ability to become consciously aware of all of these old patterns. Before this time, I had no idea that these unloving behaviors were even there.

This new awareness helped me start the healing process associated with these choices. In fact, one day I looked into Sandy's eyes and confidently said, "I never lie." I remember she looked at me with a smile and said, "We'll see." It took Step 4 to help me realize what she meant.

The first stage of any type of spiritual growth is awareness. Step 4 helped me become aware of how unloving my choices and behaviors were to others and me. I was finally able to see my part in many different situations. For the first time in my life, this step allowed me to walk out of victim-hood and start making choices for my highest good.

This step is about becoming aware of old patterns and behaviors by writing them down. It is the first real step of internal growth because it prompts personal awareness. In truth, no growth can ever happen in any arena of your life prior to becoming aware that healthy changes are needed. Step 4 is a true action step that produces a new level of consciousness regarding our old unloving patterns in our lives.

Remember that Step 4 is not about retribution; it is about self-discovery. As you see more clearly how your unloving behaviors have run your life, you will see how your choices have been made out of fear, not love. When you understand that all ego-based behaviors are consequences of a wounded inner child, you will move from helplessness to hopefulness because you will understand how to heal your inner pain each time a deeper layer appears for you. You will also learn that the consequence of crossing someone's boundaries is your own personal demise of self-value.

By working this step, I am proud to say that my self-worth, self-esteem, and personal integrity are very high. I truly love who I am today. My old feelings of constant guilt have not entered my life daily for a very long time. I remember the first day I became aware of my newly-found freedom regarding toxic shame and toxic guilt. That was the most spectacular day of my life.

When I started this process, I was spiritually bankrupt. Today I am not. And if I can achieve such high personal levels of self-love, so can you. Remember, the degree to which you love yourself is truly the degree to which you can love others.

Fearless, moral inventory is the first action step to heal our toxic shame. Find the courage to write down who you truly are. Ask for God's guidance, and with the completion of this step, you will feel as though you have walked the first mile out of the dark and into the light of your own personal reality of self-discovery. You will also know whether it is time to move on to Step 5. Don't rush yourself. Allow your inner truth to prevail and guide you. Trust that you'll know when you get the inner signal that it is time to share your fourth step with another person. And when you receive this God-given message, that will be the time to put your personal courage into action, and move on to Step 5.

Step 5: *We admitted to ourselves, to God, and to another human being the exact nature of our wrongs.*

Step 5 is the freedom step. As I mustered the courage to admit my faults to another human being, the consequence was the moving out of a lifetime of isolation. All of the old behaviors I had buried deep inside myself—the ones I thought I would never share—had me buried in my own isolated shame. My ego voices would continually tell me that if I told anyone my mistakes, they would hate me.

Step 5 is the first real step of humility because to be able to share our old behaviors with someone else, we have to be able to be open and vulnerable. The choice to be vulnerable is to crack open our hard shell of ego, and let someone really get to know us.

As I shared my deepest secrets with my first sponsor, I felt I was bearing my soul to him and God. As I looked into his loving eyes and saw his reflection of love with no judgment, I was able to start moving out of my own deep shame and into the light of my real self.

Sharing myself with another human being also started the demise of my own personal isolation. As I shared my pain with him, I was able to talk openly about my shameful past, and this helped me gain a new perspective. During my fifth step, I realized that my actions were only a reflection of a deep pain inside of me. The conclusion of my fifth step allowed me a sense of freedom, and I felt as though a thousand pounds had been lifted from my shoulders. In sharing my past behaviors with another person, I had come out of my personal hiding for the first time. This sharing was the most amazing experience of my life because I did it with the right person.

In choosing your partner for Step 5, my first suggestion would be to pick someone who has actually experienced the personal magic themselves. From their own personal experience, they will be able to guide you as you accomplish this monumental task. I also would suggest that you choose a partner with whom you feel safe. I needed someone who could listen to me with no judgment and no criticism. If necessary, I would choose someone I did not even know before I would use a personal friend or spouse.

Another important factor to consider is to allow a tremendous amount of time for this event. I needed to talk about different experiences openly and at length in order to gain the clarity needed for me to start my healing process. So please, don't rush yourself. Just take your time.

Make sure you claim a safe and quiet place to proceed with this step. I needed a place were I knew I would be uninterrupted for the duration of time I shared with my sponsor.

The last thing I needed was a conscious knowing that God was with us both. Understanding this was important because it allowed me to have the courage and strength I needed to share the in depth and detailed nature of my wrongs with another human being.

Step 5 is a mysterious event, so you may feel some fear. There is a reason it comes after the first four steps have been completed. By the time I got to Step 5, the magic of my own personal trans- formation had already happened for me. Through this process of transformation, my fear of sharing my past with another human being diminished. In the beginning, I remember feeling terrified at even the thought of this process, but on the day I accomplished this step, I had very little fear.

I currently have accomplished four different fifth steps with different people. The more I've looked inside, the keener my ability to be honest with myself has become. The deeper I share my faults with another human being, the grander my sense of freedom has grown. Step 5 has to do with integrity and freedom. Sharing my secrets has released me from my personal prison of toxic shame, and as a consequence, my ability to grow and act in a spiritual way has grown tremendously.

Today I can honestly share that I have no secrets. I have had the courage to allow another human being into my life and to know all of me. It is very humbling for me to admit that I actually was able to be vulnerable in front of another person. This still amazes me.

The natural consequence of conscious vulnerability is the ability to allow Spirit to flow in my heart. I had to be able to be open and vulnerable before I could actually feel the love of Great Spirit from my soul. For me, Step 5 was the milestone that started this opening process of vulnerability in my life. I thank Spirit each day for giving me the courage to share myself with another human being. It truly was a huge building block in repairing my relationships with myself, with others, and with Great Spirit.

After I released some of my toxic shame, I began to see myself in a totally different light. Instead of looking at myself as a loner, I started to see myself as a people person. My ability to connect with my inner child and with other people also grew. The deep feeling that there was something wrong with me started to leave little by little. As time progressed, I started to feel that I actually had something of importance to offer society. It truly felt as though I walked out of a dark closet and into a lit room.

Being released from the deep toxic shame of my past was as easy as just talking about my pain with another human being. However, as a consequence of openly talking about my deep pain, I did discover and express additional levels of grief and rage that needed to be experienced. With each new awareness I often found deeper inner wounds. As I allowed these wounds to heal, I felt the healing consequence of Step 5.

So to recap, when I was ready, I found someone I could trust who had already accomplished his or her own fifth step. I chose someone who could have compassion for me as I accomplished this step. I chose a safe, quiet place, where I knew I would not be interrupted for extended amounts of time. Then I allowed the presence of God to give me the courage and strength I needed to share my entire self with another human being. As I did this, I knew I was taking a huge step out of the depths of my isolation and into the light of Spirit.

For me, the consequence of acting upon Step 5 has been absolutely magical. My suggestion is that when you have completed your own session, stop awhile and see how you feel. I felt an immediate sense of freedom and accomplishment because I was totally relieved to be finished with such a monumental task. For some, however, the sense of relief happens over time. Either way, time is the only variable for you to see the difference in your own life.

Step 6: *We became willing to have all of our shortcomings removed.*

The first time I looked at Step 6, I thought this step would be the easiest step ever. I believed that it would be simple to choose for all of my fears to be gone. The truth is, it was much harder than it looked.

Willingness takes having the courage to change. For example, if I truly wanted to stop drinking, I had to be willing to stop going to bars and hanging around people who drank all the time. When I made the decision to stop drinking, I had to change my entire life.

The bar scene was a major part of my life, so when I stopped going out to bars, I asked myself the question, "What do I do now?" In the beginning, this change of lifestyle was very difficult for me because I had so much free time, which was a major change for me. I learned that when I said I was willing to change any old, unloving behaviors, I also had to be willing to accept the lifestyle change that would occur because of those new choices.

It took time for me to gain the willingness to change certain old behaviors. The internal pain I caused myself by acting in old ways was not deep enough to warrant facing the fear of change. So for a long time, I sat and wallowed in my self-destructive behaviors because even though I was in pain, it was not un-comfortable enough to do anything about it.

Then one day I realized that my fear of change was simply my ego acting out as a consequence of a wounded little kid underneath it. My ego was also fearful, and tried to keep me from moving forward into the void. But I had discovered how to nurture myself through either situation.

Over time, I also learned how to view my lack of willingness to change unloving behaviors as red flags. So each time I felt this fear of change inside of me, I would stop and ask my little kid what was truly going on with him. I remember numerous times using this technique to find the deeper wounded parts of me.

The other loving technique I used during Step 6 was a Higher Power. If I felt myself not being willing to change some old unloving pattern, I would ask Great Spirit to give me the willingness I needed to change. Eventually, I realized that I could truly depend on a Higher Power to help me during my scary times of change.

Willingness is something that is developed with time and practice. In the unconscious state, most people only have a willingness to change when the pain they are in is so great that they can't stand any more. Their choice to change is forced upon them because it is the only thing that brings any hope of relief for them. As we awaken, our desire to integrate the principle of willingness into our daily lives grows. For me, my ability to have willingness today is very strong because I know that Spirit is in my life to guide its direction.

In the unconscious world, the number one fear is fear of change—or fear of the unknown. In my experience, I've seen people who live paralyzed in their own fear-based egos, making any willingness to change almost impossible.

My own fear of change was continually validated by my ego, which would say, "If we stop this old behavior we can't survive." My ego would also say, "We don't deserve to be abundant, so why even try?" It would also say things like, "If we let others into our life, they will definitely leave us and hurt us." Since I had no other practical means to guide my choices in life except through my ego, I had little abundance and no real friends. In my opinion, this is where most of the unconscious world actively lives today. To verify this statement, ask yourself if you know anyone in your life who can wake up in the morning and say to themselves, "I live in total abundance." What I mean by this is, someone who can say, "I love my work; I love my family; I love my friends; and I love my life." For me, in my old state of living, I knew no one who could claim this statement as his or her truth. In fact, when I heard this statement for this first time, my ego said, "This type of living is not realistic, and no one could ever achieve it."

As a consequence of healing my inner child, all of this shifted as I started to awaken to my real self. My ability to have faith in the guidance of a Higher Power grew to such a place that even though change was uncomfortable and frightening for me, knowing that Great Spirit was in control of my life allowed a certain level of safeness to be integrated into my decision-making process regarding change. So in turn, my willingness to change old unloving patterns grew in direct proportion to my ability to experience inner faith. For me, my willingness to change was directly proportional to my ability to have faith.

As a consequence of having enough faith and willingness to change, my old limiting thoughts and beliefs naturally diminished. This was truly a spiritual experience that can only be described as human transformation of consciousness. When the willingness is there and I chose to change, Great Spirit would always remove the voices of fear that motivated the unloving behaviors in the first place. *(In Step 7 we will talk about the exact procedure that will allow the removal of all of your old voices.)*

In recap, remember that Step 6 is a step of willingness. Our willingness describes our desire to change from fear-based behaviors to new loving behaviors. The variable needed to accomplish growth through your ability to be willing is called faith. For me, knowing Great Spirit was in control of my life lessened my fear of change. As my fears diminished, my desire to be willing to change naturally grew. It's important to remember that you will establish faith and inner trust as your inner child begins trusting you and healing himself. So the more your inner child trusts you, the more faith you will have in Great Spirit.

This is when I truly realized how important it was for me to depend on a Higher Power to lessen my fears. Remember, fear of change is the greatest fear known to man; so make sure you ask and depend on your Higher Power for the courage needed in your life, and see how your willingness to change will effortlessly grow.

CHAPTER 17

Repairing the Past

Step 7: *Humbly asked that our shortcomings be removed.*
This is where I moved from living in a shame-based reality to the
experience of having healthy shame. Let me give you a couple of
examples of what I'm talking about.

A shame-based person is someone who feels they are not
good enough to receive abundance; that in order to receive
abundance, they must be perfect. This is an extreme illusion
that keeps us in a place of a total false self.

Step 7 allowed me to humbly ask Spirit to remove my
human characteristics that were not acting for my highest
good anymore. Healthy shame is experienced when we not only
realize we are powerful spiritual beings, but that we are also
human, which means we have certain limitations.

As human beings, we're going to make mistakes and fail
at certain events we pursue in life. We're going to do and say
certain things that afterwards we wish we had not done or said.
At times we will feel fear and allow it to run our lives. We will
be greedy and self-centered on occasion. We may act childishly
some days, and be very rigid on other days. The bottom line is,
as human beings we are going to act human. This means we're
neither perfect nor flawed; we are just human.

When I experienced the sensation of healthy shame, I
allowed myself to accept my limited abilities as a human being.
When I truly understood this concept of being a fully functioning
human being, my life was changed forever. Prior to learning
this concept, I was stuck in both ends of the extreme. One part
of me constantly said, "I don't deserve anything because I am
as worthless as a worm." The other part of me countered with,
"To receive any type of abundance, I have to be perfect in every
way." During my personal experience of Step 7, I finally realized
neither of these illusions were true.

As I gained some clarity on these false beliefs, I asked
myself where these illusions were developed. Looking into
my childhood, I discovered that healthy shame is something I
never learned as a child because I was so busy trying to get love
and support from my unconscious environment. My huge ego
parts, which were developed because of this environment, were
remarkable. I took on the role of being a good boy, or the perfect
one, in hopes I would earn and receive the love I needed.

Over time, the emotional support I needed in order to thrive
wasn't given to me, so my perfectionist part naturally grew. My
uneducated ego kept telling me I wasn't perfect enough, which

was why I wasn't getting the strokes and love I needed. The truth is, everyone in my life did the best they could; however, not being raised in a loved-based environment themselves, they could not give me the love I emotionally needed to thrive.

As this perpetual circle continued, seeking love through perfection and not receiving it, my fear-based ego also grew in the opposite direction. When I did not get the love and attention I needed as a child, I eventually took on the belief that I didn't deserve to be loved or have abundance. Through my eyes as a child, my parents were perfect; and since I did not feel love from them, there must naturally be something wrong with me. This is called toxic shame. The truth is, my parents did not have the internal love within themselves to give me. That is why I could not receive the emotional energy of love from them. It had nothing to do with me.

When we humbly ask God to remove the ego-based character beliefs that are just not true anymore, we shouldn't be surprised if more inner child wounds are discovered. My own shame-based self-image was truly healed after God removed the voices, and I re-experienced the pain of my neglected little kid.

The principle behind Step 7 is humility, because it takes humility to ask for help. As we accomplish this spiritual action step, we find that humility sometimes has a very vulnerable and raw feeling associated with it. It was during this step that I finally realized I could not heal these ego voices alone. Before these voices could be removed, I had to ask for help and find the courage to allow Great Spirit and all of its awesome power to support me.

As this process unfolded for me, I felt a sense of gratitude and respect for Great Spirit's power. I was amazed and humbled that Spirit would actually intervene and help me, and I finally recognized the true unconditional love for me. I consciously became aware that all I had to do was ask for Great Spirit's help, be open to that help, and know that all of my desires of internal growth could be accomplished.

The last and probably most important issue I learned during Step 7 was that I am human, and I will make mistakes. Though now in a conscious place of love, I have the ability to learn from those mistakes and move on. Step 7 brought clarity to me about being human; so in the end, I realized that I eventually could forgive myself. With this new sense of taking personal responsibility for my past actions, I was ready to do something about it. With retribution on my mind, I was ready to start Steps 8 and 9. To recap, Step 7 is about truly learning that we are human beings. We are neither perfect nor defected. We're going to make mistakes because we have limitations. Step 7 also allows us to feel some humility as we ask a higher power to help us. Last, though certainly not least, we realize that we can learn from our mistakes, choose to change, and move on into retribution.

Step 8: *Made a list of people we have harmed and became willing to make amends to them all.*

Now when it was time for me to make a list of people I had harmed, I was scared to death. It was one thing to admit my faults to another human being; it was something totally different to say I was sorry to all the people I had hurt. To be honest, when I reached this point on my path, I contemplated stopping all growth and staying on Step 7. Then when I expressed my fears to Sandy, she said, "Joe, read this step ten times slowly, then call me back." As I did this, I became aware of what this step was asking me to do.

Step 8 says to make a list, and then become willing to make amends. When I realized it was only asking me to make a list, I knew I could do this. So that day I pulled out the inventory from my fourth step, and started writing down all of the names of the people I had hurt in one fashion or another. As my list grew, so did my feelings of remorse. I literally included just about every person in my life. In that moment, I realized that because of my own fear-based nature, I had hurt a lot of people, including myself.

I remember the day I actually felt the grief of remorse regarding this step. I cried for several hours because I could not believe how many people I had really hurt in my life. My tears seemed to be some of the most healing tears I had ever felt. I could truly say to myself that I was sorry for my past behaviors. I could see how and why I had acted as I did. After this release of remorse, I began to forgive myself for all of the wrongs I had created by living an unconscious life. I really connected that day with the truth of the statement, "I didn't know I was hurting people all of this time." I just did not know!

So Step 8 is a cleansing step where healthy guilt is formed. Healthy guilt, for me, is a feeling we have prior to hurting ourselves or someone else. It is an uncomfortable sensation that helps us discern whether or not to act in a certain way. Step 8 is also where my conscience was regained; where I began to stop and think before acting in an unloving way, because I knew the consequence of choosing this old behavior was that I was going to have to feel the remorse.

Prior to experiencing the growth of Step 8, I had no internal guidance system that allowed me to know whether or not I was crossing someone else's boundaries. I was so closed down emotionally back then that I could feel no remorse in regard to any of my personal behaviors. So with no healthy fear of remorse in my life, I could act in any unhealthy way I chose and never know I was hurting others or myself. The consequence of this continual unloving behavior was that I created a massive personal experience of toxic guilt from my actions.

Let me remind you that toxic guilt is a personal experience that says no matter how loving I choose to act, I always feel as though I have done something wrong. Many times in my life my behaviors were loving, but I could not see the good in myself until I released the grief associated with the remorse surrounding the old patterns that were not loving. Step 8 was where I started to gain back my sense of internal serenity that *I have done nothing wrong today, so I can trust myself today.*

I now know intuitively if my choice of behavior is going to hurt me or someone else, but while I was learning to follow and trust my conscience, I used the Golden Rule from the Bible, "Do unto others as you would have them do unto you," (Matthew 7:12).

When it came to discerning my choices of behavior, I would ask myself this question, "How would I feel if someone chose to behave with me the way I was going to behave with them?" I would change my personal choice of action if the answer was, "I would not like for someone to treat me that way."

Here are a few examples of techniques I learned to use while I was regaining my personal conscience.

I sometimes borrowed things from family members without asking them first. I would use something for awhile, and then return it without them ever knowing it was gone. One day my sponsor asked me, "Joe, if someone walked into your house and took a personal item of yours for awhile without your permission, how would you feel?" Of course, I would not like it. So in asking this question, I was able to discern whether or not my actions were loving and trustworthy.

Whenever I chose not to pay back a debt to a friend who had lent me money, I would ask myself, "If my friend owed me money, and he or she chose not to pay me back, how would I feel?" If I would feel angry or uncomfortable, then I would choose to repay the debt.

If I were going to talk to someone in a manipulative way, I would ask myself, "How would I like it if they talked to me in the same way?" If I wouldn't like it, then I would choose different words during my conversation.

The greatest gift of Step 8 is that it is such a big step in the direction of healing our relationships with other people. It taught me to think about other people's feelings prior to choosing any action that involved someone else. The first time I changed an old behavior because I thought of someone else's feelings first was an absolute miracle for me. Allowing my conscience to be an active part of my decision-making process was a fabulous step of love, which started turning my toxic guilt into healthy guilt. Quite honestly, when it came to my behavior with another person, it allowed me to act from my Higher Self rather than my self-centered ego.

Gaining a sense of my true self was a hallmark of true spiritual growth. Choosing to live from this place of true self has brought many wonderful relationships to my life. I will be forever grateful to Spirit for providing the inner strength I needed to heal through my deep grief.

In a nutshell, Step 8 is about making a list of the people we have harmed, and becoming willing to make amends to each person on this list because we finally know it is time to right the wrongs of our past. It's important to realize that to truly take this action step of forgiveness, we first have to forgive ourselves.

My own self-forgiveness happened through my deep remorse, and feeling the true sadness from hurting myself and others because of my fear-based choices. The consequence was a true conscious-building tool. Today I am now free from my chronic toxic guilt because I regained my ability to sense the difference between loving behavior and unloving behavior prior to acting on any situation. By the grace of God, I live a guilt-free life; and to me this freedom is the greatest gift of all.

Step 9: *Made direct amends to people we have harmed, except when to do so would hurt them or others.*

The first time I saw this step I absolutely froze. I was terrified of the idea I would have to say I was sorry to someone. I felt I would never be able to do this step. In time, though, just as with every other step, when I was ready to make amends to people, I did.

Step 9 is an action step that actually starts repairing our past unloving behaviors. It is not about begging for forgiveness, or even trying to get someone to see your view. This step is strictly about having enough humility to walk up to another human being and say, "This is what I did, and I'm sorry the consequence of my actions caused you pain." This allows us to repair our wrongs, grow from our choices, and move along. By the time I did Step 9, I had come to realize that all the past behaviors for which I was making amends were behaviors based in fear. All of these choices were based on my ego, not my Spirit.

As I made my amends to people, I felt the humility I needed to allow the openness and vulnerability of Spirit to actually shine through. I will be honest with you, though; for me, feeling the depths of humility was extremely difficult. My ego fought hard inside my head, trying to keep me from righting my wrongs. My ego would say things like, "If we say we're sorry, we're being a wimp." It would also tell me, "If we admit our wrongs, no one is going to love us anymore." But the harshest words my ego ever said were, "If we are open and vulnerable with someone by admitting our wrongs, they will use this against us and shame us to death!"

It was amazing how my ego fought with me to stay closed down and wallow in the fears of my old behaviors. I asked Spirit every day during this time on my path to give me the courage I needed to move through these fears. I realized on a very deep level during the ninth step the difference between the coward and the hero. Honestly, before this time I thought the biggest difference between the two was that a hero felt no fear. The truth is, a hero feels fear, but he does not allow the fear to run his life. He sometimes has to dig deep inside, but he always finds the courage needed to act in spite of his fear.

During Step 9, I realized it was okay to be afraid. My connection with Great Spirit allowed me the true source of courage I needed to move through my fears rather than allowing my fears to run my life. Until this time, I unconsciously lived much like the coward because I had no internal tools to guide me forward. Fear ran my life, so most of my behaviors were unloving and closed down to the love of Spirit.

Through this process, I learned that it takes a tremendous amount of inner strength and courage to live an open and vulnerable life. My reward from this choice has been a very deep and grand connection to Great Spirit, which I cherish every day.

Ego and humility are two spiritual experiences that cannot be felt at the same time. The ego energy in our lives makes it difficult to feel the depth of Great Spirit's love in our hearts. During the process of Step 9, we are able to feel the humility needed to remove our ego, and allow our hearts to truly shine. So as we live a life of love and light, we naturally will feel the removal of the darkness of ego and the fear of unconsciousness.

For me, during any new experience of humility, I also felt a huge feeling of grief associated with this letting go. Step 9 literally allowed me to grow from one level of consciousness to another. During the shifts, which I call human transformation of consciousness, I felt a tremendous amount of grief surrounding the loss or transformation of my ego selves. This process literally felt as though I were dying inside. I thought of this episode as a psychic death, which allowed me a little bit of internal comfort as I experienced my massive grief.

On this path, there is no grander spiritual experience than the feeling of transforming your old consciousness. I remember numerous occasions when I was grieving from the depth of my soul, and felt gratitude at the very same time. The grief was associated with the psychic death I was feeling during my letting go process. The gratitude was associated with the awareness of the spiritual truth that with each internal death there is naturally a rebirth connection.

What I found, over time, was that the attributes of the rebirth process always gave me a deeper natural ability to love myself and remember the loving experience of Great Spirit in my heart. This happened because Step 9 caused a tremendous amount of internal humility in me, and since ego and humility cannot coexist, choosing the path of love and humility literally forces our ego self to be transformed. My own ego's job is to keep me from my true internal Spirit. With its removal in Step 9, the love of Spirit has a greater ability to consciously shine through my heart. The natural consequence of this transformation has been absolutely magical. I literally have the ability today to feel the presence of Great Spirit in my heart. The massive removal of parts of my ego through the presence of humility has truly transformed my life.

With each spiritual shift I go through, my inner child also feels more open and safe with me. The consequence of my little kid trusting me is a deep sense of love and faith inside my heart. This faith allows me to reconnect with Great Spirit on an even a deeper level.

The process of spiritual transformation, as well as internal healing of old wounds, is all tied together. The more we heal, the more we trust. The more we trust, the more our ego lets go. The more our ego lets go, the more love of Spirit can shine through us. And obviously, the more we feel Spirit in our hearts, the more we can trust.

For me, as I moved through this process, I could see more clearly how and why our spiritual path resembles a spiral rather than a straight line. It made sense to me that as long as we are still living in this existence, we will be continually growing and changing with the love of Great Spirit in our hearts.

Even though Step 9 can be extremely challenging, you might have to do its activities more than one time in your life. This happens because the deeper we go inside ourselves with Spirit, the more honest we become. We literally can wake up one day and realize that some behavior in our past, which was okay yesterday, is not okay today. This conscious shift happens as a result of our deep ability to feel safe and connected to our inner child as well as Great Spirit.

When you choose to act on your ninth step, please be very gentle with yourself. Make sure you give yourself a lot of love and praise during this process. You deserve it! I personally have a tremendous amount respect for you as you take on this challenge. In recap, Step 9 is about taking action steps to repair our past unloving behaviors. It is truly a magical step in regaining loving relationships with other people and ourselves. During the process, remember that humility will be felt and it might be challenging, but the consequence of this experience is magical. In my opinion, humility and massive ego cannot be felt at the same time, so if you take the action steps to promote humility, your ego will naturally transform. Then, with big parts of the ego transformed, your natural ability to feel and experience the internal love of Great Spirit will effortlessly be enhanced.

Regardless of what your ego is trying to tell you about this process, the natural consequence of finding the courage to repair the wreckage of your past is far beyond anything your imagination can even comprehend right now. Make your list, make your amends, and move on into a new life of love and light.

Our personal road of internal honesty becomes narrower as time goes on because of our ability to see our own unloving behaviors differently. Our human consciousness is shifting every day, and since we are going to make mistakes because we're human, Step 10 is the next logical step.

CHAPTER 18

Seeking Your Purpose

Step 10: *Took a personal daily inventory of ourselves and when we were wrong, we promptly admitted it.*

This step acknowledges the truth of life, which says we are human beings. For me, as I lived my life of toxic shame, I worked very hard at trying to be perfect or super human. My wounded little kid always acted out, trying to be a good little boy because I thought if I made no mistakes, I would be loved. Well, the truth is, it is impossible to be perfect all the time. This was impossible for me to accept until I learned the concept of Step 10, which is the tool I need to consciously be able to make my mistakes and then learn from them.

Taking a daily inventory simply means that each night before I go to bed, I recap my day's behaviors. I look at my day and see if any event pushed uncomfortable buttons inside me, or if any of my behaviors throughout the day were unloving. In the beginning, I discerned whether some activity was pushing a button by using my emotional self as my barometer. I would ask myself the question, "Did any interaction today cause my emotions to go very high with anger and fear, or did any interaction cause my emotions to go deep with grief?" If the answer was yes, I would write the situation down in detail and talk to my sponsor about it.

Spiritually, I looked at any button-pushing interaction as a God-given gift to help me grow. I remember the first time I heard the phrase, the people who cause the most discomfort in my life will be my greatest teachers. I had no idea what this meant. Over time, though, I realized that if someone was doing or saying something that pushed my buttons, I had to recognize that this wound was already inside of me, and they were not the source of my pain, only its reflection.

Before I became aware of this, I used to say, "He is such a loser because of the way he is acting," and I tried to stay away from that person. Never once did I understand that if I saw a wound in someone else, and it bothered me, it meant the wound was also inside of me on some unconscious level. I defended myself against feeling my own pain by projecting my shame on the other person and saying, "That guy is a loser." Today I acknowledge the truth that says, if I see it in you, and it bothers me, I need to look inside of myself.

Taking a daily inventory was extremely helpful in identifying my own personal needs for growth. It allowed me to quickly and consciously see uncomfortable events in my life so

I could look inside myself to heal my own issues. Many nights I looked back on my day to see how events were pushing the same inner buttons. Then as I discovered my wounds and allowed love to heal them, magically the uncomfortable events associated with this behavior stopped happening in my life. So you can see that Step 10 is a wonderful tool in your process of internal healing.

Another facet of the tenth step is taking immediate responsibility for our own personal, unloving behaviors that we performed on other people. This is where I stopped and honestly looked back upon my day to see if I unlovingly crossed anyone else's boundaries throughout the day. Boundary crossing includes such behaviors as lying to another person, stealing from another person, manipulating another person, or taking anger out on someone else. Step 10 basically asked me to be daily accountable for my unloving actions.

During our personal inventory, if we see where our behaviors have crossed another person's boundaries, the remedy is simple. We call that person up and say, "Mr. Smith, this is Joe. Yesterday my behavior was not appropriate when I was talking with you, and I am calling to make amends." That is all you have to do. This step is humbling, yet quite simple.

When I see I have wronged someone, I promptly admit to them my actions, make my amends, and move on. The consequence of making swift amends is my own peace of mind. The sooner I make amends for my unloving behavior, the sooner my internal serenity reappears.

Now the reason Step 10 is so important is because we are all human, and sooner or later we're going to act from the fear-based aspects of our self. So when we do act out of fear, Step 10 keeps the shame and guilt from building up inside of us. The act of making amends to someone replaces our ego with humility, and replaces toxic shame with the truth that as human beings we're going to make mistakes. So when I make a mistake, I admit, I make amends, and I move on.

One example of this happened for me during a period of my life when I was working part time for a friend of mine in his recruiting business. My job was to man the phones while he was out to lunch. His lunch normally lasted two hours, so on this particular day, instead of listening for the phones, I decided to watch a personal video that belonged to him. He returned early from lunch, much to my surprise, and I was busted for watching TV instead of working.

I could sense his frustration and anger with me because I had betrayed his trust. Then to make things worse, he directly asked me where I found this particular video. Well, in all of my shame and fear I lied to him, and said that I found the video sitting on top of his TV. The truth was, this video was in his personal belongings where I had no business looking. I left work that day basically with my tail between my legs.

The fact that I had betrayed my friend's trust, and lied to him, ate me up inside for two days. Finally, on the third day, I found the courage to call him up on the phone, admit my wrongs, and make my amends. It was an extremely humbling experience for me, but once I had finished, the extreme gnawing in my stomach went away.

I looked at that experience and learned a great lesson. I lost my part-time job, but I gained my own sense of self-respect by sharing my truth. So for me, as I continue to practice Step 10 daily, I find and receive a great sense of intimate relief in my life. Taking a daily inventory is about acknowledging my own personal, loving behaviors of the day. This conscious behavior of self-love is extremely important, although it is often times forgotten. It was always easier for me to criticize others and myself rather than to give praise.

Step 10 is about looking at your loving acts, as well. The loving acts that need to be acknowledged by you are things like:

- Opening the door for someone before going into a store.
- Letting someone in during rush-hour traffic.
- Listening to another person who needs to talk.
- Giving your time or money to a charity.
- Taking extra time with your inner child by journal writing or praying with him.
- Telling friends how beautiful they look or that you love them.
- etc.

Step 10 is also about daily giving yourself love, praise, and acknowledgment. It is about consciously taking the time to see your own internal glass being half-full rather than half-empty. Remember, ego always criticizes itself. Learning how to give yourself some praise is not always as easy as it seems, but if you take the time daily to recognize your own sense of loving value, your own self worth will naturally grow and prosper.

Love without personal acknowledgment is like a rosebud without water. The rose will live for awhile, but won't ever truly blossom. Self-love grows and blossoms to its fullest potential as you consciously accept loving yourself. In this self-loving behavior, you are actually living and acting as your own higher power; and the more you do this, the more love you will naturally feel in your heart.

Step 10 is about consciously acknowledging life on a daily basis. In fact, we use life situations themselves to help us grow; never criticizing ourselves for right or wrong, just allowing ourselves to be human.

The hardest thing for most people to accept is that to err is human. My friend, if you make a mistake, congratulate yourself for your humanity, make amends to anyone who was hurt, and move on. Step 10 teaches us daily to interact with life on life's terms. It tells us that situations are going to push our buttons, but to remember that all emotional buttons start within.

Last, though certainly not least, Step 10 says to list and acknowledge your own acts of love, no matter how small they may seem. Remember, giving love to yourself is God working through you. Step 10 gives us permission to be human, and for me, accepting my humanity has been a true spiritual gift of personal serenity in my life.

Step 11: *Sought, through prayer and meditation, to create a conscious contact with God; asking only for His Will for us and the courage to carry this out.*

This is a beautiful step of conscious communication with Great Spirit. It is about allowing the power of Spirit to integrate into your daily life, and to follow its direction. Step 11 has shown me that no matter what situation I create in my life, the power of Great Spirit is always there with me to provide the strength and guidance I need to thrive.

For the longest time, my ego kept me in a victim role toward life by saying, "If God loved me, He would give me a big house, a fast car, a lot of money, and the perfect woman; and since I don't have these things, God must not love me." I looked at life and the presence of God as something I would receive from my outside world as a reward for living a life of honesty and self-love. Then one day, as if struck by a lightning bolt, the truth of God's presence in my life became very clear. In that glorious instant, the source and strength of my personal, questing desire came from my inner Spirit.

It became totally clear that my conscious choice to love myself and others was God working and talking to me and through me. I became aware that I am a part of God, and God is the grander part of us all. God consciousness, for me, is not about external rewards; it is about internal recognitions. During the times in my life when the pain was so great that I wanted to die, what kept me alive was the God in me.

It finally made perfect sense why my quest to heal my inner child was so important to me. I suddenly realized that to love oneself is to love God; to heal oneself is to love oneself; and to love oneself is to act in love from the God within.

It was during Step 11 that I connected to my real truth about spirituality. To me, spirituality is about loving all of yourself without judgment or criticism. The concept of love without judgment is to love without condition. So as I prayed and asked God what His Will for me was, the only answer I received was, "Love thyself."

For me, having conscious contact with Great Spirit means that I live my life consciously looking inside for answers of love and acceptance of my total self. You'll notice I keep saying total self because there are many authors who say that spirituality is only about the emotion called love. Well, for me this is simply not true.

Real spirituality is about accepting myself and all of my emotions; anger, happiness, sorrow, and fear. Real spirituality is about discerning when each emotion is present in my life, and loving that emotion based on its truth. That means when I am angry, I don't shame myself for my anger; I own it, and feel its real spiritual power. When I am sad, I embrace my grief, and allow my soul to deepen as a consequence of this expression. And when I am afraid, I love those moments, even though it is extremely uncomfortable; and I reap the rewards of walking through the veil of fear to a life of love that resides on the other side. Real spirituality is a concept of internal acceptance, even when the only acceptance is that we can't accept ourselves.

It was during my eleventh-step prayers when I realized that all God wants for me is total abundance in my life. God wants me to live a perfect life filled with love, money, and good health. God's Will for me is to be prosperous in every way, and even though this type of reality seems to be out of reach and too far-fetched to achieve in most people's minds, it is comforting for me to know that even during my toughest times, God will give me the strength and courage I need to make it to the other side. God's Will in my life is not about the destination, it is about my growth during the journey.

It is my belief that in today's society, we have the ability to live consciously connected to God's love each minute of the day. By healing my inner child and living an honest life of love, my ability to feel God's presence in my heart is very keen. I don't have to meditate to reach a place of internal stillness anymore. I live there constantly because of my internal healing.

Books that suggest this place of internal silence is only reached during meditation or by mental mind power, quite honestly, are misleading you. The truth is, all I had to do was heal my heart in order to silence my mind. I learned and received this incredible gift of spiritual silence quite by accident, because originally I had no desire to become one with God. In fact, I hated God. Today, though, through my strong desires to heal my inner child, Great Spirit has become my closest and best friend. There is not a moment that goes by when I do not feel connected to Spirit, either through my heart or through my faith. I have absolute confidence that my life is being guided by Great Spirit. The way I know this, and can share it so boldly, is because I can feel in my heart and stomach areas the literal presence of God. This presence feels like a warm, fuzzy feeling, twenty-four hours a day, seven days a week.

This feeling allows me to live an open and vulnerable life where my internal presence of God grows. I can honestly say that regardless of what is going on in my external world, my internal world is filled with love because of the self-loving techniques in this book. The grandness of life is not measured by what we have, but how we feel.

My counselor and friend, Sandy, is the most real and loving woman I know. She lives her higher purpose every day. She gives love/support to her clients with almost no external return expected. She walks her talk and talks her walk, moment by moment, even though her external rewards are almost nil. I remember the first time I asked her why she chose to live like this and her reply was, "My heart is filled with Spirit, and this is the only reward I need." When I heard that, I honestly thought she had lost her mind. Over time, I proved myself right because she has lost her mind; however, in return she has found her spiritual heart.

For me, Step 11 is about consciously asking God on a daily basis to enter into my life moment to moment. Before I started walking this conscious path, I never considered asking God for anything. In fact, I remember becoming very angry with friends of mine because each time they got in trouble, they would ask God to get them out. That was not my case. I just wanted God to leave me alone. However, I have found through experience that when I ask God for the strength and courage to walk my path, life seems to go easier.

Now if you're reading this book and thinking that highly spiritual people have no low points in their lives, you've been misled. All people, including spiritually connected people, go through highs and lows. The only difference is that someone who has taken on the emotional challenge to heal his or her heart continually knows that with each low there is a wonderful spiritual growth toward a higher vibration which follows! Those who are connected also know consciously that God is their best friend, so their levels of fear lesson during their challenging times.

Knowing that God is on my side and in my heart creates a tremendous amount of peace in my life, regardless of what is happening in my world. It no longer matters if I am emotionally high or low. Because of Step 11, life is great!

Step 11 is about consciously becoming aware that God is in your heart. Even if you can't consciously connect to this as your truth, please have faith in my words, and keep healing yourself. Step 11 is also about understanding that real spirituality is about learning how to accept all parts of self. This means we have to acknowledge that we are mental, emotional, spiritual, and physical beings; to understand the emotions we have, and start allowing all of their vibrations to be expressed. Feeling mad, glad, sad, and scared are all God-given gifts that play a crucial roll in living a fully functioning life.

Step 11 helps us understand that Great Spirit wants total abundance for us in our lives. So as our journey takes us through lessons that challenge the depths of who we are, remember that God is the part of you that supplies the courage and strength you need to keep moving forward, and eventually feel your abundance. It is probably my favorite step because during its process of transforming me, the result was the creation of a new best friend called Great Spirit!

Step 12: *Having had a spiritual awakening as a result of these steps, had the courage to carry our message of love to the world.*

This step is the place where people allow themselves to live and work their dreams. It is a place where we walk our talk and talk our walk. As a consequence of living to our fullest internal capacity, we create a new and deeper sense of love and awareness of God in our hearts. The action portion of Step 12 is having the courage to carry our message of love to the world. This means having the insight to look into our hearts, find the love, and then have the courage to share this love with the world around us.

For me, Step 12 is about sharing the love from myself with the world by doing what I love to do. Allowing this self-loving behavior to integrate into my life also brings me great joy each day because I know that by following my heart, I am pursuing my higher purpose in life. My higher purpose, or the real reason I'm here, is to share my experience, strength, and hope with other people as they are pursuing their own inner serenity. There's no greater gift of love I can give someone else than to give him or her the gift of hope associated with my own inner peace.

In the final portion of this book, I will share in great detail the twelve common attributes associated with living as your Higher Power. For now, however, it's important to remember that you bring love to everyone around you when you let your heart lead the way. Do what you love to do, and through this action step of self-love, you will bring the greatest love to the world around you, which is the love of God.

Remember, my friend, God is love; love is an emotion; emotions are in your heart; and if you follow your heart, doing what you love to do, this connection of God's love will act through you toward the world around you. This is the greatest love of all.

The interactions of these twelve spiritual steps toward enlightenment in my daily life actually took several years to accomplish. I will share with you, however, that as I continue to walk this path of conscious enlightenment, the expression of the steps seems to extend deeper and deeper into my internal world.

These principles basically gave me a step-by-step road map by which I could guide my life. The steps are never truly completed because they are designed to take you consciously deeper into your honest levels of soulful love. For example, when I admitted for the first time that my fear-based ego ran my entire life, it was my first completely honest evaluation of my own conscious availability.

Step 1 allowed me to see my internal world more honestly.

Step 2 is about experiencing my internal world more honestly. It helped me understand that a power greater than me is the only source that can help me see my own internal Spirit more clearly.

Step 3 is when I decided it would be better to allow the choices of a power greater than me to guide my life, rather than letting my ego guide my choices. This step allowed me to feel personal surrender to a higher power with a deeper level of honesty.

Steps 4, 5, 6, and 7 allowed me to discover and discern deeper aspects of my unloved self. I admitted my wrongs, told another human being, and became willing enough and humble enough to ask for these fears to be removed.

Steps 8, 9, and 10 helped me create honest, personal relationships with myself, other human beings, and a power greater than me. I wrote a list, decided to make amends for my past, and had the courage to be human and admit my shortcomings daily whenever I made a mistake.

Steps 11 and 12 have allowed me to live my life as my Higher Power, which is the deepest level of true honesty. I continue to ask for guidance and follow that guidance by sharing my true love from God with the world through my choices of personal actions.

So as you can see, each aspect of the twelve-step concept is about living and experiencing life more honestly. As your spiral of life continues, and your ability to become more honest with yourself deepens, so will your ability to integrate these different types of honesty into your life. No matter how long you are on this conscious path, the grief you feel during this process will also deepen. However, as you begin to heal, the natural consequence of the joy and peace you feel inside will also deepen.

I am humbled to say that today I feel the peace and joy of Great Spirit in my life from a place deep in my soul. The twelve steps just seem to naturally interact with my life on a daily basis. I now intuitively know how to handle situations that would have baffled me in the past. My life today is very clear with an open path of love and abundance in front me. All aspects of my life seem to be filled with love from my personal, intimate friends to the work I do on a daily basis. I am a living example that by healing your inner child and living your life based on the twelve-step principles, all of your dreams can come true.

Sometimes I have to pinch myself in the morning because I feel so whole and complete inside. I love my life, and I thank God each day for my healing, my wholeness, and my conscious connection to Great Spirit. Today I live a life that many years ago I couldn't even imagine. The love I have found with my inner child is magical, and brings joy to me and others around me on a daily basis. Words aren't adequate to express the wonderful love I have for Great Spirit. I am humbled every day because of my ability to accept and receive the love of Great Spirit, which He chooses to give to me with no condition and with no reservation.

I love all aspects of my world because I love me. My greatest gift from God has been my newly-found ability to live in love, to give love, and to receive love from the world around me. I give thanks each day that I found the courage to feel what I needed to heal, because the consequence of this choice has allowed me a heartfelt connection I call God.

I hope that some part of you has connected to the awesome power of this twelve-step guide of living principles. Personally, I always thought that life needed to have a rule book. These twelve steps give me a daily guide for living my life in principle, and more closely to the Spirit which resides in us all.

PART FOUR

The final section of this book is called Living as Your Higher Self. It goes into great detail about what the twelfth spiritual step means for me. I hope you will discover for yourself how you, too, can live your life as your Higher Power.

CHAPTER 19

To Dream Big Dreams

Practicing these principles in all of my affairs is something I needed to learn. I thought that if I just lived a good life, and did not hurt anyone else, I was truly acting the way I was supposed to act. Today, though, I have learned that to truly live as my Higher Self, and to choose growth each and every day, I also have to allow myself to live from a higher place on a daily basis.

In the beginning, I had no idea that healing my inner child inside would allow such a wonderful internal connection to Great Spirit. My conscious intent was merely to stop hurting all the time. My reward was something much grander.

I share with those who attend my seminars that God is love; love is an emotion; and emotions are in your heart. When you heal your heart, you will feel the presence of God which resides in us all. By doing my inner child work, I basically healed my heart. I now literally feel the love of God inside of me. From this place of self-love, my life has been guided to a place where I could not have imagined it was possible for me to go.

I joked with my mother the other day by saying, "Who'd have ever thought I would be talking about God to people around the world on a daily basis? Six years ago I didn't even like God, and today I teach people about Spirit."

Her reply to me was, "Especially because you have not gone to church (a Catholic Church) in over ten years."

You see, to my mother, the only place to find God is in a church. I feel Spirit in my heart, and I see God in everything. In my opinion, most religions are just about the study of God. Spirituality is about creating a relationship between me and a Power greater than me, which I call God or Great Spirit.

So as my life continues down this path of inner child self-discovery, my awareness and conscious connection to Great Spirit continues to grow. I wasn't seeking God, but the natural consequence of healing my wounds is that I found my internal connection to Spirit.

Living my life from this place of internal connection, I make a conscious daily decision to live my life guided by the twelve spiritual steps and the principles associated with each step. Choosing to grow also means I have to be willing to stretch myself on a daily basis. This means I live a life of rigorous honesty and expanded imagination. I daily seek out the internal belief systems or old thought patterns that limit me. I am always striving to become more aware of my conscious and unconscious behaviors in order to improve my quality of life.

My feeling is that if I don't quest to be all I can be in this lifetime, I will just have to come back and do it all over again in another life. So the twelve spiritual principles of abundance were created through me to give my life a mechanism to allow me to live in principle, while expanding my horizons for today and all of the days of my future.

I begin with the first spiritual principle of abundance which says, dream big dreams! Dream big dreams for yourself and for your family. Dream big dreams for your friends, your neighbors, and your co-workers. Have the courage to dream again. As we get older, most of us forget what it feels like to dream.

We get stuck in old routines and give up on our dreams. We allow our egos to run our lives and tell us things like, "It doesn't matter anymore. I'm too old to dream." The spiritual truth is, we are never too old to dream again. We only need to ask the little kid inside to show us how to reconnect to this ability.

Dreams are part of our being. Most people close down this part because of their fear of failure or their fear of success. To allow yourself to dream again is a very liberating experience. It allows your blood to flow and your heart to open. To dream again takes courage, but as you walk through these fears, your life will be changed forever.

To get started with this process, I first needed to make a dream list. I wrote out a list of the house I wanted to own and the car I would love to drive. I committed to paper how much money I wanted to have in the bank. I also made a list of adventures I would love to experience. I wrote it all out on paper, just letting my mind wander and my pen flow.

I then allowed my inner child to create his own dream list. This meant that I literally switched hands and allowed my inner child to dream on paper. I split my list into two categories: Dreams that took money, and dreams that took little or no money. As I separated the list, I saw how easy it was to accomplish some of my dreams almost immediately.

When you are ready to begin this process, it's important to stay keenly aware of the voices in your head which are trying to limit you as your dream list is being created. These voices will sound something like this, "I could never have a house like that. I don't make enough money to drive a car like this. I don't deserve to take a vacation that nice." The list of ego voices will go on and on. So as you write your dream list, please stay aware of these voices and write them down, too.

As I wrote my lists, two things happened. First, I was able to take these limiting voices back to the first step of the twelve steps of enlightenment and plug them into that step. I had to admit to myself that I was powerless against these voices of limitation, and that my life had become unmanageable. So just as we discussed in Part Three, the second part of Step 1 says to write down our ego's limiting belief systems so we can see the insanity of it all in black and white. Obviously, as I wrote out my dream list, I was not only learning how to dream again, I was also becoming consciously aware of the limiting voices that kept me from dreaming in the first place.

By allowing the second step to help me quiet the voices, I could probe even deeper into why I had the limiting voices to begin with. When I identified and became aware of new ego-based voices or limiting belief systems, I found that its original source of creation was the wounded little kid underneath. Discovering the wounded little kid inside of myself, I began to nurture him until he felt and expressed what he needed to heal. As a consequence of his healing, the limiting voices and belief systems created by the old wounds were effortlessly transformed. As this transformation took place, a whole new type of hope was created in my heart, and I understood that all of my dreams can and will be created in my life.

I believed that if God did not want all of my dreams to come true, He would not have given me the ability to dream in the first place. All of my dreams are God-given gifts. So as I connected and healed the inner source of why my dreams were being blocked out of my life, I began to see how limitless and magical my new level of consciousness had become. Trust me, my friend, it is you and you alone who is blocking total abundance of the universe into your life. So heal the blocks by healing your inner child, and watch what happens to your world.

This is a part of my own dream list:

Money
10,000-square foot home on 20 acres
600 Mercedes SL convertible—pewter color
German shepherd
Grand piano
$3,000,000 in the bank
Complete computer system 250-gallon aquarium
60-foot sailboat
40-foot ski boat
3,000-square foot cabin on a lake
Fitness center in my home
Complete stereo system for my home

60-inch television
Buy my mother a new home
Pay college tuition for 10 friends
Visit the beaches of the world Visit Niagara Falls
Go on an African Safari
Visit the Grand Canyon
Camp in a redwood forest
Build a sweat lodge in my backyard
See every Broadway show in New York City etc.

No money
Watch the sunset Listen to the rain
Read a good book
Write 7 books
Draw
Have a lot of plants
Take long baths
Give a bath to a friend
Give and receive a massage with a friend
Listen to soft music by candlelight
Make a snowman
Lie in the sun every day etc.

My little kid's dream list
Go fishing with a new fishing pole
Fly a kite
Go roller skating Ride a bike
Go swimming
Draw pictures with crayons
Run in the park
Play with my friends
Play catch
etc.

The second spiritual principle of abundance is to do what you love to do. All successful men and women do what they love because they choose something that excites them or brings joy into their lives. How do you know if you're doing what you love? It will give you a buzz. You'll want to talk about it, to learn about it, and to tell other people about it. When you're doing what you love, the process of creation just happens freely.

Most people limit themselves because they say, "I can't do what I love to do because I can't make enough money at it." This isn't about quitting your day job. It's about guiding your life into whatever it is you love to do. When you do this, you will begin to look at your day job in a totally different way. For example, if you look at your job as a means to an end, as a God-given vehicle to pay your bills, and keep you and your inner child in a safe environment, then you'll see your job in a new light.

The majority of people look at their jobs as punishment; something they're stuck with. They see themselves as victims. Even though they hate their jobs, they keep going back because they see no other way out. If you engage in something you love to do, in addition to your job, then your vision of your job will become very different.

I understand that in the beginning, you may be limited in the amount of time you have to spend creating what you love to do and incorporating it into your life. That is totally okay. However, just by taking the action step of this integration, your life will change forever because doing what you love to do is the most self-loving behavior a person can create.

The principle behind this is awareness is God because God is love. So if you choose to do what you love to do, you're actually recognizing God's love for you. The law of cause and effect says that the more love you put out into the world, the more love you will receive from the world and from your heart.

The other thing I want to mention is that doing what you love to do does not always involve making money. In fact, most of the time the money aspect of this step is just icing on the cake. A lot of people do what they love to do by volunteering to work for a charitable cause, or by helping someone in need. Doing what you love to do means you have looked into your heart and found some behavior that gives you a feeling of joy and a sense of fulfillment toward your higher purpose.

A friend of mine earned $250,000 a year in his own business. He had plenty of time on his hands because his business was very well managed. Although he enjoyed his work, he knew there was something more for him to do in his life.

This friend has a unique talent and ability when it comes to small children. He can walk into a classroom and the children will gravitate toward him like metal filings to a magnet. Over time, he began to realize that part of his Higher Purpose was to act upon his God-given gift with children. Now he volunteers on a weekly basis to help out at his children's school, paying special attention to children of single mothers. He feels like the love of God flows to these children each time he sees them.

My friend does not earn a dollar for his efforts at the school, but ever since he opened his heart and integrated into his life something he loves to do, every other aspect of his life flows more readily. His actual business has almost doubled in size with no additional effort. His home life is more peaceful; and best of all, his feeling of self-worth has grown through the ceiling. I've personally met with him after one of his volunteer days, and the man actually glows with the love of Spirit.

Personally, I decided I love to write; so that is what I started to do. For many years I had the idea to write a book. I was motivated to get started because I did not want to look back on my life someday and say, "I wish I had written a book." So one day I just started writing. I had no idea what I was going write about or how long it was going to be. I decided to leave the details of my venture to God. Each time I was drawn to write, I would sit down at my desk and do just that.

Even though I love to write, I did not quit my day job. I wrote when I had time to write. Three years later, I'm a published author. I didn't start the book with the idea of making a lot of money. I started writing because I was drawn to integrate into my life something I love to do. The consequence of this action is earning income. How much? I don't know. I leave the outcome to Spirit. All I know is that when I do what I love to do, my life seems to be better.

I believe if everyone in the world did what they love to do on a daily basis, the world would be a totally different place. If each person gave to the world a little piece of love each day, just imagine what the world would be like. Personally, I have made the commitment to myself and to the rest of the world to share the love of God that flows through me with each person I meet by doing what I love to do.

The majority of people live their lives and die without ever sharing their true abilities with the world. Don't be one of these people. Find what you love to do and just do it. Have the courage to seek and find your own unique talents and abilities by following your heart's direction. Once you find them, take the action steps that will allow you to share your love with the rest of the world. Next, find yourself a support system of like-minded people to help you. The first word in any spiritual program is "We," which includes you, your inner child, your Higher Power, and a support system of people around you who love you.

I also will advise you not to share your dreams with people who don't have dreams themselves. It is hard enough to walk in faith and quest for your dreams to come true without having someone in your life trying to bring you down. Many people receive great pleasure out of trying to steal your dreams. A lot of these people will be very close, loving people in your life. From their perception, they're just trying to protect you from harm. The truth is, they are projecting their own fears of failure onto you.

So in the beginning, seek what you love to do and when you find it, seek a support system to help you through the tough times. My suggestion is to look in the newspaper for twelve-step groups, business clubs, or any free spiritual support group who thinks and acts as you do.

Another thing to remember is that since you are choosing to step out of your own box of life, and are choosing to quest and act on what you love to do, there will be a lot of personal growth accompanying this choice. Your ego voices will probably go crazy trying to convince you that you can't make it. Your inner child could possibly produce deeper wounds because you're adding more love into your life. With any major conscious change, there's always a state of fear.

A time of confusion always accompanies a life shift. Just keep moving through your fears one step at a time, one day at a time; continually asking Spirit to give you the strength and courage it takes to feel what you need to heal. The calm following your internal storm will be worth every moment of discomfort.

Four weeks before I did my first inner child spiritual growth seminar, all of what I just described happened for me. My fears, confusion, and emotional growth hit new levels. I felt as though I were walking into the void, backwards and blindfolded. My fear of owning and walking my truth was the biggest challenge of my life.

So I took ownership of my feelings, wrote down my limiting fear-based voices, and shared everything that was going on inside of me with my loving support system. As I integrated Step 2 into my conscious life and found my higher purpose, my awareness of God in my heart naturally grew. One day at a time I walked through my fears, and my debut seminar was an extreme success. I pursued and accomplished my dreams to do what I love to do; and my friend, so can you.

If you don't know what it is you love to do, ask every day in your prayers for God to show you, and you will definitely find what you are looking for. Once you find it, the third spiritual principle of abundance says to commit to being very good at what you love to do. Making a commitment to be very good at what you love to do is very important because so often what we love to do is not easily accomplished.

I made the commitment to myself every day that I was going to get a little better at performing my passion. Then as I hit my highs and lows on my spiritual road, I was already prepared for them. As I pursued my passions of public speaking and becoming a published author, I often hit what I call fear-based setbacks on my path.

There were many days during the process of creating this book that nothing was written down. These days I would sit down to write and nothing would come through me. My commitment to be very good at what I love to do kept me motivated to move forward even when the road seemed very dark. It was important to me to accomplish my goal of completing this book. Since I was committed to being very good at what I love to do, I never considered the possibility of failure. I never once considered that I would not finish it, or that it would not be published. The number one reason most people fail at ventures in their lives is because they believe they are supposed to fail. For some reason, they feel they don't deserve to be successful.

Many people's adult minds think they deserve success, while their little kid inside, who is still wounded and hurt, does not believe he deserves to have abundance in his life. Personally, I always connected my lack of financial abundance in my life to a wounded little kid who took on the false belief he did not deserve to be loved.

So if you hear voices in your head that say things like, "You will not be good enough at your passion to make money at it," or "You don't deserve to make money at what you love," these are all limiting beliefs of your ego. Make sure you write those limiting beliefs down and investigate their source. When you hear these voices, ask your little kid why he believes he does not deserve to be loved. Take the time to listen to his answers, and you will be totally amazed at what you will learn.

The key for moving through my own limiting beliefs—those that were keeping me from total abundance—was to find the source. In my experience, it was always my wounded little kid. When I became conscious of this source, all I had to do was listen to his needs, nurture him by supporting him through his needs, and allow him to grow by feeling what he needed to heal.

The natural consequence of allowing my inner child to heal was that all of my old, limiting beliefs went away. As my limiting voices subsided, my ability to become better and earn money at what I love to do also became more of a reality in my life.

A second avenue to discover in your quest to become the best at what you love to do is to learn how to communicate from your heart. Communication from your heart is something that naturally happens as you connect with your feelings.

Years ago, I had no idea what it meant to communicate from my heart. Whenever Sandy would ask me a question, my answer would always come out very analytical. Eventually, I learned that to answer from my heart meant to reply to a question based on how I felt about that particular topic. I learned to use words such as I love, I hate, I feel, I'm saddened, I'm angry, I'm excited, I'm passionate, etc. Using a simple guide like the feel, felt, found method is also a great way to learn how to communicate from the heart. I integrated this into my life when I was talking with someone. When someone would say something I could relate to, I would answer like this, "Mr. Smith, I know how you feel. I used to feel the same way. What I have found is...," and continue the sentence.

Using different techniques to integrate my communication effort into my heart was very important for me to learn. I knew God was in my heart, so when I learned how to communicate from my heart, my words came from a much higher place in my consciousness. As I learned how to communicate from my heart, the recipients were also receiving my words from a higher place in their hearts. The natural consequence of this is a divinely inspired conversation. Today I can actually feel another person's heart open as I communicate from my heart; so naturally, my conversations are more loving and intimate than ever before.

A life lived and communicated from the heart is a life being guided by Great Spirit. In your quest to become very good at what you love to do, learn how to communicate your passions from your heart, and watch how your new world will effortlessly open up for you, too.

CHAPTER 20

Trust

The fourth spiritual principle of abundance is to trust your higher power and the abundance of the universe. We live in an extremely abundant world. There are billions of dollars earned by people every day. Have you ever wondered why some people are prone to making money while others are not? For some people, everything they touch turns to gold. For others, it turns to dust. Why do some people seem to have everything while others seem to have nothing?

In my own life, I found that internally deep parts of me always saw the glass as half-empty. I looked at life as a struggle and an uphill battle. The reason for my dilemma was based on many variables. First, I believe that people are drawn to jobs with different levels of income based on what they feel their abilities are worth, which is an expression of self-worth; and what they're comfortable with based on familiarity or how they see themselves, which is an expression of self-esteem.

Let me give you an example of three people:
1. Corporate executive (or entrepreneur, musician, best-selling author, etc.) earning $250,000 a year.
2. Salesman (or manager, principal, executive secretary, etc.) earning $60,000 a year.
3. Cook (or custodian, carpet cleaner, etc.) earning $12.00 an hour ($24,960 a year).

Now as these individuals seek employment, where will they look for a new job? Do you think the corporate executive is going to go to a construction site to look for work? No, absolutely not. He is going to go to a high-powered recruiter who will seek jobs for big corporations.

Will the salesman look in the corporate executive management portion of the newspaper for his work? No, he is going to look in the sales section. And will the cook feel qualified for a top management position? Probably not.

All three of these people will seek employment based on their internal programming of ability and worth. This is where they feel familiar and comfortable. Many people live in that place "just over broke" because of their own fears of stepping out of their old patterns. It feels safer to wallow around in the mud of poverty thinking, purely because they feel they have no means of breaking out. In fact, most people don't even know that they're stuck in a rut. They just live their lives there because it's all they know.

For me, I realized I wanted more from life than just making ends meet. I wanted to live a life filled with abundance inside and out. I wanted to create an environment where I could have my cake and eat it too. The problem, however, was that I did not know how to accomplish this. I realized I did not know what it felt like to have abundance in my life, so this is where I started.

I asked myself the question, "Why have I never had money in my life?" The answers, I found, were quite amazing. First, I always associated having money with self-worth. Somewhere along the way I connected the two. My belief was that I would have money when I felt I deserved to be loved. The truth is, they have nothing to do with each other. There are a lot of people with a lot of money who have no self-worth.

Even though I was working out my self-worth issues by healing my inner child, I still did not have much money. So I realized there was more to creating external abundance than just self-worth. As I continued to probe into why I did not have external abundance, my answers started to flow.

For many years I looked at life and my world as being half-empty vs. half-full. This was very hard for me to admit to myself, or even see, because externally I always exhibited a very positive, upbeat attitude. However, internally my limiting voices were saying, "I can't do that," or "I don't deserve to make a lot of money." The spiritual truth is, we can create anything we choose in the abundance of the universe by learning how to be open enough to receive it.

As I learned these new visionary concepts, I asked my Higher Self how to accomplish this. The answer was one word, "Faith."
I asked, "Faith in what?"
The answer was, "Faith in myself."

I countered with, "I've had faith in myself all this time, and where has it gotten me? Nowhere!"

My Higher Power's answer to this was, "You've had faith in your false self, not your true self. You have believed the limiting voices that said you aren't deserving and you can't have things." After hearing this I became aware that my limiting beliefs came from my false self, not my true self. My true self knows that all things are possible and that God wants me to live a life of total abundance.

My next two questions were, "How do I eliminate my false beliefs?" and "How do I discover and follow my true self?" The answer to the first question was very simple. First, you heal the wounded child who created the false belief in the first place.

Second, you ask God to remove your fears in the twelve steps of enlightenment, if they don't transform themselves as a natural consequence of healing your little kid's wounds. As I experienced this healing process, I learned that identifying and eliminating my false beliefs totally coincided with the healing of my inner child.

The answer to the second question was to identify where my true self resides. My true self, or my Higher Self, is found in my heart, not my head. I need to trust my inner guide, or my intuitions. Following my Higher Self means I have the courage and the faith to follow my intuitions and dreams. All of my dreams are God-given gifts that when acknowledged, bring me a sense of total internal and external abundance.

The principle for this step is faith, and I had to trust my Higher Power to guide me to a higher level of abundance in my life. I learned to trust that the universe was a very abundant place. The universe is a place of massive wealth, and I learned that I just had to tap into my little piece of it to receive the abundance I was seeking. Faith is trust in action, so sometimes I had to walk totally into the void to find my abundance. I know the step of faith is frightening for most, but in my experience, the rewards have been absolutely amazing.

Following your Higher Self allows you to achieve anything you choose, regardless of your past programming. Think about it logically for a moment. In my original example, what is the only difference between the cook and the corporate executive? In my opinion, the only difference is their own personal perception of internal value and their courage to walk in internal faith.

Each person is given his or her own unique abilities deep inside. The question is, are you willing to do what it takes to find your unique talents, and then have the faith to act on your abilities in the world? Learning that the universe is an abundant place and that your Higher Power will always guide you to this abundance deepens the internal confidence needed to walk into the void.

Today my world is a totally different place because of this conceptual belief. I live in a place that is far beyond anything I ever could have imagined. My world is filled with creativity, spontaneity, friendships, and money. My Higher Power, or Great Spirit, wants me to live in a world of love and light, so it was my job to learn how to do this. It was up to me to find the courage to follow what I found inside my heart, and walk deep into the void. What I learned over and over again was that each time I stepped into the void, I needed to let go. Each time I took the leap of faith, God was always there to catch me.

So, my friend, please trust your Higher Power by allowing your dreams, your intuitions, and your heart to guide you. You will find and receive your magical portion of our extremely abundant universe.

Writing down your intentions and making plans for their accomplishment is the fifth spiritual principle of abundance. I feel the basis for this step, which is courage, is very fitting. It is uncomfortable for us to take the action steps in our lives that will produce change because it is scary to live out of our comfort zone. Change takes us to a place of reality where we have never been before. Comfort and safeness coincide with familiarity, so most people choose not to change unless they are absolutely forced to.

In my own case, writing my intentions down and making plans for their accomplishment allowed me a spiritual road map that guided me through my difficult times of change. In my world, it never mattered whether the change was for my highest good or not. Change was change, and I did not like it at all. So I would tell myself, "I'm going to do it tomorrow." Then tomorrow would come and I would say, "I'm going to do it tomorrow." I always procrastinated. My choice to procrastinate gave me an immediate sense of false relief; however, the long-term effect was that I would allow things to pile up until I was ready to explode. I knew it was time to change.

I have learned to avoid the paralyzing experience of being overwhelmed by first listing each task to be accomplished. The reason I put it on paper is that once something is written, it is out of my head and in the first stage of actually being completed.

I then begin the action steps toward the completion of each task. I don't choose to put a time frame on their completion because, for me, that keeps divine flow from actually intervening and supporting my accomplishments. I allow completion of each event in God's time, not mine.

Finally, I work to complete each task simply for the joy and self-pride I feel inside my heart during the start-to-finish duration. I feel great rewards inside knowing I have put my effort into something, beginning to end. I no longer choose to judge my success based on the outcome of the situation. The success is in finding the courage to act on any task, large or small.

Many people rate their success or failure based on their own projected outcome; when in fact, we only have control of our own efforts. When we find the courage inside ourselves to act on some task, completing it from start to finish, we then need to learn how to leave the final outcome to Spirit.

In reality, failure does not even exist. The concept of failure is an ego-based belief, created by a wounded little kid in us. In the eyes of Great Spirit and the perfection of divine order, there is no such thing as failure; only outcomes.

So if I accomplish something, yet feel a sense of failure because the outcome was not what I desired, two things were probably happening for me. First, I was attached to the outcome, and attachments are of my ego. Second, the situation is probably pushing a wounded inner child button inside, so I could use this God-given gift to help me discover the deeper wound of my little kid.

For example, I was in the formative stages of a relationship with a woman I met two years ago. During this time, we developed a very close and loving relationship. My ego then began attaching expectations to the outcome of this experience. My ego had convinced me that because of my feelings for her, eventually we would start to date and our relationship would grow into something more significant. I never once considered that she might feel differently because my own needy child inside blinded me.

Imagine my surprise on the day before my thirty-sixth birthday when this special friend of mine told me that not only was she intimately dating someone else, she had been dating him for over two months! I was totally blown away and shocked. The pain of hearing her truth catapulted me into the depths of my own inner child rejection issues.

Even though the pain was severe, I knew that each situation in my life is a God-given gift for me to learn and grow. After many months of grieving this new reality, I finally became clear about my God-given gift of this experience. I took action steps to create a beautiful relationship with a beautiful woman, leaving the outcome to God. Even though I hated the original outcome, I now see how and what I've learned from it.

Today, because of this experience, I have reclaimed a deeply wounded little kid, understanding that during every past experience with a woman, he would always act out. Because of the grief I released during the end of this particular relationship, my inner child is now much more healed around this issue.

So as always, I learned something and I healed something that God knew was for my highest good, even though at the time I did not. The success of this experience was not the outcome of being intimate with my friend, it was the personal growth I gained because of not being with her.

I know this concept may be very difficult to grasp, but over time, you will see that life is about personal growth and remembering your deep inner connection with the Spirit in which you truly are. So as you travel this road of enlightenment, you'll find yourself more and more able to look at life's experiences as lessons rather than conclusions.

Life's experiences don't make the person, they only describe him/her. So if you see that you continually attract the same experience over and over into your life, know that Great Spirit is trying to show you something about a wounded part of you through the consequence of each conclusion.

Another example of how this principle works is perfectly illustrated by a friend of mine who sells restaurant equipment. Seven years ago he started this business with his wife because of their dream of being financially successful and setting their own personal hours of freedom. My friend worked very hard for many years. He wrote down his plans for success and worked his plan every day. The business grew very slowly. Days turned into months, months turned into years, and my friend's business was just not taking off. Whenever we were talking, I could hear him judging his business as unsuccessful because he had not yet reached his monetary projection of success. I would listen to him talk about his situation and observe the fear-based judgment he would project.

Then one day I asked him, "Why did you start your business in the first place?"

He answered, "To pay my bills and to be my own boss."

I then asked him, "Have you accomplished this over the past five years?"

"Yes," he said.

"And what have you learned about yourself over the past five years as a consequence of choosing to be self-employed?"

He thought for a moment and said, "Well, I've learned how to be self-motivated. I've learned self-discipline and how to sell from my heart. I've learned how to manage people and how to build a small business. I've learned how to manage my own time and manage the money of the business. And I've probably learned many other things I can't think of right now."

I then pointed out to my friend, "You have just shared with me the spiritual success of your business. The personal growth you have achieved during the past five years has been God's gift to you."

As we shared that moment together, he finally got it. He realized that he was judging success or failure based on some monetary expectation that needed to be acquired in his time, not God's time. He understood that he had done everything except turn over the outcome of his business growth to God. On that day, he began to focus on all of his successes rather than his one attachment to failure. He decided to really let go of the attachment he had to the growth rate of his business, and allow this growth to happen in God's time.

My friend's business has tripled over the past two years. When he stopped holding on to control and allowed God to intervene, his business exploded. The principle behind this step is courage because it takes a lot of guts to let go and let God; but as we find this courage, the outcome in any situation will be growth for us and love from God.

Let me remind you to have the courage to change the little things every day. What this means is to start each day with the conscious attention of giving love to others all day long. For example, whenever possible, I allow someone to enter ahead of me during rush-hour traffic. When someone lets me enter in front of them, I wave and say thank you to my new friend. If I can, I will allow someone to walk through a doorway first as I hold the door for them. I will consciously choose to give cashiers a big smile and ask them how their day is going. As I found the courage to change the little things in my life and in my attitude on daily basis, my entire world changed.

I decided to stop procrastinating. I keep my car clean and write thank-you cards to people who have helped me in any way. Sometimes I'll stop in the middle of the day and take long, hot baths. I make conscious contact at least four times a year with old friends who live out-of-state, and make special efforts to listen to people's challenges, sharing my own experience, strength, and hope with them. I compliment a mother's child to show my appreciation for her choice of life. I give a smile to my world wherever I can because I know if I don't change my attitude today, nothing will be different tomorrow.

My friend, it's your turn to find the courage it takes to write down your intentions of growth and make plans for their accomplishment. When you make this choice, you'll be able to see your world change for the better.

I believe that by seeing life for its lessons, and allowing those lessons and love to be shared with the world around us, not only will we grow in love and light, we will also help the world to do the same. Life lived in love is a beautiful life. Life shared with love is a magical life with God in your heart and abundance in your world.

The sixth spiritual principle of abundance is humility. I don't care who you are or in what vibration of consciousness you live, it takes humility to ask anyone for help, even Great Spirit.

I can share from experience that the ego often says, "I don't need help. I can do this on my own." My life is a perfect example of how difficult it is trying to live life all alone with no spiritual help. Prior to asking for Great Spirit's help, I was almost homeless with no money and no friends, addicted to drugs and alcohol, totally lost inside, and spiritually bankrupt. Now that I have allowed God to guide my entire life, none of these past descriptions is my truth.

The hardest thing I had to learn when it came to asking for help was that it was appropriate. I grew up in a paradigm belief that said to ask for help and support from anyone was to show your weakness or your neediness. I believed that to be a "real man" I had to prove to myself and the world that I could do it all by myself.

The longer I walked a path of Spirit, the more clear it became to me that spirituality and personal growth are not processes that an individual experiences alone. In fact, the mere definition of spirituality says that we are creating a relationship between ourselves and a power greater than ourselves. In learning this, I started to open up to the truth that asking for guidance and support from Great Spirit on a daily basis is the most loving thing I can do for myself. During this process, I also learned how to ask for help and support from the people around me.

As I shared earlier, the first word in any twelve-step program is, "We." The "we" includes me, a Power greater than me, my inner child, and people who love me. Together we can move mountains when we understand that the mountains we are moving are the inner blocks of fear that run our lives. Today when I feel fear, I ask for guidance and support, and I am always able to walk through these fears.

The second idea I learned about asking for help is learning how to receive the help once it was presented to me. I learned that the major reason I never asked for help in my life before was because my wounded inner child told me I did not deserve to be loved or supported. Also, my fear of rejection was so big that I would rather do something all alone than take the chance of asking for help and being rejected. As I healed both of these issues by nurturing my little kid's wounds, my ability to ask for and receive help became much greater.

The third idea I learned about asking for help from Great Spirit on a daily basis was an experience called vulnerability. The times I felt most vulnerable inside always coincided with a huge grieving process of letting go.

When grieving the loss of my grandmother, the pain I felt was very intense. After this particular release, I became consciously aware of what had happened for me. During the weeks and months prior to this release, I was nurturing myself so I could grieve this major loss in my life. For three years I had experienced major blocks, or walls of ego parts, protecting me from the depths of this actual pain. With the help of Great Spirit and the nurturing of my inner child, I finally felt safe enough to experience the depth of this major loss. The only way I could feel this pain was for my ego walls to let go and allow me to experience the grief. As the process continued and I felt the pain, not only did I release the suppressed emotions, I also transformed a huge ego part that felt like a wall around my heart.

Two days after this release was complete, I felt extremely open and vulnerable because those huge walls around my heart were gone. It was very challenging dealing with this new level of openness. This experience was uncomfortable for many days because it was such a new reality for me. I remember asking Sandy about this new feeling. I wondered what I should do about it. Her reply to me was, "Joe, just take it easy and grow through it. In time you will understand what this new experience means." Eventually, I did understand what she meant.

Over the next couple of days, I came to the understanding that the more vulnerable I feel, the more open I actually am. The more open I am, the more love can flow through me. The more love that flows through me, the more I can feel the love of God, which resides my heart. It's like the spiral; the more I ask, the more I receive.

The last thing I learned from this step was how to truly ask a question of Spirit, and be consciously able to receive the answers. Before I learned this new awareness, I would ask things of Great Spirit, like:

Great Spirit, please give me a lot of money. Great Spirit, please make my job better for me.

Great Spirit, please give me a big car and a nice house. Great Spirit, please give me a lot of friends.

As you can see by my examples, I would always ask Great

Spirit for personal desires and personal attachments. Then when the things I was looking for never manifested in my world, I thought Spirit was not listening.

During my grandmother's illness, I asked Great Spirit to make my grandmother well. When she died, I felt that Great Spirit was not listening to me at all. This was very confusing for me because I thought I was doing everything right, but Great Spirit still was not listening.

Then one day it hit me. I became consciously aware that Spirit's Will for me is to grow and to feel the love of God in my heart. I realized that sometimes not receiving something I wanted from Great Spirit gave me more internal personal growth than if I had received it, and I knew I needed to change what I was asking for.

Eventually, I learned to ask for guidance and support from Great Spirit in a totally different way. The first thing I now do every day is ask Great Spirit to give me the strength and courage to feel what I need to heal today. I ask Spirit to give me the love and courage I need to allow my personal attributes and abilities to create wealth in my life. I ask Spirit to allow me the vulnerability I choose to be the best friend I can be to each person who crosses my path. I ask Spirit to give me the strength I need to move on during the completion of a loved one's life.

I ask Spirit to guide me down my spiritual road, moment by moment, especially when sometimes this road seems totally dark. I ask for the strength and courage I need to walk down the path of my highest good, even though my ego wants to walk somewhere else. I ask Great Spirit to give me the love I need to praise others and myself as we all do the best we can in walking our paths of true destiny. I ask Spirit for an inner experience rather than outside objects.

I now see how every request I make of Great Spirit is totally received. Never has there been a day go by that I have not been given the strength, courage, love, or faith I needed to continue on. The only difference is that today I have the conscious ability to see the results of what I am asking for. In years past, I was asking for support from God and looking for its results in the eyes of my ego. Today I am pleased to say that every time I ask for love and support from a Power greater than me, I am able to receive the support through the eyes of my heart.

As life goes on, and our paths continue, we intuitively know how to ask and receive guidance from Great Spirit. A friend asked me the other day if I still pray each morning to get in contact with Spirit. I told her I don't because I never live without my internal contact with Great Spirit.

This came about for me when I realized that I could communicate with Spirit, or pray, all of the time. I could do it in the morning, at breakfast, in my car, at lunch, at dinner, or during a walk. I realized I could talk to God whenever I wanted. As time passed, my conscious contact with Great Spirit in my heart became who I am, rather than something I was seeking. Having this experience of God in my heart is like having the feeling of coming home to a safe space twenty-four hours a day, seven days a week. To tell you the truth, it is absolutely blissful.

Ask and you shall receive. My friend, learn how to ask Great Spirit for support and guidance, and see how your life will be changed forever. Remember, if any voice in your head tells you, you can't do this or Spirit won't help you, know that this voice is a red flag telling you that you have a wounded inner child who needs some attention.

Feeling the openness and vulnerability associated with the true experience of humility has been, without question, my greatest gift from God. This experience allows me to feel the flow of love from God to me, and from me to others. This openness has also allowed me to feel the freedom of my spirit as my soul flies with the eagles.

My friend, words can only begin to paint the picture of what this experience truly feels like. My hope is that you will find the courage to feel the humility you need to ask and receive guidance and support from Great Spirit on a daily basis; so you, too, can feel the rewards of God in your heart.

CHAPTER 21

"I Am" Statements

The "I am" statement is the seventh spiritual principle of abundance. It is based on honesty because we are what we speak. As we learn to walk our talk and talk our walk, our ability to become honest with the true essence of who we are will naturally grow.

"I am" statements are words we speak on a daily basis affirming our beliefs and knowledge of our true selves. "I am" statements are called affirmations by some people. Personally, I used these statements as one of my best tools in becoming aware of, and healing, the deep wounds of my inner child.

Some people in the unconscious world use so-called "positive affirmations" as a scapegoat to cover up the real pain they are feeling inside. They believe if they speak loving statements long enough, eventually they will attract and feel love in their life. That is basically like saying you have the ability to talk yourself out of your own pain. The truth is, you can sweep your dust under the rug, but you will still have the dust. The same is true for affirmations. I could say, "I am love," until I was blue in the face, but if I did not feel love in my heart, I would not attract love into my life. So for me, I used "I am" statements first as an affirmation of my truth, and then as a tool to heal my inner child. Let me explain what I mean.

The concept of affirming our truth is very simple. The spiritual truth is, you are a perfect Spirit; an aspect of the divine Great Spirit having a human experience. So when you are affirming your real truth, you are affirming the spiritual aspect of self.

We must remember that we are all multidimensional beings, so besides being this perfect Spirit everyone is working to remember, we are also ego and all of its wounded, fear-based beliefs. So as I affirmed my truth and heard voices disagreeing or discarding this truth, my first step was to take the time to write down these fear-based beliefs because I knew this was my ego trying to keep me away from my truth, which is Spirit.

After writing each disagreeing statement, my second step was to communicate with each of these parts through journal writing to find out where their limiting beliefs originated. In my experience, I normally found that most of these voices were always attached to a wounded little kid inside of myself. For example, when I would make the statement, "I am loved,"

I always heard an additional voice that would say, "No, I am not loved." Every time I chose to take the time to ask that part of me why he felt that way, I would discover a little kid inside who had developed the belief that he does not deserve to be loved because of his wounds.

My third step was to give that wounded part of me love until he felt whatever he needed to heal. As a natural consequence of allowing this part of me the time to heal and feel loved, I was able to eventually make the statement, "I am love, and I also feel loved." You can choose to do this exercise with any or all "I am" statements. Here are a few of the statements I used: I am love.

I am abundant.

I am God, and God is grander.

I am a world-known seminar speaker.

I am a world-known published author. I am healthy, wealthy, and wise.

I am totally connected to Great Spirit.

Remember, you are Spirit; even though your ego will do anything it can to convince you otherwise. It takes a lot of courage to own your truth. To be able to be totally honest with yourself, you have to take the time to heal those wounded inner aspects and transform your ego.

I can share from experience that time is the only variable for this freedom process of transformation to be created for anyone. In the beginning, every time I spoke an honest "I am" statement, I had a hundred voices screaming at me that they were not true. Eventually, the voices became less and less vocal, and now I have no voices of denial at all. As a consequence of this new freedom, I now can feel and own my real truth.

We are all pure love, but some people just have not been able to completely remember it, yet. For me, the longer I gave my discarding this truth, my first step was to take the time to write down these fear-based beliefs because I knew this was my ego trying to keep me away from my truth, which is Spirit.

After writing each disagreeing statement, my second step was to communicate with each of these parts through journal writing to find out where their limiting beliefs originated. In my experience, I normally found that most of these voices were always attached to a wounded little kid inside of myself. For example, when I would make the statement, "I am loved," I always heard an additional voice that would say, "No, I am not loved." Every time I chose to take the time to ask that part of me why he felt that way, I would discover a little kid inside who had developed the belief that he does not deserve to be loved because of his wounds.

Remember, my friend, thoughts as well as emotions are pure energy that flows through us. As you learn to give nonjudgmental affirmations to all aspects of yourself, you will feel the consequence of giving yourself unconditional love. Love without judgment, in my opinion, is love from God. So when you learn not to judge yourself, you'll feel the unconditional love of Great Spirit in your own personal heart.

On my path, I have learned how to affirm all aspects of self; and I will tell you truthfully, it was not easy. Many times the uncomfortable feelings were so big, I wanted to stuff them back inside with personal judgment or criticism. Now that I have healed the depths of my inner world because I chose not to stuff my feelings inside, the freedom of flowing energy I feel is absolutely magical.

My ability to feel love and compassion for others and myself is identical to the love I receive from Great Spirit. My desire to live in flow and stay in flow is also very great. The more I affirm all aspects of self, and allow all aspects of self to be expressed, the more whole I truly feel. It is in this experience of being totally whole where I feel and know my conscious and emotional connection with Great Spirit. I now live in a place of wholeness which allows me to feel the love of God in my heart every day. I have a sense of serenity and freedom that before, I could only dream about. I live my life at one with God because I have learned how to affirm all parts of myself, and have taken the time to allow all aspects to express themselves.

I thank God each day for giving me the strength and courage to be able to feel what I have needed to heal. So, my friend, know that if I, who was once a spiritually bankrupted drug addict, can reconnect with God's love in my heart, so can you. My prayer each day also asks Spirit to give you the strength and courage you need to heal your wounds and find the love of God which resides in your heart, too.

The law of giving, or brotherly love, is the eighth spiritual principle of abundance. This is a very important principle to live and learn because this is the aspect of love and life that will eventually heal the wounds of the world.

The law of giving basically says that the more you give, the more you will receive. This spiritual concept has been described in many different arenas of spiritual literature including the Bible. The truth of this law is absolutely amazing as we learn how to apply this action step so that all parties involved receive love.

When I first heard this law and started to practice this concept in my world of activities, I viewed it as a superficial idea. I thought that if I gave some money to a charity or individual, my reward would be that someone would give me money back. I thought that by helping someone with a particular project, they would automatically help me with my projects. If I loved and cared for someone, I assumed that they would love and care for me.

Well, my friend, I was deeply disappointed when none of my assumptions came true. I couldn't figure out why I was not receiving back what I was giving out. Eventually, I came to understand the truth behind giving and receiving.

The first thing I had to learn was how to love and honor myself. In doing this, I learned what it felt like to truly feel love. I learned that one of the keys to the law of giving is that you have to be able to give without any need of return. This is called unconditional giving.

For me, this wasn't possible at first because my wounded little kid was so needy. He needed to be loved and cared for all the time. The challenge for me was learning that the answer wasn't in the illusion of someone outside of myself loving me. I learned that I have to love all parts of me; the wounded parts as well as the happy parts. I learned that the law of giving has to start at home. Before I could truly give love to my outside world without condition, I had to learn how to give love to my inner child first so he could heal.

Prior to learning this self-loving activity, my wounded little kid very often felt left out each time I was giving some type of love in an external fashion. He was the reason I could not give any type of love to someone else without having attachments or expectations of return.

I am not telling you to stop giving money where money is needed, or to stop helping people when help is needed. What I am saying is that you can stop shaming yourself for the voices in your head that tell you, "There must be something wrong with me because I give all the time and never seem to receive what I want in return." You can, however, use this voice as a red flag to warn you that your little kid needs something from you.

Each time I heard this voice, I would stop and write in my journal to find out what my little kid needed from me. As I used this technique and healed my inner child wounds, eventually I was able to give money, love, or time to someone else with no voices and no need of any external return.

Let me also share with you the true meaning of the receiving part of this law. I thought that if I gave money, I would receive money. I thought my reward, or what I would receive in return, was always exactly what I had given. I learned this was not the case. I learned that my reward for giving without condition was the glorified feeling of joy I felt in my heart and soul. I learned, through experience, that my reward for giving love to myself and to others is the feeling of love I have in my heart. I stopped looking externally for what I was supposed to receive, and started looking inside. This is when I truly found the actual meaning of the law of giving. The more I give, the more love I feel inside; and the more love I feel inside, the more love I have to give.

My life has been truly blessed with love. I now have the ability to give without condition of return because my little kid is healed with our own love. Receiving love from outside sources is an enhancement in my world, not a need. The law of giving allows us to see how much love we need to give our inner child first, then how much love we have to give to the world.

I can also share that I want and need nothing. I receive more love and abundance in my world around me because of my ability to give to my world without condition. My ability to receive external abundance is truly proportional to my little kid's ability to receive love from me. The more healed inside I become, the more I am able to receive external abundance.

So many people get lost in the false illusion that says if they give to their external world, they'll automatically receive from it. Well, in my experience, this is just not the case. The easiest way to receive from your external world is to heal your internal world first. Abundance comes from within, not from without. So heal your heart and watch how the rest of your world will effortlessly change for the better.

The last thing I will share with you is the idea associated with the biblical passage, "...love your neighbor as yourself," (Leviticus 19:18). To tell you the truth, for the longest time I had no idea what this meant. For many years, my true self-worth was so low that if I had treated my neighbors the way I treated myself, my list of enemies would have been a mile long. Over time, though, I learned the meaning of this spiritual statement.

As a natural consequence of loving myself and healing my little kid's wounds, I found the love of God in my heart. This love was not something I was originally seeking, but it was something that just appeared. As a consequence of feeling and experiencing Great Spirit's love in my heart, I now feel the oneness of love that resides in all living things. I can see, feel, and experience the love of God that is in each human being. I can see and feel the loving presence of Great Spirit in all animals and plants. I have the intuitive ability to feel the oneness of Spirit in all beings.

I remember the first time I heard about the concept of all living things being as one. I had no idea what this meant. I looked around the world and asked myself how that could be. If I'm standing here and my friend is standing twenty feet away from me, how could we possibly be connected in any way? How could we possibly be one?

You see, my friend, back then I was looking at the world through the limiting beliefs of my ego. I saw the world through my eyes rather than my heart. The whole concept of all things being one does not coincide with our physical human self. It coincides with our spiritual self; the part of us we can't see, yet most people can feel. It's the aspect of life that all questers on a path of enlightenment are trying to remember. It is the "you," as you identify yourself as Spirit, rather than your body or ego. It is the part of us that knows all things and remembers oneness. It is our piece of the awesomeness of this force called Great Spirit, which is in each one of us. In fact, it is this spiritual aspect of us that allows us to actually live and breathe.

Most people still identify themselves with their ego self because that's all they know. This does not make a person good or bad, right or wrong. It is just where most people consciously reside.

By embracing my childlike essence inside, I have been able to connect and identify myself as Spirit, which resides within me. As a natural consequence of my internal spiritual knowings, I live life from a totally different place than I did in my past. Today I don't have to meditate or go into some unconscious trance to feel and experience Spirit in my heart. This feeling is who I am; it's not something I am seeking. I have the ability to see, feel, and experience the oneness because I am consciously connected to this oneness. I continue to have experience after experience where Great Spirit has communicated with me through this oneness by sending me signs and signals.

A specific example of this is with my own patience level and an experience with "ant medicine," about which several books have been written. For three months my house was covered with ants. I knew, through my oneness with all things, that God was sending me the message to be patient. To be honest with you, when I feel good, patience is easy, but when I am hurting and anxious inside, I really have to work on the quality of my patience. Whenever a God-given sign is so apparent in my world,

I immediately go inside and ask, "Who is not being patient?" Over time, I receive my answers.

As I found the patience I needed and worked through my issues, my ant friends completely disappeared. Now I know most people would say that this is impossible, or it is just a coincidence. My response is to communicate with the aspect of yourself that doubts the authenticity of oneness by writing with yourself in your journal. Also, I would suggest that you do the same with the aspect of yourself that doubts the power of God's ability to communicate with us.

Another example of oneness happened for me after one of my routine walks. I live in Atlanta, Georgia, so I frequently jog up a solid rock trail called Stone Mountain. This rock is the largest single piece of granite in the country. It is five miles around, and a mile and a half high. It is a very spiritual place for me, so I frequently visit it for my exercise.

On this particular afternoon, as I proceeded down the hill, the sky was black with thunderstorms. The winds came out of nowhere and picked up speeds over sixty miles an hour. I was totally enjoying the awesome power of Great Spirit as Mother Nature was displaying all of her fury.

On my way down, I encountered a four-year-old boy named Tommy and his mother. These two people had never walked the mountain before, so as the storm moved in, they were terrified and exhausted by their climb. I asked Tommy's mother if she wanted me to help them reach safety at the top of the hill. She told me she did, and I picked up Tommy, grabbed her hand, and proceeded to pull them both to the top of this very steep mountain.

We walked for over twenty-five minutes while we were assaulted by sixty-mile-an-hour winds, heavy rain, and pea-sized hail. I held Tommy close to my chest, reassuring him that I loved him, and that God loved him, and that everything was going to be okay. As I pulled this stranger and her son to safety, I realized my gift was my internal ability to love a stranger as if she were my best friend. I hugged little Tommy and loved him as if he were my own child. My ability to truly feel brotherly love for complete strangers was an absolutely awesome gift from Great Spirit on that day.

Through the feeling of oneness, I could feel and express the reality of loving my neighbor as myself. As I have healed my heart, the love I feel for myself now can also be felt for my neighbor. When I told Sandy how I truly felt love for these two strangers as if they were connected to me, she lovingly smiled and said, "Joe, that is the oneness I've been telling you about."

So remember, the law of giving starts with giving love to your little kid. As a natural consequence of this self-love, I believe that you will be able to give love to your world without condition. The reward of giving love without condition is a glorious feeling of love in your heart.

Self-love produces the ability of conscious connection with the true you, which is Spirit having a human experience. Knowing and living this truth has given me a sense of safeness and a feeling of freedom that words cannot express. To feel and experience the connection to Great Spirit on a conscious level is absolutely magical. It allows me to totally walk my talk, as well as talk my walk. I absolutely know that I am connected to the whole, which is called Great Spirit. I have a sense of great safeness in my world today because of this internal knowing.

Today I fly with the eagles because I have embraced my inner child, and have allowed that love to flow freely into the world. What goes around, comes around is the easiest way to share the truth of the law of giving. When you feel love in your heart and you allow that love to flow into the world, you will effortlessly attract love into your world. Today my life is lived in a place of total abundance because of the law of giving and brotherly love. I feel very blessed for this loving reality, and I thank Great Spirit every day.

Committing your own emotional, personal, and professional inner growth is the ninth spiritual principle of abundance. Its foundation is discipline because that is exactly what it takes to be able to grow on a daily basis. Quality of persistence is the tenth spiritual principle of abundance. Its basis is perseverance, and it is also a very important quality to integrate into your life to be able to grow on a daily basis. Let's examine these two principles.

For me to grow on a daily basis, I had to be willing to look inside myself each day and see what I could find. For many years, every time I wrote in my journal, all I found were wounded little kid parts who were either angry, lonely, sad, or scared. I went many years before I ever felt the joy of a happy, contented little kid in me. So I can speak from total experience about how important the ninth and tenth principles were for me to stay focused on my healing process.

During my quest to become one with God, my intention was to reach a place in my life where I could be all alone and feel no pain. I just wanted to stop hurting all the time. My commitment to inner personal emotional growth was paramount in my life.

My quest, and in fact, my entire life, was dedicated to healing my inner child's wounds. My life was completely out of balance for a long time because of this strong quest for healing. However, I was totally committed to go to any lengths to heal my little kid.

I asked myself many times over the years where this huge commitment to personal growth came from. It was many years into my path before I realized that the source of this commitment was God. The strength and courage I needed to go to any length to heal came straight from Great Spirit. My commitment to my little kid to do whatever I could to heal his wounds also came from Spirit.

My entire world changed on the day I connected with the wounded little kid in me who was sexually abused. I could feel how emotionally neglected this part of me was, and in turn, I felt an overwhelming desire to give him all of my love so he could heal.

Now if you are reading this book and thinking, "I lived a pretty good childhood, and I don't feel necessarily wounded inside," consider yourself very lucky; but please don't make the mistake of not committing to your own personal growth. I honestly don't believe there's a person alive who somehow, somewhere, was not neglected or abandoned as a child. Our world was designed at the core of our social belief system to do just that to children. So even though your mind might say that your childhood was okay, please commit to yourself daily to look inside and grow. You never know what you might find until you have the courage to look inside and see what is there.

For me, making this commitment also meant I had to be very persistent. It is easy to do any activity for a day, a week, or even a month; but understand that inner child questing to become one with God takes a lifetime of commitment. The quality of persistence allows us to persevere even when our world seems so dark that we truly don't feel we can make it any longer. The quality of persistence allows us time to heal all wounds. You see, each time you discover something new about yourself, you have to allow time to pass for this new aspect of self to integrate into the whole. Quality of persistence allows us to keep on keeping on. It allows us to say, "I will never give up. I will never stop doing whatever I can to heal my little kid and become one with God."

The quality of persistence is especially important in today's society where there are millions of things to divert you from your internal world. Personally, I had to close down my entire external world for almost five years while I was healing the depths of my inner child's wounds. I've heard this phase of our spiritual development referred to as the dark nights of the soul. When I first heard this term, I shouted with agreement because that was exactly how I felt. I, myself, had felt like I lived in a totally dark cloud.

Many of my friends who have traveled down the same road have been able to have jobs and raise children at the same time. I tip my hat to these brave souls because healing our inner world is hard enough, let alone raising a child in our outside world, too.

It's important to keep in mind that no matter what the current situation is, you have the internal ability to keep moving forward. Remember the phrase, Rome was not built in a day. The wounds of your inner world are not going to be healed in a day, either. In fact, some of your wounds might take many years to heal completely. Spiritual growth is like a spinning spiral. It has no beginning and it has no end. Your commitment to yourself to grow every day must be a lifelong commitment. You must never give up because the more truth you find, the more freedom of truth you will see. I don't know how else to explain this concept except by sharing my truth and suggesting that you integrate these aspects into your own world so that you, too, can experience the freedom of spiritual truth.

The best way for me to personally stay motivated on my daily self-discovery was to surround myself with other people who were doing the same thing. I chose to associate myself with a good counselor who could help me see my life patterns that don't work for me anymore. I joined any twelve-step program that fit my own personal needs. I took classes and seminars like the one I have created called, Creating Heaven on Earth, where I talk about all of these concepts in detail. There are literally hundreds of books like this one, where people share their own experiences around some type of personal growth.

Allow yourself to be supported during your personal quest to become one with God. Everybody needs somebody during the highs and lows of this process. So seek out support systems to help you persist on a daily basis.

One last suggestion regarding these two principles is to wake up each day knowing it is the first day of the rest of your life. So many people, including me, tend to hold on to yesterday's mistakes and dwell on them. When you realize you can start your process fresh each day, you will have a new way to look at your entire life. Each day when you release your suppressed emotions, you will be one day closer to remembering the grandness of Spirit within you.

It took me a long time to learn this concept, so I stayed stuck in the misery of hopelessness for many years. Then one day it hit me; every tear I shed brought me a little closer to feeling the wholeness residing underneath my pain. Now, with every expression of anger I exhibit, I'm able to feel and connect a little more closely to the awesome strength and power inside me, which I call Great Spirit. Learning this philosophy gave me internal hope to know that each day of my dark-night experience I was walking a little closer to my truth of internal spiritual connection.

Many nights I lay in bed feeling lost, alone, and filled with fear; but I knew that tomorrow was a new day, and I would be one day closer to remembering my true connection. This new insight gave me the ounce of hope I needed to persevere. It gave me the glimmer of light at the end of the tunnel that allowed me to keep on keeping on.

Today I live a life of joy and abundance because of my personal commitment to growth and my continual perseverance through all of the tough times. I still have the same commitment to grow each day, but the things I am learning about myself are associated with the awesome attributes of our inner connection with Great Spirit. Rarely do I look inside anymore and find a wounded little kid. Now I look inside to find a grander aspect of my spiritual self.

It is said that Great Spirit has no beginning and no end, and that this force is associated with all that is. So as we see inside ourselves how we relate to and connect with Great Spirit, our glorious process of enlightenment also has no beginning and no end. The more you look, the more you see the truth of how awesome you are inside.

Since I've reached this awesome place of connection, it is much easier for me to want to look inside and learn more about myself on a daily basis. It is my hope that you, too, will reach this place of enlightenment.

I know, my friend, that if your path right now seems dark and scary, it is hard to imagine there is any relief in sight. But take it from me, you are much closer than you can imagine. God is in you guiding you the whole time. During our dark times of pain, it certainly does not seem like God is there helping us. I used to say, "If God loves me so much, why do I hurt so much?" I never received the answer to that question at the moment I asked it, but over time, I came to realize the only way I made it through those dark times was because God was with me, supporting me through the awful pain.

So if you are one of those souls who is being led down a very challenging road, remember you have the courage and the strength you need to make it through all levels of pain. God never gives us more than we can handle. I used to hate that phrase, but now I can say that the personal inner strength I have gained during my deepest times of grief and pain is a glorious attribute of empowerment that I enjoy every day. When you commit to yourself to keep on keeping on, you will find that time is the only variable in taking you to the place of remembering the glory of who you truly are.

DON'T QUIT

When things go wrong, as they sometimes will, When the road
you're trudging seems all uphill, When the funds are low and
the debts are high, And you want to smile, but you have to sigh,
When care is pressing you down a bit–
Rest if you must, but don't you quit.

Life is queer with its twists and turns, As every one of us
sometimes learns, And many a person turns about
When they might have won had they stuck it out.
Don't give up though the pace seems slow– You may succeed
with another blow.

Often the struggler has given up
When he might have captured the victor's cup; And he learned
too late when the night came down How close he was to the
golden crown.

Success is failure turned inside out, It's the silver tint of the
clouds of doubt; And you never can tell how close you are,
It may be near when it seems so far.

So stick to the fight when you're hardest hit, It's when things
seem worst that you mustn't quit.

–Author Unknown

CHAPTER 22

The Spiritual State of Abundance

Flexibility is the eleventh spiritual principle of abundance and in my opinion, one of the most important attributes we possess. The principle associated with flexibility is willingness, which is the ability or desire to allow change. In a life of continual growth, if we're not willing to change, basically we are saying that we are not willing to grow. As I mustered the courage necessary to allow my world to change internally as well as externally, I also allowed my world to function much more in a state of flow. Today I trust that whatever is supposed to be in my life and on my path will be. I don't worry anymore if people leave my life or if I need to change careers, because I allow my internal sense of knowingness to guide my way.

When I was drinking and taking drugs all the time, there was a huge internal sense of neglect felt by my inner child. The universal truth that like energy attracts like energy meant that every woman I attracted into my life had the same type of inner wounds that I had. We would literally mirror each other's inner wounded worlds. Then as I got sober and started paying more attention to my inner child so he could heal, my internal world started to change. I effortlessly started to attract different types of loving people into my external world.

I had to be willing to allow my external world to change, or I would find myself stuck back in the old reality of drug addicts and alcoholics. I became flexible with my external world, and it is now a very different place for me.

We have to understand that as we grow and change inside ourselves, our outside world is also going to grow and change. We have to learn to accept and understand that what is right for us today might not be right for us tomorrow. Being flexible allows us to be in flow with the world rather than against it. This attitude allows us to accept life on life's terms and to be much more readily available for it.

Although I make these statements very easily today, believe me, I know it isn't always so simple. I personally outgrew three different female experiences in my life, which were all with wonderful and caring women. I also had to let go of three different business opportunities in which I had invested thousands of dollars and thousands of hours because they just did not fit into my world anymore. Sometimes I had to be willing to stop everything in my life for a period of time while I figured out what was right for me on that day. Trust me, I know from experience how difficult this can be; but if I can do it, so can you.

Several years ago, a friend of mine left a twelve-year marriage, both of her children, her job, and the state in which she was born to give herself the space she needed to heal and grow. Another friend left his high-paying job to check himself into a treatment center to give himself a chance to heal. Still another friend finally said enough was enough, and left an abusive husband with a multi-million dollar business in order for her to heal.

No matter where you are on your path right now, if you have to change your world so you can heal, then do it! I know it is scary; but many people, including myself, have walked through our fears to find peace and joy on the other side.

Not all paths take such drastic changes toward internal growth. Some people just change jobs because the job they are in is not fun anymore. Other people start to pursue their passion in life because it feels good for them to do so. Other people walk through their fears and actually get married to someone they love because the personal rejection issues have been healed as a consequence of their personal inner growth. I don't know what will happen for you, but as you heal inside, I'm sure some change in your external world will probably happen.

Spirituality is about living life to its fullest capacity. At one time in my life, I was afraid to seek and quest to be all I could be. Today I am living a life in light, and each day is a new adventure. I cherish the idea of change and growth because I love the idea of becoming better and better. I'm totally flexible and willing to change moment to moment in whatever way God sees fit for me. I truly believe that God knows what's best for me, so I allow the flow of God's love to manifest in my world each and every day.

I honestly don't know how I'm going to feel or experience any situation until that situation is upon me. I allow my world to come to me rather than me going after my world. I allow the flow of life to co-create my world one moment at a time, so I choose to be extremely flexible. Sometimes this way of life is more difficult than others, but I can tell you it is always exciting regardless of the challenges I face. Today my world flows because I am willing to change any situation that is not for my highest good.

The only real challenge I continue to have is knowing when to make a conscious change around any uncomfortable situation. The process I use is very simple:

- First, I check in with my little kid, and I never do anything to put him in an uncomfortable position. So if my little kid does not like something, I change course.
- Second, I talk with my counselor, Sandy, and the other loving people in my support system about all uncomfortable situations in my life. They help me see all sides of any situation so I can grow from this lesson. Then I can make a personal decision whether or not to make a change.
- Third, I ask Great Spirit for guidance daily to advise me on all things. I ask for help, and then I allow time for my answers to come. Invariably, Great Spirit always replies with a profound higher consciousness reality.

My ability to be flexible is easy because I have no attachments to any outside things. My desire and trust in following my internal guidance system is so strong, it is easy to change things that don't work for me anymore. However, I will tell you that in the beginning, I would not change anything in my world unless my life depended upon it. Over time, though, I learned it was much easier to change than to fight the Will of God.

Flexibility is an amazing concept. It allows us to live in flow and abundance quite effortlessly. It also allows our external world to manifest itself without condition; to mirror our internal world. So remember, as you heal and change inside yourself, you have to be willing to allow your outside world to change and catch up with you.

I went from being almost homeless—with a car that did not work, and with no friends and no money—to living in a world of total abundance. I thank God I had the courage and the flexibility to allow my world to change for the better.

଼

Doing something to help others is the twelfth and most important spiritual principle of abundance. It is based on service. There is no greater gift of love you can give to another human being than the gift of service. As you travel down your path of spiritual strengths and real-life experiences, there's no finer gift than to share your hope with another person. I believe that it is every human being's highest purpose in this existence to share his or her love and light with someone else; to be there for people when they need a helping hand or a pat on the back. This is what it means to live in service.

There is no greater gift of personal abundance than the gift of watching the people we love and support on a daily basis grow in the eyes of their own Higher Power. By just taking the time to share my own experience, strength, and hope with people, I've watched them go from totally unconscious to super conscious awareness of their entire inner world. I've seen myself shift and change a thousand times by listening to people as they have shared their experience with me.

Allowing someone to talk with us, or cry with us, or just sit with us when they are in need of support is a magical expression of God that we all have the ability to display. As we heal ourselves and allow our love to grow inside, we heal our inner world; and the love we feel inside naturally and effortlessly flows out into the world around us.

I imagine a world someday where every human being has the conscious attitude of wanting to give love to their neighbor. I see a world where anger is replaced with empowerment; where fear is transformed to love. I see a world where people are respected for their uniqueness, as they are honored for their oneness. I see a world where hate, crime, and poverty are things our children will have to read about in their history books. I see a world full of happiness, hope, and joy.

I have great confidence in mankind and the goodness of heart. At this particular time, I know few people who truly remember their own oneness or their own personal greatness. However, I believe with all the conviction of my heart that each day, more and more people are waking up to their real truth; the truth that we are Spirit having a human experience. We all have the personal ability to achieve personal greatness in whatever we choose, as long as we allow the greatness of God and time to be our variables.

I see a world where children are taught empowerment techniques in order to seek their own glory and magnificence. I see a world were love rules, and where God is not only sought, but felt and experienced by all. I see a world where the statement, I am God and God is greater, is a philosophy taught by all. I see a world were spiritual attributes like the ones I have just described are used by all people in all languages. I see a world where our personal glory is acknowledged by the number of people we supported that day, as they individually seek their own love and light.

I see a world where each person I see sees me as their friend because they have reached a place of inner peace which allows them to see themselves as a friend. I see a world where each person feels the innocence in their heart and the love of God in their soul. And I see a world where people will find the courage within themselves to seek their own truth, and to share from their heart the love of God which resides in us all.

My friend, if I can do it, so can you. Allow yourself to dream again, allow yourself to heal, allow yourself to remember who you truly are. God loves you and so do I for having the courage to follow your destiny.

CR

To dream impossible dreams is the perfect description of how I felt when I first started this emotional release portion of my spiritual path. All I could see through my pain inside was a little flicker of light. All I could hear was a tiny voice saying, "Help me." At the time, I could only imagine what each of the signs meant. All I knew was that I had to keep moving forward with blind faith until all of my answers were clear. In time, I found out the meaning to each of these God-given signs.

The little flicker of light was a symbol of God's love that burns brightly in all of us. The tiny voice was my inner child; lost, alone, and surrounded by fear–mustering the courage each day to ask me for help. Finding my child within and sharing my love with him has led me to God's love, which resides in us all. I feel I have reached the reachable star of Spirit. My hope is that you will do the same.

CONCLUSION

I've been in the creation stages of this book for over two and half years. I hope that by reading my story, you have learned some things that can enhance the quality of your own path. Obviously, I know from experience that if you heal your child within, your reward will be a glorious reconnection to Great Spirit. Sometimes I feel I've been walking this conscious road forever. Other times, it feels like the first day. Looking back, I can honestly say from the bottom of my heart that every dark day was worth the glory I feel in my experience of today. I hope that your world has become a little brighter with a little more hope because of this book.

I can't express to you in words how proud of you I am for having the courage to walk your path. You have read this book because you are seeking answers. All of my answers were found inside of myself, and all of yours are within you.

God is love, love is an emotion, and emotions are in your heart. So as you heal your heart, you will reconnect to the love of God which resides in us all.

My friend, please know that I love you, and Great Spirit loves you. Trust that all of your dreams will come true as you seek and find the love of your inner child. May God's Love shine on you and through you as you find your own internal truth; and may the miracle of God be with you always.

God speed,
Joe

The following is my gift for you, my friend. I pray that the words will express your own truth as you make your journey toward healing.

♦ ♦ ♦

As my life's path takes me down another road, I've reached a place of new beginnings. My heart has opened to the truth of my Spirit. Everything that was true for me yesterday is an illusion today. Even though I am in the light, my world still seems very dark and new.

That which I called truth, now is false. That which I called love, now is not. My world is open to new a reality with no beginnings and no endings; where today does not exist, and only now is recognized.

I feel as though I have awakened from a deep sleep mourning the loss of my favorite dream. My days feel real, although no part of me sees through the same eyes. My truth has deepened from dark to light, encompassing all beings of life in between.

Today I meet the beginning of a new tomorrow—filled with life, love, and lessons. I can see, even though my eyes are blinded by the light and love of Great Spirit. I can feel, even though my senses are numbed by the warmth of my inner love. I now live as never before, free to be all I can be. In this moment, I am all that I am—love, life, joy.

Today I will find a new truth that allows all to flow with the divine rights of Spirit and all that is. My life has passed from dark to light, from beliefs to knowings, from personality to soul. I know with a comfortable level of certainty that all I have to give is me, and all I will receive is thee.

Today I live a life from a place of inner peace that all beings need to find. I choose light over dark, life over death, and truth over ego. I now know that I don't know, yet I feel safe in the faith of Great Spirit. My life moves forward by myself, though never alone; to seek, to find, and to remember.

Today is my day that all mankind needs to find; the day of peace, love, and the grace of Great Spirit. I have finished a long journey seeking and finding a lost part of me. My journey ends to begin a new freedom of soul. My path never ends, as a spiral never reaches itself. I glide with such a feeling of ease that I know the winds of time and the breeze of Spirit guide me to a grander place in life. My Spirit sings with the joy of new life. My soul soars in the sense of accomplishment needed to find a level of life which is true to that of the spiritual warrior. My heart is filled with the love of a child within, precious in all ways, safe in the womb of my own sacred love.

Today I thank God for the miracles of life, the blessings of love, and the gratitude of grace. I claim my need and desire to share my truth with the world. I walk my talk and talk my walk; and I live life from a place of soul that I've never known before.

Today is the first moment of the rest of my time, and I thank God for my strength, my courage, and my willingness to feel what I need to heal. I quest to share my love with others as I soar with the eagles, having innocence of the butterfly and wisdom of the owl. I am love, I am Spirit; and Spirit is one with all.

This day is a moment to cherish, to love, and to live. I thank Great Spirit for being my guide, my strength, and my inner courage. I thank myself for seeking my truth, finding my little kid's love, and having the courage to share with others.

◆ ◆ ◆

Joe Mittiga is also available to share his message of hope and self-discovery from the platform at your next association conference, corporate event, or church retreat.

Joe@MyInnerChildBook.com
Joe@InnerChild.info

For more information visit:
www.InnerChild.info

www.ingramcontent.com/pod-product-compliance
Lightning Source LLC
Chambersburg PA
CBHW030923090426
42737CB00007B/297